Of HEROIC PROPORTION

An American Story
of Patriotism and Survival in the Soviet Union During the Cold War

Mary Bruno Friedman

It was their great misfortune to have lived at a time when the worst were in power and the best among men were considered their greatest threats. May they find peace knowing that, of all, Stalin feared them most.

~

Edited by Adam Friedman

First Editions:

Paperback: *ISBN* 9798329720334 (Amazon KDP)
Paperback: *ISBN* 979-8-991-61291-3 (Barnes & Noble)
eBook: *ISBN* 979-8-9916129-0-6

Second Editions:

Paperback: *ISBN* 979-8-991-6129-6-8
Hardcover: *ISBN* 979-8-9916129-4-4
eBook: *ISBN* 979-8-9916129-5-1

Title:

Of HEROIC PROPORTION: An American Story of Patriotism and Survival in the Soviet Union During the Cold War

Published by *Mary Bruno Friedman*
https://www.of-heroic-proportion.com

Published in the United States of America.

This book is available for library purchase.

Disclaimer:
This is a work of narrative nonfiction. Names, characters, and incidents are portrayed accurately to the best of the author's knowledge and research, as well as the protagonist's memory. Every effort has been made to ensure the accuracy of the information presented.

In Dedication and Memory

*...for Danny, who sacrificed so much because
he treasured being and remaining an American.
Unfortunately, Danyk Szafranski passed away on
April 21, 2018, and his devoted wife, Olga passed
on March 6, 2022. It had been my greatest
desire that he could have seen his book in print.*

*... for Pat Hughes and Joe Bruno,
my sister and brother, who did not have enough
time to grow old but will remain young
in our hearts forever.*

—Mary Bruno Friedman

Contents

Notable People

Listed in general order of sequence:
(*Note: not all records recorded names consistently, some may vary:
ex. 1: Szafraski /Szafransky / Shafranski ex. 2: village of
Gorodnitski/Horonitza*)

Danyk Szafranski (also known as Danny after he arrives in America)

Olga Shevchuk (Danny's wife)

Maria, Oksana, Mykhailo, Bogdan (Danny and Olga's children. Once in America, Bogdan will go by the name, Danny Jr.)

Szymon Szafranski (Danyk's father, also known as Sam once in America)

Nyky Szafransky (Sam's father)

Paranka Czornij Szafransky (Sam's mother)

Iwan or Ivan or Evon (Sam's older brother, captured in Kiev by Germans, believed he died in battle)

Mykhailo (Sam's brother, member of Insurgent Liberation army, and a hero to his people

Wasy or Vasil (Sam's brother, dies at 19, was used as cover by the Soviets)

Paraskevia (Sam's sister)

Mariya (Mary) Slobodzian Szafranski (Sam's first wife, Danny's mother)

Paulo/Paul (Mariya's brother, lives in France)

Maria (Paulo's wife, who Marion meets in France)

Marion (Mariya's brother, goes into Polish army, becomes German POW)

Anastasia (Marion's wife)

Anna (Marion's daughter)

Anna and Volodymr Romanuke (Mariya's bosses in NYC)

Mike Shegren, Charles Biermak, Stephen Leko (Sam's friends in NYC

Miss Larned (Sam's counsel from the International Migration Service)

Kupetsky Alexa (Danyk's loyal neighbor in his village)

Joe Malaznick (American staff member at American embassy in Moscow that befriended Danyk)

Jim Mahoney (American staff member at American embassy in Moscow that befriended Danyk)

Satner Powell (Marion's loyal friend in the German POW camp)

Otto Lang (German farmer that nurses Marion)

Shetnuks (Danyk's kind neighbors who offered aid when Danyk returns after being arrested)

Doskoczyniskis (the family who had a sister-in-law leaving for Moscow. Kupetsky asked her to guide Danyk to Moscow)

Tessie (Sam's supportive second wife)

Vyktoria Henchuk (Sam's third wife)

Miss Maria Zemba (the threatening teacher that was keeping track of Danyk's family)

Sergeant Carber (one of the embassy staff members that had Danyk's photo taken the day he arrived at the American embassy in 1947)

Rick Firstman (the journalist that researched Danny's story and presented it in a nine-page feature article in Newsday, September 27, 1998)

Anna and Walter Romanuk (the Syosset couple that took Danny and Olga in once they reached America)

Bogdan and Olha Perito Shafranski (Danny's son and granddaughter who helped with translations)

Chapter 1

The Soviet Union, Post WWII, First Trip to Moscow

The boy tried to disguise his nervousness with a jaw that stood tight and eyes that narrowed to keep watch. He had good reason to compensate. He was pale and thin with a vulnerable posture that exaggerated his adolescent youth. The dark circles beneath his telling eyes were drawn there by his exhaustion and hunger.

There was one wisp of color, the luminous blue eyes that radiated despite their guarded caution. The rest of him though was lost in a drab mixture of browns and sun-bleached grays that covered his thread-worn garb.

Deep wrinkles etched his bent elbows, knees and crotch from sitting too long. An opportunity to soothe them... and his cramped muscles was long overdue. But he dare not stand and risk losing his seat.

The train, almost always crowded, was overstuffed with people. Some, literally hanging on, barely found enough footing on the steps of the train's entry way to remain on. Two women monitors shared a twenty-four hour shift guarding the train from vagabonds and urchin boys who hoped to board or ride the brake beams without tickets. At each stop, they would exit and merge carrying red flags as they detected the scoundrels and chased them away.

Each time the train approached another station, he found and held dear to his ticket which he had bought with his own hard work and meager savings. It was his only proof that he belonged on the train and did not deserve to be ejected along with the other orphans and beggars. Then, he'd sit tight and wait for the people and dust to settle, so the train would move again.

The ride had been a stagnant, boring existence for a fourteen-year-old boy, even for one with as dreary a past as his. He had survived mainly on a ration of sugar-water and dry bread, as had many of the other passengers.

A few more fortunate travelers had been able to buy an occasional cup of hot tea made by the women monitors, who would scavenge bits of wood to boil water and then mix it with samovar leaves. Or they had been able to scurry off the train at one of the stops and purchase kvass, mineral water or milk from barefoot children eager to sell their wares. Of course, each passenger had to provide their own receptacle, usually a small metal pail or empty vodka bottle to get their fill.

Over his grueling two-week journey, there had been little else to do but study Stalin's masterpiece through the train's cracked, smudged window. As the locomotive clanged, hiccupped, hissed and moaned its way over the Soviet countryside, they would occasionally pass a tank trapped in a trench or weathered sandbags sheltering a fox hole. These were all abandoned artifacts of history and the nation's trauma and war with Germany.

Fast moving rivers turned into swamp land and rolling hills rose up into dense forests only to wither away into patches of cut-over or burnt oak and spruce trees. Ash and alder renewed the earth with shrubs determined to live, though the land grieved for what it had seen.

Everywhere drained, worn faces mourned, and stared back in the same unfocused, haggard way. At once, they blended in with the backdrop of Stalin's Russia and contrasted with nature's beauty which, with a mind of its own, still exuded from the evergreen forests and tall grassed meadows that grew vibrantly without human tending.

The people's pain, so visible, had a color all its own and it spoke too, calling out.

Humiliation. Hopelessness. Agony... perfectly captured on the human canvas.

All credit went to Stalin. While the war had drained them, it was Stalin who had enslaved them. Their condition was their dictator's creation, a vision of his perfect world held still as if by an artist's stroke in perfect portrayal of mass human degradation.

It went against the heart of all people to witness such tragic devastation and loss of free will, yet live... but millions had, some-how... including the boy. Such is the power of the human spirit to go on. Such is the irony of history.

Each face had their own story to tell, and the boy's was no less revealing... just less noticed. So goes human nature throughout time and place, we rarely turn the pages of another's story when we are overwhelmed with our own. This was one slight fortune for him as he was determined... rather desperate to keep his story hidden ... at least until he was safely within the keep of the American Embassy in Moscow.

Occasionally, a fellow passenger would speak to him, usually in an authoritative tone.

He would answer in a respectful and humble manner reflecting his Ukrainian upbringing and the history of repression against his people. Really though, neither he nor they had much desire for conversation.

No one asked who he was, where he was going or why. No one cared. It felt both usual and unnatural at the same time. Of course, it could also have been the paranoia that seemed to grip the country, caused by neighbor betraying neighbor, a symptom of Stalin's repression, which had left his own people deeply scarred, guarded and alienated.

Danyk was finally approaching the Moscow train station. For him, it would be the last of many stops that the train had made since leaving his small village of Gorodnitsa, once part of Poland, but now part of the Soviet Union post World War II.

The train slowed, then jerked to a stop, but Danyk knew they were not yet at the station. It was a familiar routine that did, however, warn him and the other passengers that their arrival was imminent. Those whose final destination was within sight began to stir.

Adrenalin commenced his heart to hammer, and he jittered, distracted by the pounding in his chest. Perhaps it was the anticipation of the journey's end, the sugar-water diet or simply overwhelming fear that made him feel like a dry twig, crisp and ripe to snap. It was difficult to remain seated. But he did. It was difficult not to look at the other passengers. But he didn't.

This was how he had spent much of his life. Doing... that which he should not have been able to do.

It had made him resourceful, mature beyond his years, but still the fearfulness, the vulnerability never left him. He measured it with every breath he took.

The activity in the car began to rise as the train jerked forward and stopped, then jerked forward again. The jolt had caused a stringy strand of blond hair, browned by weeks without soap to land mid right eye. He wiped it away, but it annoyingly bounced right back. Absent-mindedly, he chewed his right thumbnail until his teeth felt gritty from the dislodged dirt.

Until recently, his secret had been well kept, but as it unraveled... so had his world. Once dreary but predictable, it had altered the day the Soviet soldiers had come to arrest his mother and grandmother after learning of their western ties. No greater sin could have been committed in Stalin's Russia. The consequences of this had spun out of control and had had an effect on every member of his family who had managed to survive WWII or The Great Patriotic War as it was known to the average Soviet citizen.

With the threads of his existence untwined, there seemed little else to do but put one foot in front of the other and keep going. Millions of other Soviets had done it before him. They were all a part of the sea of sad faces that seemed to be everywhere he looked at every train station, at every village and farm.

When the train took one last jolt and came to a final stop, he stood and at once became part of the cattle drive that moved forward, down the aisle and off the train. His last step was a leap onto a crude wooden crate that gave way and squeaked to the bounce of his unsteady footing.

After weeks of sitting with barely any movement at all, he was suddenly caught up in a frenzy of activity. A train whistle blew in the distance urging him forward and it seemed to stir energy into the otherwise lifeless and bleak-looking passengers. Within moments they converged to become one wall of bodies that moved in unison, dragging him determinedly along to follow the path of the rushing current.

He suddenly felt weak and dazed. The physical demands of the long trip with almost no sleep and little food to sustain him, were taking their toll. He quite literally could have dropped from the exhaustion... certainly physical but mental as well.

To his surprise and against his will...his body slowed becoming a frictional force that worked against the rushing crowd and suddenly he stilled. Just like a protruding rock in a flowing river, the stream began to divide and rush by and around him. The force, still moving, lifted his elbow and pushed forward his right shoulder. He was barely aware of it though, until his stillness, contrasted to the wind created by the rushing crowd, forced him to gulp for air to fill his lungs.

Frantically, he looked for refuge and eyed a quiet cobbled area off to the side. He scrambled against legs and limbs headed else-where, until he reached the tiny, paved area. There he was able to squat his body and rest his head on his knees. Within minutes the station quieted, and for the first time in weeks he was once again, all alone.

No less fearful or drained than he was moments before, he rose to his feet unsteadily, knowing there were no choices to make. He needed to be on his way and face whatever lay ahead of him.

Just put one foot in front of the other, then again, then again...

He meandered through the streets of Moscow in the direction of Red Square, vaguely aware of his right foot developing a blister from its constant rubbing and knocking about in an overly large boot. The footwear was his most valuable possession and had served his family during the war as their only pair. He asked anyone who gave him a second glance the same question.

"Kah dojty do Amerikanskojo posolstra?"

"How do I get to the American Embassy?"

Recognizing a Ukrainian accent, many only frowned annoyance and continued on their way. Some pointed, giving a vague indication of which way he should continue.

He made his way down Mochovaya, until finally, just across from the Kremlin, the embassy came into view... along with the endless line of people waiting to get into it! Were they Americans, too?

An armed Soviet guard stood at the entrance door checking papers that people had anxiously readied and held in hand. Most were turned away even though they had waited long hours. Their faces were marked with raw grief. Rarely, however, did the guard get an argument. Soviets were long used to being ruled by a sole authority. To argue usually meant severe consequences. Danyk was sure many had come a long way just as he had, only to be turned away. Even after many brutal years of war, his heart was still a soft place and it squeezed tight with compassion to see such despair and mass helplessness.

Patiently, he took his place at the far end of the line and began his laggard wait. Time ticked by sluggishly, while his heartbeat quickened. Bravely, he reined in his trembling apprehension with a pretense of youthful boredom and spent his restless energy sliding his weight from side to side.

Finally, when it was his turn to hand over his papers, the guard took all of five seconds to review them. Danyk knew the guard couldn't possibly be able to read them as they were in English, sent to him from his American father back in the United States of America. But he looked to be reviewing them anyway. He looked from top to bottom, then he turned them over and frowned when they were blank on the back. Other than that, he gave little reaction to indicate what he was thinking, one way or the other... and it was an endless moment before his verdict was ultimately revealed.

With little more than a wave of his hand, he indicated that Danyk must move on like the others. Danyk would not be getting Soviet permission to enter the American Embassy, at least not today!

The shock of it was numbing. He had been so desperate; he had not allowed himself to even consider the possibility that he would be turned away, as the many others had been.

But I'm an American citizen! I was born in America!!! I have documents! I belong with my father in America... and I have no place else to go!

He wanted to shout into the guard's face, to shake him, to demand that he let him into the embassy... but of course he did not. He had had many childhood experiences with war and bad men, and one did not ever expose his anger to someone holding a gun.

Still his mind raced...

I have no food! No family... no place to go! Only a father in America!

He froze, uncertain of what to do next.

All he could think to do was go back to the end of the line. Maybe a new guard would be here by the time he reached the front again and ...

The boy's anguish did not go unnoticed by the guard whose next impulsive move demonstrated either great human kindness or Soviet disinterest and apathy.

Suddenly... the guard walked away leaving a clear path into the embassy! If Danyk took a second to think it would be too late.

Run. Runnnnnnnnnnnn!!! Run as fast as you can!

Danyk seized the moment.

Off he ran for the over-large, arched Embassy door. Flinging it open, he scrambled as deep into the belly of the United States Embassy as he could.

For the next ten months, this would be home.

Chapter 2

Arrival at the Embassy

"You are an American citizen?" the clerk asked Danyk in Russian with an odd accent that he had never heard before.

"Yes." He bent forward mildly hopeful.

It felt good to admit it out loud to someone who would not think it a bad thing.

The clerk was not really asking. He was confirming it, after reviewing the papers Danyk had produced for him.

"We'll contact your father... we'll handle everything." He said with authority.

It was too wonderful to believe! He was safe. He was in the American Embassy in Moscow. He was safe. They would contact his father and he would be on his way back to America. Finally, finally... he was safe!

His mother had described America as a heaven on earth.

His mother...

Where was she...?

Was she alive...?

Would he ever see her again?

His young mind could not process it all. For now, it had to be enough to feel safe. "Come, we are going to take your picture for your father."

The uniformed soldier motioned to the entrance of the Embassy. Why was the soldier going that way?

No. No. That was not a way he dared to go! He was still shaking, still struggling to catch his breath from his dash into the embassy. He was being asked to do the unthinkable! The clerk was gesturing to go back outside the embassy.

Moments before he had snuck by the Soviet guard. If he saw him now, wouldn't he shoot him?

The clerk seemed to read Danyk's mind. Putting a fatherly hand on his shoulder, he reassured, "It's fine." Then, he leaned into Danyk's ear to whisper, "You didn't sneak by that Soviet guard. Every once in a while, when he stands alone and no supervisors can see...," he continued in an even lower whisper as though he was letting Danyk in on a huge secret, which in fact it was, "... he lets someone in. This time he allowed you!"

Danyk gulped in a huge mass of air at the surprise. Wouldn't the guard be at least a little angry at his disrespect? He had disobeyed. Never before had such disobedience to a Soviet soldier gone unpunished.

There seemed to be no choice as the clerk continued to lead him out of the Embassy and to the iron gates that surrounded it. His knees, quite literally, shook with fear and hesitancy. In truth, his compliance was showing more bravery and courage than his run into the Embassy had.

Deciding to trust... yet not... he made ready to run again at a moment's notice. He felt a degree of anger at the clerk as he pushed unrelentingly further in the direction that Danyk had no desire to go. Of course, he was careful not to show his anger to the clerk, who seemed a bit amused at his resistance. Hiding anger well was a practiced skill for a child of war.

Perhaps Americans were fools; perhaps they too could not be trusted.

This was odd and terribly confusing because it contradicted everything his mother had ever told him throughout his childhood.

The clerk searched about the area first and then made ready to approach the guard. By the time they stood a foot away and made eye contact, Danyk's face was drained of all color and his severely bent head had made his jaw sink tightly into his chest. His eyes were forced to arrow upward, like a puppy dog obediently submitting to its trainer.

A moment later a camera flashed and captured for history the day Danyk Szafranski would become known to the government of the United States of America as an American child trapped in the Soviet Union. Also captured would be the image of the Soviet soldier whose great compassion, so historically unexpected, had given Danyk access to the American Embassy.

Through all of World War II, Danyk had never found another Soviet soldier whose kindness and mercy had matched this one's. How lucky I am, he thought, that today of all days, was the one when our paths should cross.

Danyk would now become one of some 1,900 American citizens who would find themselves in a similar position. Twenty-one of them would be children like him, separated from their American parents and, like them, his story is no longer a personal one, it is historical.

For now, though he would be a sole American child tucked behind the gates and protection of the American Embassy in Moscow.

Once the deed was done and he was safely back behind the Embassy walls, he felt a tremendous sense of satisfaction, closure, relief and exhaustion. He sank into the comfortable chair, listening to the click of the typewriter keys as the papers were readied to contact his father in New York and process his claim to American citizenship.

This is a miracle!

What would his mother think? After all they had been through. If only she were there with him.

No.

She was not. He was alone.

But...at least, now there was hope.

He woke to a strange sound. A muffled moan... was someone sick? Danyk rose from the cot. The Embassy had assigned him a room in the basement, which though small, was grander than anything he had ever slept in. Before he could poke his head out the door, an American appeared.

He knew because he appeared somewhat different from other adult men that he had been familiar with. He was...healthy! His skin was pink. His hair was clean and shiny though thinning and showing slight signs that it was beginning to recede. Still, he looked youthful, somewhat tall with broad shoulders and a thin fit waist.

"Hello, young man, where are you going?" It was strange but the American spoke impeccable Russian. He had expected some kind of accent, but he couldn't detect even the slightest one.

"I heard someone moaning, is someone sick?"

"Um, I'll check into it," he said with a hint of authority, "but you just go back to sleep."

Danyk felt vaguely reassured and trusted that the American would see to whomever it was that seemed to need some help.

The moans continued through the night. But there was little Danyk could do about it for he fell into a deep sleep. The next morning when he woke, the American returned again.

As though he had greeted Danyk "Good morning," a thousand times before, the American plunked his six-foot plus frame down at the foot of the cot with easy familiarity, leaning casually against the back wall.

"Got you something."

"Excuse me?" Danyk responded politely. "I got you something. You want it?"

Danyk nodded slowly, unsure of what it could be.

The American reached into his shirt pocket and pulled out a brown bar. Perhaps a bar of soap? Danyk immediately felt gratitude for such a precious gift. Then the American flipped it into the air, caught it and presented it to Danyk in one quick, graceful movement.

Danyk reached for it, only to have the American pull it out of his way. Something in the American's manner and the gleam of his eye let Danyk know the man was no threat. He was being playful and teasing. He wanted to have fun!

"You're not even going to tell me your name first?"

"My name is Danyk, Danyk Szafranski." His soft-spoken tone and respectful manner helped the American settle on a first impression quickly.

"Actually, I knew that already," the American confessed.

He handed the bar to Danyk who examined it cautiously. He had never seen such a thing before and could only think to bring it to his nose for a quick sniff. It looked edible.

"This is choc-o-late... a choc-o-late candy bar... take a bite."

Danyk hesitated, unsure of what it would taste like, but he didn't want to offend the nice American who seemed to like him.

"Try it. Trust me, you will like it."

He took a nibble, waited to process the taste and then gave a huge, relieved smile. It felt strange to smile, and he was overwhelmingly aware of the muscles that stretched to do so. When was the last time he had had reason to smile? He couldn't remember.

"I told you."

"It is very good." Then, he took a huge bite, as though it was necessary to finish it all in one swoop. Displaying good manners, he then offered the American a bite.

As his chocolate-filled mouth chomped away, the American felt an endearing pang for the boy.

"It's all yours, Pal." Then he stood up and took two more bars out of his pockets and slapped them down on the cot. Danyk's eyes went wide, forcing the American to chuckle easily and delightedly.

"Pal?" Danyk did not recognize the word.

"It's an American word. It means friend. Should we be friends?"

Danyk's mouth was yet too filled to answer, so he nodded his head up and down in a huge, swinging motion.

"Take it easy there, Pal. You'll make yourself dizzy... and don't eat all the chocolate at once. You'll get sick."

Danyk didn't answer. He didn't want to lie to his new friend. He knew as soon as the American left that those other two chocolate bars were the rest of his breakfast.

The American turned to the doorway.

Danyk's airway cleared of chocolate just enough to ask with some gulping, "Is the man alright?"

"What man?"

"The man I heard. He moaned all night."

"Kept you up, huh?" the American asked apologetically.

Somewhat embarrassed, Danyk admitted, "No, not really... but I felt badly for him."

"Well..." the American hesitated, giving thought about how much to say, "...he's out of pain now, Pal."

Was there remorse in his tone? Danyk's question had disturbed the American. It was best not to ask him anything more.

"Enjoy your candy bar, Pal. I've got to go, but maybe I'll see you when I get back in a few days. Should I bring you more candy bars?"

"Yes, please." Danyk nodded and hoped the American did not think he was greedy, but he could not possibly turn down the candy bars. They were the most delicious thing he had ever tasted!

"Wait!" Danyk sprang up in after-thought just as the American started to disappear.

Suddenly, Danyk turned shy and hesitated; then, he found enough courage to ask his question. "What...is your name?"

"My name? It's...Joe, Joe... Malaznik...but you just call me Joe." Then he winked and left.

Danyk settled back on the comfortable pillow satisfied with his morning. Not only was he now under the influence of a chocolate high, but he had met and befriended a real American Joe!

A warm, cozy security blanketed Danyk his first few days at the embassy. He was the center of attention, and it seemed all the Americans wanted to make him welcome and comfortable.

His whole life had been centered around the two women in his life, his mother and his grandmother. His deep love for them could not be questioned, but he had often envied other boys who had a father and he had a strong inclination to make up for lost time with as much male attention as he could attract.

If he shined a shoe or swept the floor, he was rewarded with a tousled head, a wink or tossed a coin. If the Americans were making breakfast in the embassy's kitchen, they made extra for him and as soon as he cleaned his plate, they shoveled more on telling him to eat, so he would build his muscles. They'd flex their own and point, but their attempts to motivate him weren't needed.

He'd already decided that he wanted to be just like them. Healthy and strong and American.

Of all the Americans that made the embassy feel like home, there were two that took a special interest in his care. They were Joe Malaznick, who Danyk had met on his first night in the embassy and Joe's good friend, Jim Mahoney.

Jim's attentions, at first, were at Joe's request, but both had taken an immediate liking to the boy who they found polite, well-mannered and in serious need of some good fortune. It gave them both a sense of satisfaction to oversee his care and keep his spirits up, while they waited... and waited for arrangements to be made to send the boy to his father in New York.

Danyk never asked, but it was conveyed that Joe held a higher authority position than Jim. Joe was always writing or working on a draft or some report and was regularly called away on important business or "missions" that could require him to be away for days or even weeks. He was sure to have a special treat for Danyk upon his return.

This always got him a warm welcome home response, but he would have gotten one anyway even if Joe had returned empty-handed. He was fast becoming Danyk's idol.

While Danyk had only spent a little time in school, he was astute enough to recognize that Joe exuded distinction. It wasn't only the way Danyk observed how Joe spent his time reviewing important, official-looking papers and documents or that he spent his evenings reading thick intimidating books. Nor was it the way he shared interesting stories of his travels and the various people he'd met along the way; all of which brought great excitement and adventure into Danyk's rather bland existence.

Mostly, it was that he understood a lot about people, not just the Soviet people, but the Ukrainian and Polish people, as well. Not much ever had to be explained to Joe about the Soviet people's history or customs. Not only did he know about them, he delighted in them and enjoyed all the flavors and variations of people that humankind had to offer.

There was something in the way that Joe lived and viewed life that was altogether soothing, nurturing, hopeful ...and alluring to a boy whose life lacked all the aforementioned. It was a strong attraction and mutually satisfying. It provided Danyk with the presence of a much-needed parental figure and Joe, an intimate, compassionate connection to real people whose real situations and problems he, as a member of the Foreign Service since 1926, was more than aware.

Joe had long served his country and been an eyewitness to the rise and fall of Nazism as a member of the Foreign Service in Germany, even at one point becoming a German prisoner while in that service.

He'd met Stalin face-to-face and watched the purges of the 1930's, knowing personally some of those who were persecuted for nothing more than Stalin's whim. He'd studied the faces of these men, seen them up-close, at their trials, ashen and grief-stricken knowing they'd done nothing wrong but that no defense could save them.

Of course, young Danyk knew none of this history. These were not the stories Joe shared with him as they talked and laughed and ate popcorn together on his bed in the basement of the embassy. Instead, he spoke of his home back in the Midwest and his exciting travels where he connected with the people, enjoyed amazing scenery or the tranquility of sitting on a rock and watching a moving river until sundown.

However, these atrocities were the things that Joe knew existed in Danyk's world, knew he'd been exposed to and wished...with a father's desire, that he could protect him from. If only he could?

Perhaps it was the reason he had bonded with Danyk so. He wasn't typically a sentimental person, just a very honorable one... and honorable men protect the helpless... and children... and try to make the world a better place.

Joe was committed to that and being a spiritual person believed he needed to use his innate nature intelligently and never lose sight of his ultimate purpose. His ability to think clearly under pressure, his talent to write and communicate concisely, his easily acquired language skills, his intense curiosity and appreciation of people were all leading him somewhere. As was his nature, he was letting them take him.

Jim's staff position, on the other hand, kept him closer to home, and while Danyk had come to rely on and appreciate him as the steady, everyday caregiver, it was Joe who captured Danyk's adoration and worship. Jim knew there was no way to compete with the spell Joe had cast on Danyk, and he never attempted to persuade him otherwise. Instead, he sat back and observed, marveling and appreciating Joe's ability to lure people in...even an adolescent boy, with his soothing, steady attentiveness. After all, he couldn't blame the boy. He too, was in awe of the man who persuaded respect from everyone he encountered. Besides, Jim wasn't the kind to feel so easily threatened and he knew where he stood with Danyk.

It wasn't as though these grown men, with specialized and important jobs, revolved their lives around the boy, but he had certainly helped fill a crevice created by long periods away from family and life back in the States.

Jim and Joe's small "Moscow" community consisted of the limited diplomatic entourage, Foreign Service Agents and military personnel, a few select Soviet officials and to a lesser extent a few locals (including the "boiler men" who regularly visited to fix the furnace and update the embassy's bugging devices for Stalin, of which, the embassy pretended they didn't know anything about).

There weren't many players because of where they were in the world. Since the United States had returned to diplomatic relations with the Soviet Union in 1933, the country had grown more and more isolating with Stalin's growing paranoia of the west. It was not only seriously frowned upon for Soviets to spend time with Americans, but it was also considered a criminal activity. If Soviets were in the company of Americans, it was because Stalin wanted them there keeping as close a watch on them as he believed they were on him.

This meant work and recreation hours were generally spent amongst themselves while they were in Moscow. It also meant Joe and Jim had gotten to know each other quite well, despite a difference in their rank.

Joe's cool exterior didn't fool Jim one bit. You had to be tough... able to take it, just to be doing the job they did. They were well trained, knew their job well and were respected by their superiors or they wouldn't have ever been assigned to the Soviet Union. But it wasn't a job you actually got used to doing or necessarily even liked. A shadow of danger always hung over you. Stalin knew you were there, just out of his reach. Or were you? He didn't always play by the rules. You just took a deep breath, held it as long as you were ordered, and did your job because your country needed you to.

Just like the boy, they often took it day by day and did their best hoping nobody too powerful or frightening took too great a notice of them. They were just like a couple of million other people, shaking their heads at the turbulent times.

Jim knew Joe's sensitive side had been captivated by the boy's innocence and likeability.

They both had grown to really care about the boy; he'd become part of their daily routine, a bright light over the months they spent within the dim embassy walls waiting for new orders or another mission.

They were always checking in on him, surprising him with treats and trinkets. They'd gotten him an American flag that now draped the back wall of Danyk's quarters and given him framed pictures of themselves taken while back home.

They were, in a sense... a family, and did the typical things a family would do. They talked over their day at supper and reminded Danyk to keep his room tidy. They weren't sure why they gave the boy rules; just somehow instinct told them he needed them. As best they could, they tried to give his life order. They even saw to it that he got a job sweeping the embassy floors to help him make some money.

Their bond had been built over the many weeks that were turning into months, while Danyk and the rest of the embassy waited to be advised about Danyk's American citizenship being recognized by Soviet authority and his return to his father in America.

It was a time of hope and anticipation not only for Danyk but post-war Soviet citizens and American diplomats as well. Surely, a world war won on the sacrifice and cooperation of Allied Forces... Soviet isolation and distrust would be over.

Joe and Danyk represented the melting of different worlds that suddenly decided to smile at each other. But perhaps, Joe and Jim were beginning to care about Danyk a bit too much, considering Stalin had not yet confirmed the world's assumptions.

It had already occurred to them both that Danyk might never make it back to the states to meet up with his father. To date, they couldn't recollect any applicant who had been released by Stalin. But the hope was there as the world was changing a bit every day in these post-war times... just a lot slower here in Moscow.

Maybe soon, it would shift a bit in this boy's favor.

Chapter 3

Life at the Embassy

"Hey Joe, look at me!" Danyk, the boy who was mature beyond his years, called out with the glee of a five-year old.

A giddy feeling came over Joe to see Danyk so excited and thrilled, just to sit on top of a dilapidated motorcycle, looking like he was king of the world. But that was part of the delight of sharing his world with Danyk. There was nothing in life to take for granted.

Joe had borrowed the motorcycle from a visiting dentist, thinking it would be a great treat for Danyk. It proved to be that and more for the boy.

"O.K. Pal, I'm ready...smile!" Joe clicked the picture like a father at his son's graduation. They were just outside Spaso House about fifteen minutes from the embassy where the Ambassador and most of the embassy's personnel lived. He'd wanted to get his camera after he'd realized how charged up riding the motorcycle had made Danyk. Joe wanted him to remember the day... a happy one amongst so many that had been disappointing. Each day began with the boy expecting it to be the day he would be allowed to go to his father in America and each day ended with him realizing it would not. But today would be a good day, a diversion, and they would share it together.

After taking the photograph, he brought Danyk, who had been reluctant to get off the bike, into Spaso House to play a game of pool. The boy had observed Joe with wide-eyes for a time as he angled and thrust the pole, this way and that over the green table, striking the ball that made the others dance and roll into deep pockets. Mixed with the knocking and swishing of the balls as they rolled over the soft surface was a background of American music.

Everything was a first for Danyk. The motorcycle ride, the playful excursion, the grandeur of Spaso House surrounding him as he played a game of pool... everything was new and absolutely delightful. He didn't need the photograph to remember it all, as Joe might have thought. It was all burned in his mind and as 'firsts' tend to be recorded; they were mental keepsakes that would stay with him forever.

At first, Danyk used the pole more like a hockey stick than a cue stick. But soon, under Joe's tutorage and patience, he was angling it this way and that just like Joe, sliding and thrusting and hitting his mark.

It was exhilarating for both of them. One loved to learn, the other loved to teach. One had almost no schooling, the other had scholarly credentials. Both needed human tending and each was willing to give it. It was rather simple really, the fit worked. The bonding benefited them both.

From then on, they'd gotten into the habit of spending even more time together, and Joe used the time to teach Danyk American things. He gave him magazines about fancy American cars and baseball, and they'd discuss it while practicing Danyk's English. Or he'd teach him how to play cards or chess. Simple things... just to pass the time, so the boy didn't feel so lonely or dwell on missing his mother, Mariya. They'd still not gotten any updated information on her, and it was not yet known if she had survived or was dead.

Many other Americans, now claimed by Stalin as Soviet citizens, had come and gone from the embassy in their attempts to get home to America, and Joe had felt sympathy for them all. However, the boy, probably because of his age or maybe just his eternal enthusiasm had captured not only Joe's attention but his devotion. He knew, eventually, life was going to catch up with his emotions, and in the end, it was going to hurt. Sometimes though, even when we know what is coming, we do things anyway. It's a human factor that sometimes amuses God; at others it compels him to hold our hand with pride and love.

Joe would manage to salvage many days for Danyk during his stay at the American Embassy. But they would not all be good days... soon to come... would be one of the worst for both of them!

Finally, the inevitable occurred and it was devastating news that Jim wanted to share with Joe quickly... before he saw Danyk.

The minute Joe returned from his mission, Jim was notified, and he immediately went to search Joe out.

Jim didn't want Joe to find out by coming upon the boy himself and he knew that the first place Joe would head after settling in at his residence in Spaso House would be Danyk's room in the basement of the embassy.

"Joe?" Jim was looking up as he stood nearly a foot shorter than Joe.

"Yeah...Jim." Joe looked over his shoulder, shifting through his hand-drawn sketches and various correspondence and telegrams that had piled up on his desk while he was gone. His greeting held a distracted edge. "How is it going?" Then he continued on, not yet aware of the weight that Jim's answer would carry.

"Well...," was all that Jim said. It was enough to get Joe's attention. He startled, catching Jim's hesitation like a curveball.

"What?" It came out more like a command.

"It's Danyk...they...", Jim choked, unable to finish.

The moment filled with silence and stilled. It was thick in the air as Joe's eyes locked with Jim's while he read his mind.

It was too indecent to be spoken aloud. No matter how often it happened, neither Joe nor Jim could stomach the inhumane treatment dished out by the KGB to those in residence at the embassy.

Danyk had not been the only American residing there. There were others, too. Many, Danyk had gotten to know and watched as the KGB regularly visited and took them in for "questioning".

This questioning was a form of interrogation, or more descriptively put, a type of torture that was inflicted on those claiming American citizenship. The intent was to get the subjects to sign away their American citizenship.

This would happen repeatedly until one of a few things happened: they signed away their U.S. citizenship thereby losing it forever, they were executed or they returned to the embassy and committed suicide. The latter was quite common and seen by some as the only way to avoid additional torture or a life of total submission to Soviet dominance. Not only did Jim and Joe witness this, but Danyk did as well.

When would it be Danyk's turn? This was simply a discussion they never had. All three remained in denial for months, hoping that Danyk's young age would see him spared.

The American Embassy was quite powerless to stop the Soviet authorities from questioning Americans or offer any protection or asylum whatsoever. The KGB retained the right, claiming the subjects were Soviet citizens and under Soviet jurisdiction, not American.

American officials, having full knowledge of what was happening, were forbidden to interfere, not only by Soviet authority... but by American as well.

Once the torturous episode was over, the subjects were returned to the American embassy, without an apology for their battered state. The embassy would patch them up as best they could. How could they not. After all, they were fully recognized American citizens. The only one denying it and refusing to release them... was Stalin.

But this time they'd done it to a child... to their Danyk.

~

"Noooo!" The wall shook to the intensity of Joe's last and very physical denial. It was so loud that Jim hoped Danyk had not heard it from the floor below.

But it wasn't really a denial at all! It was a moan of pain in utter understanding and acceptance of the tragedy that had passed.

It eventually happened to all of them.

He must have blocked that fact out and he was amazed by the raw power of his own unconscientious denial of reality.

It was the reason grown men crumbled, cried like babies, moaned through the night. It was the dark, hidden secret of the embassy and no one... not he... not Jim... not President Harry S. Truman, could do a blessed thing about it.

It took everything in Jim to get the words out, but still they were delivered in choked, choppy breaths.

"They took him last night... returned him this morning."

"The damn KGB! What could they possibly want with a fourteen-year-old kid?"

Joe hit the wall and a puff of white chalky dust clouded the air. Then, he sat down and cried with such force that it made Jim turn away.

Jim had done nearly the same thing after he'd tended Danyk's wounds and tucked him into bed. Seeing Joe's reaction made him revisit his own initial emotions and he too watered up.

This was probably the most putrid moment Joe had ever endured because his expertise in the KGB and methods of torture gave him a vivid picture of exactly what had happened to Danyk and the degree of physical abuse and degradation he'd probably endured.

Joe couldn't remember a time he'd cried with such ferocity... ten, fifteen years ago maybe, but once he started, he wasn't going to recover easily. Not pride, not embarrassment, not his foreign service training was going to stop the volatile, explosive flow of anger, helplessness and guilt that poured out of him.

The boy was special. He broke the monotony of Moscow's bleakness and the long weeks between assignments with his curiosity, energy, cheerfulness and his eagerness to please. He was a human element in a time of guns and barbed wire. No denying it, he'd been touched by the boy. There was a bond and somehow, he'd let the boy down.

As irrational as the guilt was, it returned in wave after wave as the pictures kept coming, replays of torturous acts so vile, so monstrous, yet typical of the methods used by the KGB to bend the will of their citizens, all in the name of the motherland, Stalin's Russia.

Finally, when there was nothing left in him, he found himself staring at a wall in a crumbled mess on the floor. He wasn't sure if it had been a minute or ten or twenty that had gone by, but he knew he didn't want another second to go by before he saw Danyk.

As he stood up, somewhat like an old man stiff with arthritis, he used the back of his hand to awkwardly wipe his eyes. It was obvious that it wasn't a natural or familiar gesture. He staggered hurriedly on his way to Danyk's room, then stopped when he got there. He took a deep breath and then another before he poked his head in. He wasn't sure at all what he would see.

At once, he realized he wouldn't need to hide the red rim around his eyes. Danyk was in no shape to notice.

He lay perfectly still underneath the neatly tucked blankets which he was sure were Jim's handiwork. His eyes were swollen shut and his chin was tilted up to the ceiling as though he had found one comfortable position and did not dare move from it. He was stiff and rigid, but he looked oddly at peace. An imprint of a hand stained Danyk's left cheek. Joe began to reach for it as though he could wipe the welt away, then stopped short realizing it was a silly notion and that the touch might disturb him.

Joe didn't dare lift the blanket to see the rest of his condition. He knew he'd find more bruises there, and he didn't know if he could bear it.

Danyk's slight stir let Joe know he was aware of his presence.

"Hey, Pal."

Danyk reached out and Joe grabbed gently, cautious not to hurt him.

His hands were warm and pliable. Joe felt safe to touch him there, so his thumb began a back-and-forth motion to soothe him.

Danyk swallowed hard once, then again as though he was trying to speak. Joe shushed him softly, letting him know there was no need to say anything.

It was a long time before either one spoke. They just sat quietly letting their company comfort each other.

Besides, what was Joe to say? Should he tell the boy this was routine? If you wanted to claim American citizenship, you had to endure torture by the KGB, even if you were under the protection of the United States Embassy? Even if you were just a kid?

Should he tell him about the others? Most were adult men, but there had also been other children. All claimed western ties and American citizenship.

Unfortunately, Stalin simply didn't recognize American citizenship. Anyone living in the Soviet Union's claimed territory as a result of boundary changes after WWII, lost all rights to other citizenship. Any other citizenship was simply overruled. Case closed.

"Joe?" Danyk finally whispered, barely moving his mouth. "They wanted me to give up my American citizenship."

"What did you tell them?" Joe bit his lip preparing for the impact of the bad news.

Danyk's eyes flickered open wide at the ridiculousness of the question. "What do you ask me?"

"What did you tell them?" Joe repeated solemnly with the certainty of his reply. Giving up his citizenship meant no going back. Once it was lost, it was gone forever. Stalin didn't give second chances.

"I tell them, no! I tell them... I am an American...right Joe?"

Joe had been ready to comfort him... to help him accept signing away his citizenship and the loss of all his hopes and dreams. This... he had not expected. His breath was swept away.

Perhaps, Danyk was not remembering correctly because he was in shock. It just couldn't be. He was still alive... and that just wasn't the way the KGB worked.

Silently, his thoughts whirled as he waited for Danyk to fall into a deep sleep.

Never before had Joe seen Danyk without his wits about him. For all his mild, timid appearance, he was as quick as a whip. His instincts had all been sharpened by war; his mere survival to date, proof.

Perhaps it was faith, maybe a bit of pride... but somehow, he concluded that without a doubt this gentle, unassuming kid had done just what he'd said.

To the sleeping child, he softly spoke his praise.

"Right, Danyk... you are an American... of heroic proportion... and I'm proud to know you, Pal!"

He kissed Danyk's forehead gently, as those who had also loved this child before had done. Then, he stood. For a brief moment, he was lost in his own reflection, and then he knew what he had to do. He gave a soft well-deserved salute and was then ready to start another mission ...this time just for Danyk.

Through the night Joe used any and all connections he had to make the arrangements.

By morning, he was sitting beside Danyk's bed waiting for him to wake... so that he could say good-bye.

Chapter 4

Joe Meets Danyk's Father in America

"You will see my father?" Danyk asked incredulously!

"Within 72 hours I'll be sitting with your dad in a diner on 1st Avenue in your hometown. It's all set." He gave Danyk a confident wink then added, "This is for you, Pal!"

"Joe..." Danyk began gratefully. He raised himself up from his bed on his elbows and then winced when his bruised body reminded him that he had a long way to go in his recovery.

"Yeah, Pal?" Joe winked and drew closer. "You are the best pal... I ever had!"

"You...you deserve better Danyk but I'm doing my best."

"You will help my father bring me to America!" Danyk sounded a bit too assured for Joe's conscience.

"Pal... I wish we lived in a better world." He meant it with all his heart. "I don't want to make promises I can't keep. What I can promise is... I'll do my best."

That was enough for Danyk and his eyes looked adoringly back at Joe, wide and open with relief and trust that Joe prayed was not misplaced.

If nothing else, he had rekindled Danyk's hope.

Was that a good thing?

Was he being smart about this?

He hoped this wouldn't become one big regret.

But then he figured... the biggest regret of all would have been to never even have tried.

Soon after, he was on a military plane headed for a short layover in Germany and then back to the United States. When the plane landed in Washington D.C., he was ready to kiss the ground.

He'd spent so much of his adult life outside the United States, not because he didn't love it, but because he felt duty bound to serve it. Joe's unique intellect and talents hadn't gone unnoticed, and they had gotten him to a unique position and place in history. They were leading him to his destiny, and he knew it with every fiber of his being.

It had been his own decision years before not to attend law school after graduating from Princeton and do the expected... return to the quieter life that awaited him back in his hometown, Milwaukee. Instead, he'd chosen to join the Foreign Service. He didn't, in any way, resent serving the agency so far from home. In fact, he was easily bored and his international travels, even throughout a world war, helped him to remain feeling vital and engaged. But, returning always made him realize how much he missed the states.

God love the USA he thought to himself over and over again.

His appreciation of a world seemingly taken for granted by the average Joes he passed left him feeling strangely out of place. He couldn't help but compare the world from which he had just come, to the one in which he had just arrived. For the moment at least, he felt he didn't belong in either.

After finishing up official business, he was off to New York to meet Danyk's father, the real reason he had returned to the states.

He'd stepped from a dreary place that seemed stuck in time in every way, from toilets to haircuts, into post-war Manhattan, primed and ready to move on into the future, away from war, army life and foxholes. Emotionally, however, he was still stuck somewhere in the middle.

But he was on a mission, and it wasn't time for reflection or making sense of the world. He needed to stay grounded on the very task which had brought him to this time and place. There was an American child in Moscow who longed to return to his father and no one, not even the President of the United States of America, seemed to know how to make that happen.

What was he going to do about it? He didn't have a darn clue!

He just knew that the KGB only tolerated those making a request for just so long before they lost all patience. It was a mind game that the Soviet Union played with their citizens, allowing them to build hope, to think they had some control over their destiny, before humiliating and degrading them to such a great extent that they would collapse in acceptance of their own total powerlessness. If they didn't... they were destroyed... one way or another.

In Stalin's Russia, no one had control but Stalin. Even his own generals knew they weren't secure. It created a fear so alive, it almost breathed. In its grip it held a nation of men and women squirming for mere survival. It swallowed people up and made them senseless. Stalin's tight hold was so deliberately suffocating to his citizens, that it was almost incomprehensible to the western mind. But its intensity was so great that it made a generation of its citizens give up free will. It also made a small, courageous minority fight knowingly to their deaths. He didn't want one of them to be Danyk!

Joe's superiors, particularly those who had never themselves been to the Soviet Union, had great difficulty conceiving the depth and breadth of what was Stalin. Likewise, acknowledging to a significant degree that it had been the forces of Stalin's army that had endured and prevailed against Hitler's relentless advances, they had difficulty grasping what a weakened, backward and messy state of affairs Stalin's country actually was in. Instead of playing their upper hand while they might, they often backed down, at least in Joe's opinion...

too easily and unnecessarily, leery and concerned about Stalin's reaction.

If they would just play his bluff..., Joe thought.

Stalin would go running with his tail between his legs!

But that wasn't the way the State Department saw it. And it wasn't really his job to convince them otherwise, unless he was asked.

Sometimes if an opportunity doesn't come to you, you have to go to it.

Maybe that was what Joe was doing here, back in the United States. Or maybe, he just didn't know what else to do.

Joe's bus made its way down 34th street and he got off just before 1st Avenue. He walked a block or two before he found the diner where he had arranged to meet Danyk's father. He was seated quickly and took the side of the booth facing the door.

He didn't wait; he ordered coffee, black, no sugar.

It wasn't long after he'd slid into the booth that a man walked in. He recognized him as Danyk's father more by the bend of his back than anything else. He'd seen that posture more times than he would have liked. It was the posture of men whose hearts had sunk low, whose chests were too heavy to lift up anymore; they were battle worn but still going through the motions. Then there was the look as they made eye contact and it spoke to him like a whisper given too close to his ear. It made him shiver. Was Danyk's father also sizing him up the same way?

Sam Szafranski didn't hesitate. He walked directly to Joe's booth after he identified the only patron who could have been the American official that had contacted him.

There wasn't anyone else around who quite fit the bill. Though he wasn't wearing a uniform he looked statesmanlike and welcoming at the same time. Then there was the look of someone who knew all of his business... and understood his pain. He needed to explain nothing. When Sam shook Joe's hand, a burden was lifted. Its weight was shared for a moment, and he straightened, acknowledging the relief.

Instantly, they knew they were on the same team, and neither was as alone as they had been moments before.

"I am Sam," he introduced himself with a strong Ukrainian accent yet a gentle manner, using much of the same, familiar tone his son often used.

"I'm Joe Malaznik... a good friend of your son." Joe motioned for Sam to sit down. "Yes," Sam nodded and then closed his eyes briefly as he took a deep breath. His chest rose fully as though he had just taken in the fragrance of fresh flowers. As he sighed outwardly, tension left his body, and his shoulders dropped an inch. Then, he added, "...and a good friend of mine as well." He took the seat across from Joe.

He has been with my son, Sam thought.

He has heard his voice. Perhaps he has tousled his hair or patted his shoulder. Maybe he has seen his smile. Sam regretted the pang of jealousy he felt and quickly wished it away.

He replaced it with such gratitude toward this man that he almost felt he should bow before him. He wanted to get up and kiss the man's feet, instead he said, "Bless you for making this trip ... for coming to see me... the care and concern you give my son." Tears came to Sam's eyes and as unbelievable as it was to Joe, they came to his eyes as well.

Joe began to clear his throat. "Your son..." he began and then abruptly stopped.

What could he say... that Danyk was well? He was far from it. In fact, he was still recovering from his last beating given by the KGB. He couldn't bring himself to explain the degree of torture Danyik had endured. And would endure again. It seemed unspeakable and cruel.

"Your son," he began again, "is a fine young man."

"His mother would have seen to that." he acknowledged lovingly. "She is...was?" he hesitated and gestured his confusion with a shake of his hand, "a strong woman... a loving mother." For a moment he seemed lost in another place, somewhere in the past. He was remembering the woman who had raised his son without him, whose fate he still did not know. Perhaps he never would.

"I...I am a bad father... I can't protect my son."

Joe knew that Sam wasn't looking for false reassurances.

No one can, not you, not me, not the United States of America. Everyone is powerless in Stalin's Russia. This is what Joe wanted to say.

Instead, he gave comforting words. "He doesn't blame you, you know. He loves you very much."

"He loves a father he doesn't even know?" Sam couldn't help but question him. He needed to know the truth.

"His mother spoke of you often. He cherished every word." Joe smiled remembering Danyk's enthusiasm when he would get caught up in his daydreams and share his mother's recollections of her former life in New York with her young husband.

"You are very kind to tell me this. I wish very much he could know me, as a boy should know his father." Sam gestured with his hands as though he wished his son were between them so he could grab and hold him. His teeth clenched at his desire, his face flushed, and his eyes once again squeezed shut in utter frustration.

Again, silence. But it was not uncomfortable. Both had thoughts that trailed and needed to be considered before continuing. They each respected the other's distraction and allowed for it.

"I have a letter from your son. He reads and writes well... he tells me your Mariya made sure of it!" Joe broke out into a smile and Sam followed with a half-hearted one, remembering her determined presence. Joe winced slightly realizing how quickly he had brought up Mariya again. He hadn't meant to, but then again it had made Sam's face soften for a moment.

"The letters aren't censored. I smuggled them out".

All other letters between Sam and his family had been censored since the war. Sometimes, entire pages were blocked out. Sam couldn't imagine what had been in them to make Soviet Union officials feel so threatened that they had to take away from him his wife's precious words. What threat could his little peasant family be?

Sam reached to behold them, his hands shaking and tender as though he were about to hold a fragile artifact.

"Many years went by without a single word..." he reminisced. My life stopped when I thought I had lost them both." Vacant eyes showed a man so filled with hurt for so long that he dare not feel.

"But now I have hope..."

Joe wasn't so sure. He didn't know of any other American who had made it out alive. They had either died from interrogation, another name for torture, or had given up their American citizenship.

Even by now, Danyk could have been taken for another interrogation and have given in and signed it away. Once that happened there was no way to reclaim it. As far as the Soviets were concerned, it was a closed case.

But... how could Danyk's father understand this? He had never known Stalin's Russia, having left what was then Poland nearly twenty years before WWII.

He began to doubt why he had come. Now, if he failed there would be two faces to haunt him instead of one.

But Danyk could not remain at the American Embassy if, in reality, his dreams and those of his father, Sam, were not to come to pass. It would kill him! That was just the way it was. The embassy could house him, but it couldn't protect him.

"How far have you gotten, in the process?" Joe's voice was sterner than he meant it to be.

"I had all the papers together and managed to get them to our village and to Mariya. But she was afraid to bring them to Moscow. So, she waited... perhaps she knew best...look what has happened to her...to my family...to my Danyk! All because of their western ties, their relationship to me!"

Sam gestured and pointed an accusing finger that now rested on his own heart. "Every day I wake and ask God the same question... will I ever see them again? Sometimes I think he answers me...and the answer is no. In my heart, I think no. This makes me a bad father? I am weak."

Perhaps Danyk's father was more realistic than Joe had given him credit for.

"I cooperate fully. The United States government has asked me to pay for Danyk's board which I am glad to pay. But I am not a wealthy man. Soon, I will have nothing left to pay with. I keep asking, "Soon maybe my son will come home?"

"What do they tell you?"

"They say first the Soviet government must give permission. You understand, when Poland was claimed by the Soviet Union, they made all the people citizens. They do not recognize Polish citizenship...or American citizenship. This is mad...but Stalin is a madman! And my family is in his hands!"

Joe shook his head acknowledging more than perhaps even Sam knew, the insanity of it all!

"Oh... if I could do things over, so much I would change, so much I would do differently. I was so young and in such a hurry for my new life." Sam could not hide his own disgust with himself. Regrets are what make young men old, not time.

Then... he began from the beginning.

Speaking of it was therapeutic and once he began, he could not stop. Joe could have interrupted; he could have found an excuse to go. Instead, he listened intently, respectfully, as the puzzle pieces of this American story came together.

When he could, Joe filled in the gaps for Sam from recollections Danyk had shared with him of his mother's memories and from Danyk's own life living through a difficult time in world history as it unfolded. Sam absorbed every detail with rapt attention. Although Sam prayed otherwise, he knew that this conversation might be the most intimate contact he would ever have with his son. And so began the give and take.

Sam spoke first and began from the very beginning. It was necessary. He needed Joe to understand. He needed to speak of it all.

Finally, in one nutshell, so maybe he himself would understand and come to terms with what he had done.

This man carries a heavy load of guilt, Joe thought as he listened and read between the lines. It occurred to him that this American story was not just Danyk's, nor Sam's... nor even his wife, Mariya's. It was every American's. Imperfect, generated by hope for a better life and filled with human complexities.

"I was born Szymon Szafransky to Nyky Szafransky and Paranka Czornij on October 15, 1902, in Kobylija Poland. Or perhaps it was August 15th? Or maybe it was September? Well, it was one of them. Such a fact had not been important in my small village of Horonitza from which I had come.

Making it through the first year of life was important. Remaining strong and healthy to support one's family was important. Hard work, too. However, I had never given it much thought. For me, it was a way of life. It was the way men kept their pride in the struggle to get through each day. It was my way and my father's way... and his father's way before him.

Someday, it would be my children's way. I had never known anything else, nor thought to question it. Did I question the need to breathe air? To scratch an itch? Such questions would have been just as silly as questioning a man's duty and right to work hard for himself and for his family.

My village of Gorodnitsa, Province of Galicia (outside the provincial center of Ternopol) was once part of Austria-Hungry. The Polish victory led by Pilsudski during the Polish-Soviet War (1919-1920) had extended Poland's boundaries eastward after defeating the Red Army and now my Ukrainian village and homeland was under Polish jurisdiction.

Generation after generation had cleared the region's center of trees unveiling vast stretches of rich fertile soil that yielded a surplus of crops, grain, potatoes, sugar beets and rye. Herds of cattle, sheep, hogs and horses grazed the rolling, easy hills, the open meadows and the streams that meandered and flowed as crisp and clear and natural as the day God had created them.

There, I worked the land as a farmer and made $35 a month supporting myself and my young wife, Mariya. We had one child. But she had only lived a few days...

I did not have much education... a total of six years maybe in the village schoolhouse. But I did not feel uneducated. I was as educated as any other man of my class in my village.

I had built my own home from mud bricks that I had dried myself and I grew my own food. These were the everyday things that a man did to sustain himself and his family... perhaps you would not know from this...it is different in America.

I had married a sensible woman... my Mariya was a good wife...I loved her, and we were happy, but...I was informed enough about Polish politics to be quietly concerned. It made me think.

Which was where my troubles began!"

The Polish Royals had long maintained privilege and authority, restricting Ukrainian freedoms and expression of language and customs. For the most part the Royals remained the landowners and required the Ukrainian population, with limited prosperity, to pay high taxes. It was a difficult and at times resented but accepted way of life.

When Marshal Josef Pilsudski ruled as dictator, he allowed the Polish Royals to keep their status but also began economic and social reforms in education, transportation and communication. This allowed the long-suffering Ukrainian peasantry to recognize a world and way of life other than what they had known for so long. When Pilsudski retired in 1922 a series of coalitions arose but quickly fell, unable to meet and deal with the rising social and economic issues of the time. By 1926 Pilsudski had returned as a result of a military coup.

A new generation was awakening, not only to the unsteady beat of social and economic change in their own country but also to the music of the outside world industrializing. How did a small Polish farmer of Ukrainian descent fit into this changing world?

These things Szymon questioned. These things made him think. Was he destined to remain the subject of Polish royals who repressed his heritage, while he, a proud Ukrainian, worked their land only to be charged exorbitant rates to do so and with little profit or gain?

From June to December 1923, Szymon had fulfilled his obligation to serve Poland as a private in the cavalry. Now, four years later, he was a married man and though he had seemed to have begun the traditional path expected for a typical, young, Ukrainian farmer, he had never let go of a hope to change the direction of expectations for his life by following through on a dramatic decision.

The death of his first-born had been the sign he had needed. It justified and gave meaning to his dreams. This naturally conservative, cautious man made a bold decision; he must take the steps needed to provide better for his family.

In May 1927, following the footsteps of some other 200,000 Poles, Szymon Szafranski, then aged twenty-five, took what money he and his twenty-three-year-old wife, Mariya had managed to save and left Poland. Mariya stayed behind. They had only been married three years and like any other young couple, they did not like being separated, but it was only to be until Szymon got settled in Canada.

On May 27, 1927, the SS "Scotland" landed in Quebec and Szymon, a third-class passenger, stepped off to begin a new life among Ukrainian immigrants who had arrived earlier after WWI.

Like many other new immigrants, he found employment working for Gunderson Lloydminster in Alta, Canada doing what he knew best, farming. It required little English or French, though he used every opportunity to learn and master these new languages.

By the end of October, he was able to find work cleaning

windows with Swift and Company. Things seemed on schedule. He was now making $25 a week compared to the $35 a month he had made as a farmer in the old county. He filed an application for the immigration of his wife to Canada and sent for her. By July 1928 Mariya was on her way to join her husband in Montreal, Canada.

Just before Mariya's imminent arrival, Swift and Company ran into financial difficulty. Szymon, along with approximately twenty other employees, was laid off. How could he face his wife?

Unemployment lines were growing, and he had no way to support them. They had no family here. No real friends to turn to. Were they to find themselves worse off here than they had been back in the old country? He felt a growing sense of panic.

Then, he was presented with an idea. For $200 he could be smuggled into the United States. That was a lot of money, nearly two months' pay...but he had been assured that jobs were plentiful for hard-working foreigners in New York City. The long-term consequences were a cloud barely casting a shadow.

After living twenty-five years as the son of a Polish farmer who lived each day as it came, leaving Poland had been the biggest stretch of planning ahead he could manage. He turned to his youth and innocence to help him make his decision.

Americans themselves were also still at an innocent stage. It had only been four years earlier that firmer immigration laws had come into effect requiring visas to enter the country.

He came from honest people. He wondered ... why was it necessary to do something deceptive just to earn a living? Wasn't it his right to support his family? What else could a man do?

These complex questions were disguised by the simple workings of a young man's mind.

Thus, they received simple answers.

He was a man. A man did what a man must...he worked hard and provided for his family. They would go to America! It would be the point of no return for his family and for all the generations to follow him.

Would the answer have been as simple for his Mariya? Would she have felt the same?

He knew in his heart that she would do as he said. She had already left her homeland and widowed mother to follow him.

Forever, he would know that he alone had chosen their path. He alone would carry the way in which he had answered these questions for his family upon his shoulders, as though they were bags filled with the weight of the world. As time passed, he would wonder...try to remember... question his unsettled soul...had he even asked her?

As he spoke, he remembered. He wanted Joe to understand.

Then, maybe he too, could understand... and forgive himself.

Chapter 5

Szymom and Mariya Begin Life in America

I n August of 1928 they were smuggled in separately, first Szymon, then two weeks later, Mariya; both entered by way of Rouses Point, Niagara Falls without inspection.

By October 1928 they were both steadily employed and living in an apartment on 1st Avenue in New York City. Szymon was now working for Beaver Window Cleaning at 15 Whithall Street making $45.00 a week.

Mariya began working by cleaning houses. Shortly after, a wealthy Jewish family hired her as their housekeeper.

Szymon had spent a year in Canada, but Mariya's first taste of a new life was in America.

She found there was little here not to like.

As part of a Ukrainian enclave she found the comforts of both worlds. But most importantly she had been reunited with her handsome, young husband whom she had missed dearly. That alone made her new life colorful and alluring.

One could not miss the obvious differences in day-to-day life. Here, she did not live in a clay house with poor lighting and work a potato farm that left her muscles aching at day's end. Rather, she contributed to the income of her small family by caring for a kind-hearted employer and her husband. They often treated her to unexpected days off and generous gifts.

She found herself making friends and feeling as though she belonged. How needlessly worried her husband had been, when at first, she had been homesick. Eager to Americanize, she began going by the name of "Mary".

Back in the old country Mariya had buried her first child, a girl. She had lived for only a few days. Here, in America, "Mary" would deliver a strong healthy son...Danyk. He would be the first of her many children to be born in America, she was certain. Danyk was an American, natural born.

He had been given a strong Ukrainian name, a small connection to his heritage. But it was her full intent to extend their family's Americanization by nicknaming him Dan or Danny as soon as he grew into it. She would teach him and the other children that were sure to follow to serve America well. After all, America had done so much for them and she and her Szymon... her Sam, as he was now calling himself, were people that always repaid their debts.

Once there had been little opportunity for her husband to be anything more than a potato farmer...but here in America, hard work paid off far more quickly and assuredly than it did in the old country. Here her husband could be and do anything. The opportunity and pride shown in the way he held his shoulders back...his head high...carried his son, and even in the way she caught him gazing at her now and then.

Her handsome young husband was more beautiful now that their future held so much promise. Perhaps, now she too looked more beautiful to him, if that were possible.

Hope seemed to grow in this land of abounding prosperity as though it were a muscle, a part of them that they could exercise and stretch. With it came a growing strength to meet all the days to follow with confidence. As it bulged for the world to see, a sense of accomplishment and pride made them work harder still. This new life was one to grip hold of and not let go. And so, they did.

They would teach their children to embrace it too, yet also maintain and carry on the work ethic they had brought with them from the old country. And their children would teach their children. So, it would be as it always had been... for future generations to carry on the traditions of those who had come before them. Hard work had always been their way but here in America it was not just a means to survive. It meant profit and prosperity that one could touch and feel, and it generated a deep love and respect for a country that had given them precious opportunities. Endless hope... promise... strength...what greater gift could they have been given! What greater gift could they leave their children? America was the land that had blessed them!

By 1933, Danyk was two years old, and the Great Depression was on. It was not the best time for a young immigrant family trying to grab hold in an economically troubled country, but Europe's depression had hit a decade earlier and they were used to hard work and a simpler life already. It had prepared them to cope and make do with what they had... even appreciate it, while natural born Americans seemed flustered and even embarrassed by their new poverty.

"Sam" had been able to remain steadily employed as a window cleaner. Skyscrapers were popping up all over Manhattan and someone fearless enough to hang outside the building sixty stories up was needed to keep the windows clean. It was good pay for an immigrant; in fact, anything was good pay for an immigrant when so many were out of work.

It confused Mary to see so much luxury and fuss in a world that cried "DEPRESSION!" It seemed there were still a number of people that wanted and were able to enjoy the good life.

Her old-country upbringing told her she should not be impressed by new modern conveniences and the freer life-style which America offered.

But for a brief time, they were hers in which to experience awe and delight! She would lock them in her mind as treasured mementos, to later share with her child, after they'd aged and turned to memories, as the evidence, precious evidence... there was always hope of a better life.

She could spend hours looking out from their high apartment window with a view of the avenue below. At home in her village of Gorodnitski, the windows in her house were cutouts that barely let the outside light in, let alone the air. If someone had windows that were covered by glass, they would be considered especially fortunate, very well off.

In contrast to the primitive paths she'd walked on throughout her youth which became muddy and dough-like when it rained or covered over with slick sheets of ice in the winter, the tree-lined streets below were paved and lined with freshly lumbered telephone poles. Painted parking spaces were filled with automobiles.

Ford Model A's with beige leather seats, Blackhawk Sedans, Bianchi S5's, Morgan Three Wheelers, Bentley convertibles and most outstanding and impressive, the Piera Arrow models lined the streets and avenues. She, of course, did not know the name of even one. But each fine detail was recorded to memory as though she were looking at rare and fine museum pieces.

Back home they had one horse. If a heavy load needed to be moved, nearby farmers would pool their horses until the horsepower was adequate to complete the task.

Before coming to America, Mary had traveled everywhere by foot. Now she traveled in an underground train to work each day.

Food? One could now buy that in a store! No crops to plant and harvest! In fact, now she did not even have a place to grow a garden. But food was not only plentiful; there was tremendous variety from which to choose. Not only vegetables could be bought but delicious plump fruit, many she had never seen or eaten before. Her favorite was oranges. She could buy a dozen for 57 cents. There were strawberries and peaches, too. For as long as she lived, she would never forget the sweet juiciness of a perfectly ripe peach or the delicious punch that dripped down her cheeks as it was devoured!

There was also no need to milk a cow any longer to make butter. One could buy it at the store. A pound was 46 cents and worth every penny.

No longer did she need to climb down a root cellar to preserve food in its cool dampness.

Now, she marched up to her apartment and put it in a Leonard electric refrigerator. It had a small freezer compartment, no less. She had worried at first at its small size. How could one used to storing food in a large root cellar now store everything in such a small box? How quickly she learned to manage. In fact, she learned quickly with everything, it seemed.

Each morning, she now woke to an alarm clock. It not only told her exactly what time it was, it told her when to wake up. She no longer depended on a slight strip of light to make its way through the two small windows of her mud brick house, to tell that her day had started. Now she had a set time to start work...and more amazingly...a time to STOP work!

Anna and Volodymr Romanuke were kind employers, fortunate to still be wealthy when so many of their peers had faced financial ruin. Why they were spared, Mary would never have presumed to ask. She only knew they were charitable Jewish people who seemed to keep an eye on her and watch out for her during these difficult and vulnerable times.

Mary was a good and cheerful worker, proud to wear the starched black and white uniform they gave her to wear.

They rewarded her often. If she looked tired, they would treat her to a paid day off or a shortened work day on a Friday. Always, Mrs. Romanuke was mindful that Mary was a young mother and careful not to require her one moment longer than necessary. As it was, Mrs. Romanuke felt terrible that a young mother would have to leave her baby to work. As a general rule for the times, it simply wasn't done, but she understood Mary's circumstances and was as supportive as she could be.

When it was time to give away clothes, she gave Mary first choice. When she was done reading her magazine subscriptions such as Harper's Bazaar or Woman's Magazine, she gave them to Mary. Mary could not yet manage reading English, but Mrs. Romanuke knew how the young woman loved to look at the beautiful pictures. Mrs. Romanuke, being a sensitive woman, felt it was Mary's way of studying American culture. She was not only sometimes amused but also impressed with Mary's deductions.

When she, for a moment, would see the world through Mary's eyes, she too became befuddled at how a full-scale depression had not stopped Americans from focusing on what others might have considered frivolous. Fashion, music, movie stars? But did Mary really consider them frivolous? Sometimes, both she and Mrs. Romanuke wondered what she really thought.

It was difficult to remain closed and unchanged when the world one lived in was open-minded and in constant transformation. As one spun on, turning to and fro to the tides as they came and went, where was one to stop and self-reflect? When did one decide who they were or who they wished to become? What was to mold them, their past, their present or a bit of each? It was difficult enough just to be young, but to be a young, immigrant woman could be like trying to whistle and sing at the same time.

Always it seemed to be the old way versus the new. Here, women did not just put on a peasant dress and wrap a shawl over their shoulders. Shoes were not made simply to make one's way through the mud and snow. For women especially, they were delicate and sometimes awkward things, sometimes with high spiked heels. But...how attractive...how fun!

Cocktail dresses, satin evening gowns, slit skirts, hairpieces, pillbox hats and toques (small hats worn on the side of the head) were all the rage! Mrs. Romanuke occasionally even had her hair styled to go with a new toque. Browns and pinks, prune and turquoise, gray and powdered blue were the popular mixes of colors. Everything seemed to matter and make a statement... at least as to how fashion was portrayed in the magazines Mrs. Romanuke gave Mary.

Even underwear mattered! Mrs. Romanuke had drawers filled to match outfits. They often came in sets with lavish embroidery. Mary's hands often smoothed over the soft silk as she stacked them in the drawers. Catching herself, she would think, "What would my mother say, back in the old country?" Yet, she could not help having the dreamy girlish longings, though she hid them well, underneath her rational, practical immigrant sensibilities.

Joan Crawford? Greta Garbo? Bette Davis? Marlene Dietrich? Who was prettier?

More mysterious? Who would she choose to be if she could?

None of course. She was very happy with her life as it was. So happy... and so appreciative! But it was fun to dream and pretend, now that there were fun things to pretend and dream about.

Maybe she should treat herself to a nourishing night cream like Mrs. Romanuke used.

Could it really stop wrinkles? Should she consider lipstick? Should she pluck her eyebrows to a thin line? Mrs. Romanuke had trays filled with make-up, face powders, lanoline, tonics and nail polish. Most women, not just the wealthy, were considering them, too. The 1920's natural look was out. Make-up was in... for everyone!

Five and Dime stores carried the cheaper version of what used to be the wealthy's indulgences. She'd ask Sam what he thought...or maybe she wouldn't. In America a woman could have a mind of her own.

With savings Sam bought her a used, fairly new Tailor and Cutter 1931 sewing machine.

It even had a buttonhole maker. Now she could send away for Vogue, Butterick and Weldon patterns and make fashionable dresses for herself. Her first one would be a flowered print dress. Next would be a sailor suit for her Danyk. She would make him one larger than he needed now, to ensure room for growth.

It was exciting to know that one could be fashionable inexpensively in America...what a wonderful country! In America, even poor people could live rich lives.

For just a brief moment in time her dreams and reality had met. They had intertwined and been one. One was seemingly no different from the other. And as impressions of youth are known to do, they strongly imprinted on her the realness that heaven on earth did exist. Heaven could be found...in America.

Sam too, was invigorated here in America. Here, he felt like a man. Capable.

Confident. There was a security he felt like no other time in his life.

They liked him very much at his job. He had proven that he was responsible and could be trusted.

Life seemed almost perfect but for one thing.

They missed their families. Before America, the family had been a central part of their daily lives. Three brothers and one sister remained with Sam's mother and father. He was uneasy about them remaining there. Inflation and unemployment were high but his family, feeling no threat, had chosen not to come. Not yet anyway. Perhaps in time he could convince them.

Certainly, it was the one thing that did not delight his Mariya about coming to America. She did not like leaving her smaller family behind, especially her widowed mother. Although she never complained, Szymon knew it bothered her that her mother had never seen their son, Danyk.

Though they never spoke of it, he knew at times that both of them could not help but think of the baby girl they had left behind in the old country. She had not lived long past her birth and now rested in the slope of a hill by his village, amongst her many ancestors. It would be the only grandchild Mariya's mother might have to visit as she aged.

Conflicting emotions left him confused and unable to sort out or fully explain why he felt a sense of shame. Shame over her death?

Shame for leaving her behind? Or was the shame for selfishly bringing with him what he had... his wife, their promise of a joyous future... together, without those they'd left behind in the old country? It was an odd mix of emotions that he could not put into words, nor did he ever try to. Szymon was not a man to wear his heart on his sleeve.

Before Mariya had left for America she had given her brother, Marion, strict instructions concerning his care of their mother. He had properly nodded in assurance, smiled and vowed to follow her directions to the exact word. Of course, both knew that carefree, bold Marion would handle the affairs of his mother's aging in manly awkwardness.

Mariya had sighed heavily realizing their only hope was that Marion would marry a sensitive woman who would dote on her mother-in-law. Her brother, Paul, had left for France in the 1920's, leaving behind a depressed Poland for a chance at prosperity. Mariya often shared his letters home with Szymon. His words painted a colorful, exciting life beyond bleak Poland. In part, it was Paul's written words always murmuring themselves over and over in a young Szymon's mind that urged him to throw caution to the wind and pursue going to North America!

It had been a contradiction of his generally serious, always-two feet-on-the-ground persona that at first, had Mariya not taken his decision to immigrate seriously. She had laughed light-heartedly, as was her way, thinking that he was sharing some unattainable, wishful dream.

When he further announced that it was not to France to join her brother that he had in mind, but to Canada in North America, an ocean and a continent away, she realized she had better pay closer attention. Which she did, as he further explained the other details, large and small, that he had worked out carefully and meticulously.

Of course they would ask her mother to come, too. He had hoped that would be a convincing point, so he had left that for last. Then, he met her eye to eye and waited.

She knew this was her cue. The silence meant that he was asking, not telling her. She appreciated the courtesy, as it was not expected that a husband would ask his wife anything.

~

"I don't know if she'll be willing to go with us."

He gave her back a smile that she had never seen before and she took a long moment to admire and study it... remember it for always. He had just said, "Thank you!"

"But we will ask her anyway." Szymon had hoped to sound commanding, but he knew his perceptive wife had picked up the relief in his voice, as well.

When at first Mariya's mother had refused, he had given her credit for using common sense. After all, she was aging and not only would the adjustment to a new place be difficult but the journey itself would. He worried that she was too frail to make the trip, but most of all he worried that she wouldn't make it through customs. Once they had made it all that way, he would have hated to have to turn back. Better, he thought that they should establish themselves and then send for her later.

Only now there were unforeseen complications.

They had not remained in Canada. They had moved on to the United States of America.

Here, they were illegal.

He barely believed such a term could apply to his wife and himself, but in truth it did. Most days, it had no effect whatsoever on their lives. They went about their business. They worked hard, made friends with their neighbors and went about the day-to-day events of life as most decent people did. They had even had a new addition to their family, Danyk. Just like any other parents, they were anxious to give him a better life.

However, when Mariya reminded him of his promise to eventually send for her mother, it was a problem. They were better off, yes.

They were settled, yes. But still they were illegal and that meant they could not make an application for her mother's immigration.

Sam could sense Mariya's growing anxiousness. He worried that it was only the newness and excitement of this country that was distracting her and that a time would come when she would express her regrets and blame him. He believed in the back of his mind that her rush to replace their old life with a new one was her way of filling the emptiness that so many changes had created.

One did not give up all that they had ever known without a price. It was not that simple. For a time, it would help her accept their new life. But for how long before she resented him? Of course, they had both tried to convince her mother to come with them, but perhaps, should he have tried harder?

It was a hot summer night in 1933 when his regret would confront him...

Chapter 6

Beginnings of an Unsettled Soul

Sam took out his handkerchief and wiped the sweat from his neck as he climbed his way up the many steps of his 1st Avenue apartment. He'd done it so many times; he no longer gave each step any thought. When finally, he reached the last one, he returned the cloth to his pocket and began to stretch his muscles and arms in anticipation of his arrival home. It was always the brightest part of his day and a reason, in and of itself, for the day's tension to leave his body.

Danyk, Sam's two-year-old son, had already been seated for his dinner and was licking a slice of hard bread. A hearty potato soup boiled on the stove and after bending to kiss the top of his son's head he reached for a wooden spoon to stir and then taste the creamy delicious broth.

Mariya seemed oblivious, until he approached her, one hand cupping the spoon beneath and the other outstretched offering her a sampling. He watched as her mouth formed a delicate circle and blew at the steaming air rising from the mushy soup. She took a small taste all the while continuing to cut a large carrot. Only when he bent to kiss her neck did she stop. She looked up but not at him. Her head tilted just so, releasing a playful giggle and smile.

Ah, her smile! It did so comfort him and warm his heart. It was like a hearth that kept his home a cozy place, a haven to renew and refresh weary muscles and mental unrest.

It was a quiet uneventful evening. They had made their way through dinner with odd bits and pieces of conversation, usual things for a husband and wife to discuss. Danyk provided the only bit of excitement when he dropped mashed carrots on the floor and then gleefully pointed it out to his parents. One stooped to pick up a portion of the mess, the other reached to kiss his messy outreached orange palm and scold him simultaneously. Such was the way they worked together to teach and guide their young son.

It was a perfect evening. Messy carrots and all! It all just seemed to be the easiest part of life; the sharing of whatever came, being a family, feeling and giving love.

Keeping to the beat of their routine, the dishes were done, Danyk readied for bed and a calm darkness fell over the apartment. Propped before the apartment's oversized window were two chairs, one that rocked with a pitiful squeak and another with a straight high back, Mariya and Sam looked out on the avenue below, still steady with city life on a hot summer's night.

This was when she chose to tell him.

However, she said nothing. With her head lowered she pulled a familiar-looking piece of paper from her apron's pocket. It was a letter from her mother.

He could tell from the slant of her handwriting. What news did she have to tell? He had always looked forward to letters from Mariya's mother. She would update them on Mariya's brother, Marion, a big strapping young man who was most surely catching the eye of every marriageable young lady in the Village of Gorodnitsa.

Impatiently he grabbed the letter, eager to hear news from the old country. But there was something in the way Mariya had let go of the letter. Something in the way she kept her head lowered. He was not going to like what was in the letter, somehow, he was sure.

After he was done reading it, he stared out into the night. It was a while before he spoke.

"You're going back, aren't you?"

Her silence, as always, spoke to him and confirmed his fear.

"I don't understand why. Your mother has been ill before, she probably has already recovered." But the words were not meant to change her mind for he knew it was impossible to change a stubborn woman's mind. And his Mariya was a stubborn woman. She was also a kind and devoted daughter, a sweet and loving mother, a generous and giving wife...and she deserved more than him. Somehow, he knew he had failed her.

"My mother is alone now and needs me."

Already he was shaking his head, hoping that she would understand that there was no real need for her to explain herself. How selfish and ashamed he was to even consider asking her to stay. She whispered her last words so softly that the last could barely be heard. "But you are right, she will recover...it would only be one reason for me to return."

Yes, there was another reason. He knew how it hung over her, especially now because she was a mother herself. As a mother should...her child was now her first concern.

Mariya had not been certain that he had caught her last words but then... his back straightened just before he began and with a thick guttural accent, he spoke the charge in English so crisply that it hung in the air for a few moments before it evaporated away enough for her to respond.

"It ...is... be...cause ... we are il...legal." His tongue rolled out the words as if he were keeping to the beat of a drum. His face was firm and revealed much. She was startled to realize that he knew, had known for perhaps some time, enough to give it great thought. His understanding settled within her, and she felt a momentary relief until she realized she must confirm what he had deduced.

"Yes", she whispered.

Then, she spoke aloud her greatest fear.

"I'm afraid they will arrest you where you work." For the slightest instant her voice quivered but then she bravely regained her determination. "...And...Danyk and I would be left alone...or perhaps they would arrest me too, and no one would be here to take care of our son."

Both turned back to the room where their son slept as though they had suddenly been alerted to some danger from which they must protect him.

"If it were only me..." she hesitated, seeing how these words, known but never before spoken between them, wounded her husband, "...but it isn't just me and I fear for our son."

There was no argument in him, for he knew she was right. This very truth was the shadow that had hung over him like an evasive vision for many months.

"We are good people. We should not be living our lives in hiding. You know I love America, but this is not how our life should be. Not for us, not for Danyk."

He had done this, forced his family to separate again. He could blame no one but himself. His impatience was going to cost them greatly.

"You seemed to love America so." His voice trailed off with evident regret.

"I do. If I felt I had a choice, I would not go. When you've taken care of things, we will return".

We. Mariya and their son would both go of course. His heart ached. "Maybe, I will return with you."

It was an impulsive thought. Mariya knew he would too, if she accepted his offer. In the end, however, he would hate himself and perhaps her, as well. No, they must not make a foolish decision. He must stay for himself... and their son...and for her, as well. For she too loved America, it was her home now. In fact, she already ached to return to the home she had not yet even left.

"No!" she commanded softly. "You must stay. This is your dream, but mine too. You will stay and make our dreams come true. You will stay for both of us. When the time is right, you will send for us."

Her hand reached out and caressed his stubbled cheek as though it were smooth silk. Her eyes, too, caressed as they met his.

"But you will not wait too long?" She hid a smile as though to tease him.

"And you will promise that you will return?" His eyes, too, smiled, but in afterthought they grew quite serious.

Mariya backed away in shock and pushed him playfully to help him regain his common sense. How could he think that she would not return to him! But then, she also realized how his male pride was hurt. For him to have failed his family was a great shame. How could she reassure him that he had not failed her or their son? Neither of them could help their circumstances. They were just two people making their way in the world as best as they could.

"Remember...I love America, too! More importantly, I love you. This is not what I want. This is just what must be. It is what is right."

He held her tightly, cherishing her softness, as well as her incredible strength. That night, like no other before or since, he cradled his blessings.

He held and beheld. He stroked. He committed to memory.

He took in his fill of the tiny, rounded form beneath the blanket that slept. He breathed in the sweet smell of his son's hair as though it would be his last breath. He fingered the soft, warm curl of his young palm as it rested and flexed in sleepy innocence upon the crisp linen crib sheets. He molded Danyk's plump firm little cheeks with his thumb tenderly stroking with paternal pride and gentleness until he feared waking him.

Every detail mattered. Even the steady slumbering breath of his son was part of this song he must memorize and be the music in his life which would carry him, when what he cherished most was far from him.

And as for his young wife...he would surround her with

husbandly gentleness, as he had so many times before...and as he never had before! For she, in her selfless strong way, had given him a sense of home, order and determination.

When it seemed that the rest of the world was fast asleep, she would turn to him and snuggle in the closeness and safety of his arms. Pulling just far enough away for their eyes to meet, outlined by the streetlight shadows cast upon them, he would at once be struck by what he had wished most to find there and that which would break his heart!

Mariya's eyes spoke the truth he had sought these last few months. His Mariya did not want to leave!

What should have lightened his heart only made it sink to the depths of despair. What kind of husband puts his wife in such a position! Which decision was it that he alone had made to finalize his family's destiny? Was it the decision to leave Poland? The one to come to America? What moment or choice was it that he would take back if only he could? Of course, it didn't matter now. Destiny had been chartered. There would be no going off course.

A powerless, helpless feeling settled in his gut, and he knew it would remain there until his family returned. Until can sometimes be a very long time. He would need to be patient.

Never again, he vowed, would his boyish dreams and impatience cloud his judgments. Youth was now an old shoe that had worn thin.

All this, he froze forever as a memory, which he would revisit many times over the years to come. It would need to serve and satisfy him. As memories are known to do, it would bring him great comfort, as well as great pain. For in knowing all he had had, he would also know all too well, all he had lost.

It would be the beginnings of his unsettled soul.

Chapter 7

Mariya and Danyk Return to Poland

I t was Poland 1933. Mariya, now back in her native Poland and surrounded by people she had known since her childhood, returned to using the name she had been known by all her life.

The village women gathered to admire the photograph that Mariya now held in her outstretched hand. The attention made her feel an odd mixture of pride and shameful extravagance. Her young son looked so handsome in his white starched suit and the photograph would make a precious gift to her husband back in America. Still, she knew those gathered around her would not have thought to open their pocketbooks for such a frivolous commodity.

Well, she thought as she threw her shoulders back to receive their compliments and appreciation of her son, Danyk's captivating smile and well-mannered pose, my husband has no son to tuck into bed each night, as theirs do. But... he will have this beautiful photograph to touch and hold close to his heart.

She tried only to think of Sam's loss, but she could not help but to reflect on her own, as well. She was a mother raising a son alone, at least for now. How she wished it could be otherwise!

Tonight, she would write to Sam and tell him that all was well with them. The photograph, of course, would also help assure him of that.

She would tell him how the money he faithfully sent took care of all their needs and more! Indeed, it helped with their comfort greatly and she wanted him to know that.

His sensitive Ukrainian male pride had been hurt before she had left America, and she knew he would need to be reassured that his family still needed and depended on him. Which in truth, it greatly did. The support Sam sent, helped them live a privileged existence, at least compared to the average Ukrainian farmer, and other than the typical responsibilities of being a good mother to her young son, a caring daughter to her ailing mother and an overseer to a hired hand, she had little else with which to concern herself, besides of course missing her husband.

Over the many pages of her letter, she would remind her husband over and over again, how much she and Danyk missed him. She would never write the words she wished to ask most... have things been made right? When may we return? For she knew if he had answers, he would send them in his next letter. She was a good and understanding wife. She never asked for that which he might not be able to give, in every way she thought how not to offend his pride.

Mariya was always careful to include good news; she knew how Sam depended on her cheerfulness. This time her news would be very joyous! Her brother Marion had found a wife. Now when she and Danyk returned to America, her mother would have a daughter-in-law to pamper her. It would be one less worry for Mariya ... and one less reason for Sam to feel guilty.

In addition to sharing news with him of his mother, father, sister and brothers, she would also ask Sam's advice on everything just as she might if they were sharing their daily lives together. These questions mostly made Sam chuckle and endeared her further to him, as he knew she was just venting, thinking something through or perhaps just being polite. His Mariya had a mind of her own and although she always dutifully listened to his words of wisdom in the end, her decisions were generally independently and smartly made. For all her sweetness, she was a strong woman with a strong mind, and he wouldn't have her any other way.

Mariya always updated Sam on her mother's recovery, and he could sense that she did not feel burdened with the care her mother required, even when she remained ill for some time and in need of what seemed like constant care. She did wish there was better access to doctors here, as there existed in America. She had to depend on the older woman of her village to give her nursing instructions and advice. Thoughts that perhaps she should spend some of the money Sam faithfully sent her (approximately $35 to $50), on a doctor in the big city were quickly and repeatedly doused by her mother's insistence that she follow the old ways and practices.

She shared with him that there were things to appreciate in returning to one's homeland after one had left and thought never to return, especially when one returns with a bit of independence and the greater financial security that Sam's monthly allowances provided.

The countryside felt familiar as she compared it to the busy streets just out her apartment window back in New York. The people's smiles seemed friendlier as they were connected to her past and pulled the strings of her childhood memories. Day-to-day tasks reminded her of how eager she always had been to finish her chores so that she could visit with the other girls in the village or to meet Sam in the days when they were courting.

Was it better to let him know that there were benefits to returning to the old country, so he would feel less guilty? Or would it be better not to bring up such memories, which might make him dwell on a longing for home and family so far away? She was not always certain. So, her letters tottered back and forth between being heartfelt and revealing to being diplomatic and tactful. Sam, of course, could detect and appreciate both.

The Village of Goronitsa (also known as Horonitza) in which they lived was four kilometers east of Skalat. Through the village ran a river and next to the village was a big and beautiful, surrounding forest.

In addition to its 1,500 residences was a Greek Catholic Church, one store, a smith shop and one school. There was no electricity. People used kerosene lamps or just plain candles.

There was no natural gas to heat the houses or cook the meals. People had to use straw, wood or if they were lucky, coal to prepare their food and keep their houses warm.

There was no technology of any magnitude whatsoever. All farm work, the planting of seeds, working the land and harvesting the crops, which usually consisted of potatoes, wheat, rye, beets and buckwheat, was done by hand.

There were no factories in the village. People had to do everything themselves. They made thread from plants, then made the clothes by binding the cloth. It was a simple place, with simple ways, shared by a simple people.

It was not the life that Sam and Mariya now saw for themselves, but as a visitor, it was a way of life to appreciate.

Every family had a few chickens, perhaps a duck or a goose and a horse. The cow was considered the most important animal for the family as it provided most of the food, like milk, sour cream and cheese. The horse was used to help work the land and transport heavy material from place to place. Of course, Mariya and her mother did not have a horse, as there was no man to manage it. If there were a need, they would borrow one from the neighbors, offering some kind of trade in return for its use. Seldom was real money used.

Money could only be earned at the Polish Royal House. Twelve people and their families lived on the Royal property and worked full-time for the head of the village. He had a big piece of land with a forest and a mountain as well as a huge farm. At times, people from the village worked for him when it was time to harvest. In this way, they could earn money needed to pay their taxes and insurance.

The village Royal's job was to enforce all the laws and make sure everything in the village was managed well. He was also the local teacher. There were four classes in the school, and he taught them all.

At this time, when western Ukraine was colonized by Poland, Polish Royals were living in every village and city. In schools only the Polish language was permitted or taught. A student could be severely beaten for using the Ukrainian language. All books had to be written in Polish. Likewise, only Poles could be teachers. Hard measures were used to outlaw Ukrainian traditions, national clothing, holidays, and other forms of Ukrainian culture.

However, if one followed the rules and paid his taxes, one could sustain a meager existence as had generations of Ukrainians before him.

Most lived in a one-room mud house, where they cooked, slept and performed their other daily activities. The houses were old and patched, reflecting the generations who had lived in them before the present one. Often, there were no chimneys so many smelled of smoke and ash.

Limited supplies of food were stored in a side closet or storage room under the ground where it was to be cool all year round.

In the house they had a few pots and a few wooden utensils like spoons and forks. Generally, they didn't have tables, but they had a bench and a wooden bed, which could be covered by straw to make it more comfortable. Those particularly industrious might make a bed of feathers.

Mariya's father had been one such industrious peasant who took pride in his home and providing for his family. She thought of him when she opened the front door to her mother's home. She remembered the day her father, now long dead, had proudly placed it on its hinges after a day of sawing, carving and sanding. Everywhere she turned there was a face or a memory bringing comfort. Yes, it was good to be able to return to the land one had come from. At an odd moment she might even wonder why she had once longed to leave.

Why had she hurried away so quickly... from her mother, who now seemed so all alone... from her helpful neighbors... from this simpler life, where she did not have to leave her household and work for another? Here she could stay home and tend to her young son herself. Yes, she saw things from a different perspective now. It must be motherhood that gave her these insights.

She remembered now that there had been moments of doubt when she questioned the decision to leave all she had ever known, but she had wanted to join her young husband in his new life of opportunity. She had done her best to leave without looking back. How odd, that she had to return home before she would permit herself to be homesick!

However, these thoughts were only fleeting, not enduring. For just as she had felt attachment for her homeland, she heard her new home calling her back, anxious for her return. There too, awaited her husband ... and her bond to him, she felt even more strongly. Life was not simple, was it? For such a young woman, her life was filled with many questions.

She missed her husband dearly! How could they continue to grow their family if they were separated? As much as this old world offered, her new world offered change and challenges... and a new life, with the husband that she was so anxious to begin it with.

She was not a fool and she realized that the life she now had in her village was somewhat different from the one she once had, before she'd left. Now, she had the money that Sam faithfully sent her. It gave her security, as well as respect. Without it, life would have been uncertain.

She would have had constant worry. Would the winter be too harsh? Would they be able to afford the coal that would be needed to stay warm? Would the summer be too dry and yield a poor harvest?

Life's events and celebrations continued to happen. She did her best to make Sam feel a part of it, but she also knew in doing so, she was telling him what he was missing. There was no easy answer.

In Sam's letters he expressed growing concern for the mounting unrest growing throughout Europe. Certainly, Mariya thought American newspapers had to be exaggerating the threat.

Here, in their little village of Gorodnitsa, little had changed. In fact, with the money Sam sent, life was quite comfortable.

She was more concerned with the reports of massive starvation just over the border in the USSR, just a few kilometers away. Stalin had imposed a "five-year plan" on the Soviet people beginning in 1928 and ordered that private farm be organized into collectives. These were large farms where everyone worked together...for the state.

Kulaks, the rich peasants, were not happy to comply. They did not want to lose their farms, some of which had been in their families for generations to the communist government. They had tried to resist by under-producing or killing off livestock rather than handing a profit to the state and receiving little for themselves in return. The price for their resistance was a heavy one indeed...massive starvation.

Disturbing reports circulated that the famine had been so great that some had even turned to cannibalism, but it was difficult to be sure what was true and what was not. Communication with the area was difficult.

Laborers were restricted to the farm on which they were assigned and were severely punished if they talked to foreigners. Any such reports had to be smuggled out at great risk.

If they were smuggled out, the USSR shrugged off the reports, responding that they were a progressive nation on the verge of a great industrial modernization.

The rest of the world had to be satisfied with the USSR's response. What else could they do? But local people, protected only by an invisible border, found mounting evidence that their fears were true. They, like the rest of the world, did not want to believe that such a fertile land within kilometers of their own was not producing enough to keep its people from starving. It simply didn't make sense!

But they, like the rest of the world, were learning what the Soviet Union under the tight control of Stalin was like. In years to come, Stalin would remember that the area was a vulnerable one, as it was difficult to maintain or minimize outside contact or influence. He would hold it with obsessive suspicion and paranoid control.

Mariya always tried to reassure Sam in his letters. Surely, he had to see that Poland's strength and national pride were growing stronger, not weaker. She had hoped that the 1933 Non-aggressive Act between Poland and the USSR would ease his fears and concerns about their strange and secretive neighbor to the east, but of course she knew it would not, as his worrying was nothing new between them.

He had always been the more serious of the two. Easily she interpreted his carefully expressed concerns, worded to minimize the chance of frightening her and detected that his political barometer was irritated. Sam, she was sure, was keeping a watchful eye on the Soviet Union from America, for all the good it would do him...or her!

As Mariya would have guessed Sam filled his days with working and his nights thinking about his family. He read the Ukrainian/Polish newspaper meticulously each night dissecting news about his country, as well as various reports measuring Hitler's aggression. He knew that Poland was once again very vulnerable, just as it had been during World War I, a war from which it had not even yet fully recovered.

Each night, as his eyes scanned the reports of the mounting tensions in Europe, the news left a gnawing uneasy pain which stayed with him throughout the following day and into the next. His stomach churned like winds foretelling a coming storm.

If his Mariya were there with him she would have cautioned him that his wayward thoughts only stirred up trouble particularly for his sensitive stomach. She would have teased him and made him laugh. Oh, how he missed the way her presence seemed always to dissolve life's problems. How he missed her humor and strength!

While thoughts of his homeland and his family made him spin with contradictions of a man with a purpose, to a man set apart from what made him whole, his feelings about America continued to grow steadily.

Ever since Franklin Delano Roosevelt had been elected, the economy had continued to strengthen. He liked the way President Roosevelt had set a good example for the rest of the county. Instead of going to his Inaugural Ball he'd gone straight to work. That was a work ethic and a man he could respect. President Roosevelt worked for the people, all the people, even a regular working man like himself. That said something for this great country, which was now his, too ...almost.

He continued to submerge himself in his work, faithfully sending Mariya and Danyk an allowance each month. He hoped that somehow providing them with a comfortable life back in the old country would make up for the fact that he had not yet been able to send for them. It was not going to be as easy as he had hoped to make things right. If they had arrived in America just four years earlier it would have been different, but they had not, and the new immigration laws were not going to be as forgiving about their illegal entry as those which applied to the many who had come before them.

It bothered him terribly that he was missing Danyk's earliest years, but what else was he to do? Return? His heart knew this was not the answer for himself or his family. He must forge on and somehow fulfill his promise...meet his destiny, their destiny. It was a course set, with no path to alter it.

Driven by terrible loneliness for his family and hope of saving enough money to hire an immigration attorney, he worked extra hours and began an apprenticeship to learn how to be a shoemaker. His employer was an older man and he hoped that at some point he could buy the business from him. That would make him an established businessman. Then America would want him! Then he would have proven he was worth having.

After a while, the weeks became months... and the months became years. His long-distance relationship with his family was just a fact of life, one shared with the many other immigrants who had come during this time period, determined to work hard, sacrifice for their families and make the most of this wonderful, once-in-a-lifetime opportunity.

Meanwhile, his eye was ever watchful on what was happening in Europe, particularly in his homeland, Poland. He couldn't help but note that with Pilsudski's death came a more authoritarian constitution. Pilsudski had been a heavy-handed dictator. However, he had been respected as a patriot and had brought enormous and much needed social and economic reform. With him the country saw improvement in agriculture and communication. Now that he was gone, it seemed the government was regressing to the traditional forces of the army. It was these steady changes and unexpected dynamics that had prompted him to leave Poland in the first place and left many Ukrainian Poles desirous of an independent Ukraine.

The rest of Europe, too, was seeing changes. Germany had enacted the Nuremberg laws taking citizenship away from Jews. Jews could no longer marry or do business with non-Jews.

Back in the old country, in Sam's village there had been only five scattered Jewish families.

Events in history, hundreds of years long past, when Jews were forbidden to own property and forced to live in designated areas had limited or perhaps more accurately, dictated to a large extent the economic, social and political structuring of the Jewish population in his homeland.

Jews had been forced to turn from farming to other means of earning a living, most often relying on an innovative kind of trading structure, using bargaining and negotiating to trade up for profit of crafts or handy works. Later, with industrialization and periods of tolerance and acceptance, their products had become more sophisticated and worldly. To maintain this structure, the Jews tended to live close together in contained areas not only maintaining their culture and traditions but flourishing.

The Jews that Sam had known were farmers as he had been. Their families had, generations before, somehow managed to go unnoticed during anti-Semitic sweeps and had kept hold of their properties and farms perhaps because of the remoteness of their location. They struggled with their daily existence as he and his family had. Their families shared intertwined histories and neighborly concerns.

A much larger population of Jews, approximately 7,000 lived near a synagogue in Skalat. Historical necessity had made them a prosperous business community.

Since the beginning of civilization man had farmed, using the land to materialize and provide for his needs. The Jews, like most of the population of the world, were also farmers. They might have been satisfied to remain so, had various challenges not been put before them time and time again, due to the whims and anti-Semitic dictates of the various powers that had been throughout history.

In 1825, Nicholas I began a particularly difficult time for Jews, taking large numbers and relocating them to Pales, and displacing them from their traditional occupations. Jews, forced to be creative and cunning, began to develop a system of pedaling and trading to survive and eventually even prosper.

Fifty years later an enlightened Russian society began to coax Jews from isolation where a unique culture, form of education and networking had begun to develop. Remaining suspicious and guarded to maintain their own values, the Jewish community began to integrate and contribute to the general society. Individuals even began to drift and rebel from the strict influence of their Jewish communities as they became more comfortable with the outside world.

The networking, such as credit and loan associations established by the Jews earlier to support each other and maintain their survival in a hostile world was beginning to be appreciated and adapted to the infrastructures of mass movements. Young Jews looked to follow their own aspirations and started to move out of their Pale settlements, which felt restrictive and forbidding. However, following the death of Tsar Alexander II the hopes for escape and enlightenment were lost.

Anti-Semitic feeling was revived and encouraged. Jews were once again restricted and forced back into the Pales, which were to become known as ghettoes, shtetlekh (shtetlach or shtetel) or hamlets. Once again, laws restricting them would threaten their livelihood. The Jews who had turned from a livelihood of farming, when laws restricted them from owning land to occupations in business, were now barred from heavy industry.

Again, how was the Jew to earn a living? A cottage industry was to develop. As the political borderlines between Russia, Poland, Hungary and Austria were redrawn time and again, the Jews were to form pockets, cohesive communities aware of the outside world, but largely unto themselves in terms of values, culture and adaptability. Their cottage industries would turn into small thriving workshops specializing in handicrafts and later, with modern industrialization, they would grow into modest factories, tanneries, lumber mills and machine shops. The Jewish labor force would flourish due to their own resourcefulness as traders, storekeepers, peddlers and money managers. By the end of the century the typical Jew lived in an urban, though self-contained, area.

Sam's neighbors then, were not typical. However, these few Jewish farming families of Sam's village that seemed to be more like him than not, had given him his only reference or view of what or who a Jew was before he had left Poland for North America. Those that lived in his village were simple farmers like him. No better... no worse. Generations had lived side by side. Their lives had intertwined as those of all neighbors did, and much was taken for granted. Births and marriages were celebrated; deaths were mourned. The important events of everyday life, they shared together except for one. The Christians went to one church, the Jews to the synagogue. It was not such a big difference.

Once a month, his neighbor Kupetsky traveled to the industrial regions of Poland to trade with Jewish businessmen. For his farm products he could negotiate fair bargains and return with ready-made products which otherwise would take his wife many hours of hard work to produce. His friend Kopetsky seemed to have no problem with these Jews.

His Mariya had worked for a wealthy Jewish family as their housekeeper before she had returned to the old country. She would sometimes return with stories of their customs and holidays that were different from their own. However, after living amongst immigrants from all over Europe and even elsewhere, everyone's customs were different. They seemed to be very good to his Mariya. That was good enough for him.

He did not understand these Nuremberg laws. What was the purpose? He knew he was a simple Polish immigrant of Ukrainian heritage. He only had six years of education. Still, he shook his head with the stupidity of it.

On March 16, 1935, Hitler announced the military draft and the world, now alerted, seriously contemplated his design and purpose. He would deny aggressive intentions. However, his actions indicated otherwise.

In 1937, Sam received news that his father, Nyky Szafranski, had died.

The news left a hole in Sam's heart. By the time he read the letter he knew his father had already been buried on the slope of the hill near his village, where his ancestors and baby girl also rested in eternal peace. His family would have already gathered to share support and comfort his gentle mother.

She would be left with a young daughter to raise, though he was certain his young strong brothers would step in to care for and help them both. He, far away, a world away, would grieve alone. He would not be able to offer comfort or receive it.

The rough paper he held tightly in his calloused hands was his only connection to them. "He had not suffered; it had been quick," Mariya had consoled him. He read the words over and over, hoping they would fill him, and the hurtful emptiness would be eased. They only made him hunger for his family more.

He had not seen his father since the spring of 1927, but it was not the image of their final farewell that crowded his mind, as he, in solitude, mourned his death. His father had been a small man in stature but had had broad muscular shoulders upon which Sam had been carried often as a small child. There had been no safer place to view the world than from that throne. His father had been a wise man of few words, who had a way of summing up life's complexities and challenges simply, to keep their weight in proper perspective.

He had understood his son's desire to leave the old country and search for a better way of life perhaps more than anyone else, including Mariya. He had not been happy to see his son go but he had understood. It was probably the best gift his father or anyone could ever have given him.

Sam would miss this small man whose patted assurances were enough to send him across an ocean to fulfill his dreams.

This terrible grief, he would bear alone. It wasn't that Sam had not made good friends. He had found a circle of hard-working Ukrainian immigrants like himself. They shared their common concerns about establishing themselves and their families in a new community.

They could remember the old country together and understood the "old ways" that were sometimes relied upon because of their familiarity or habit. They were a comfort to be with and allowed him to retain some sense of home and the past. But with little exception, he had been the only one with no family member in America.

At this time, especially with the world events which were about to surround him, it was a lonesome time.

On March 17, 1936, Hitler took Rhineland, disregarding the 1920 Treaty of Versailles.

Hitler had already rearmed Germany and now appeared to be pursuing fulfillment of his plan outlined earlier in the text of his book, Mein Kampf. It foretold of rebuilding Germany, reduced significantly as a result of losses after World War I, by a series of German conquests.

Was Hitler next intending to reclaim land lost after World War I, including his homeland of Austria? Then, move on to the Polish corridor of Czechoslovakia's and the Russian Ukraine?

Hitler would deny it all, but a suspicious world did not believe him. Nor were they courageous enough to confront him.

In 1938, Hitler, using intimidation, issued an ultimatum to avoid bloodshed and forced Austria's President Miklas to order Chancellor Kurt Schuschnigg to resign and leave the country.

Hitler's troops marched in without resistance. Austria was now his.

The Jewish pogroms would begin.

Chapter 8

Waiting for News

Mariya now addressed Sam's letters to 433 East 15th Street. He no longer lived on 1st Ave. in the apartment they had shared together as a family.

The extra space was no longer needed as it was only for him, and he wanted to save as much money as he could. Leaving it however, was difficult. Before making his final exit he had taken a moment to survey the room and allow it to freely conjure up memories of his Mariya and Danyk, when they had last shared a life together. It was beginning to seem like many lifetimes ago.

It was around this time that Sam's letters began to change. They became gentler and reassuring which for his wife, Mariya who knew him so well, was a red flag that something was terribly wrong. Sam was not one to put his emotions on a page. His usual letters asked about their son and her mother. He'd offer advice about the crops and tell her how he was working long hours and saving money "to work things out" as he would put it.

She knew his general nature was to worry, this she expected. But she was now concerned that his worrying was getting the best of him.

Only she, who understood him before he spoke, could have read between the lines.

The news he was hearing back in America was surely exaggerated. Sam was frightened for her, Danyk and the rest of their family! Between each line she read that he was asking her to leave the area and somehow come to him. His sense of helplessness and powerlessness was evident, though he had tried to conceal it. These would not be easy emotions for a proud Polish farmer of Ukrainian descent to endure. It broke Mariya's heart and reminded her of the great distance there was between them as well as the years that had passed separating them further.

Though Mariya intuitively picked up much of what Sam did not tell her directly, there was still much she did not know. There were some things, at least, from which he could protect her.

In April of 1938, he had heard that Immigration authorities were making inquiries about him. The time had come, he'd thought, to let his whereabouts be known. At worst, he would be sent back home, and as current events were unraveling daily perhaps, it was where he could best serve his family. He would leave it to America to decide for him. Was he worth having or not? Finally, he would know.

Almost five years after Mariya and Danyk returned to Poland, Szymon Szafransky turned himself in to Ellis Island. Later that same day, he was released on a $500 bond.

Also, what Mariya did not know was that Sam was being treated for a "nervous stomach" and had been hospitalized in August of 1938 for an emergency appendicitis.

At an August 17th Immigration hearing on Ellis Island he weighed only 140 lbs., 30 less than his usual weight. She also might have been startled to see that his brown hair was now gray.

Sam followed the clerk into the hearing room. A neat looking woman was stationed to the side and as Inspector King began his questioning, the woman began to lightly tap on the keys of the machine. It made a tick-tick-tack sound responding to the gracefully flowing movements of her hands which were centered into place by unmoving wrists.

For a moment he was distracted. Then, the questioning began and he was startled to full attention. He needed to concentrate intensely to make sure he interpreted what was being said accurately.

As he did so, the clerk relentlessly taped out and recorded his exact words for official documentation. Had Sam realized how precisely she was transcribing, it would have challenged his nerves even more.

The drill began.

~

"What is your full name and correct name?"

"Sam Szafransky." (Spelled Sem Szofransky in original documents) "Have you ever used or were you ever known by any other name?" "No."

"Where were you residing at the time of your arrest?"

"33 East 15th Street, New York City."

"When were you born, and what is your race and nationality?"

"Horonitza, Province of Galicia, Poland, in August or September 1902, Ukrainian race, Polish nationality."

"When, where, and how did you last enter the United St

"August or September 1928, at Niagara Falls, New York, without inspection."

"I now show, and serve upon you, read and explain to you Department Warrant of Arrest No. 55983/643, dated August 17, 1938, and advise you that you are now in custody charged as follows: that you have been found in the United States in violation of the Immigration Act of an unexpected immigration visa. You are advised that you will be granted a hearing under this warrant to enable you to show causes, if any there be, why you should not be deported. At this hearing you will have the privilege to be represented by counsel, at your own expense and of your own selection, which counsel may be an attorney at law or any person of good character and reputation. Do you fully understand the charge in the warrant and your right to representation?"

"I understand. I don't want a lawyer."

"The warrant for your arrest provides for your release from custody pending final determination of your case, upon furnishing a bond in the sum of $500. Do you understand?"

"Yes, I understand."

"At the time you entered the United States from Canada in 1928, were you in possession of an unexpired immigration visa?"

"No."

"Have you resided in the United States continuously since your arrival in 1928?

"Yes."

"Were you ever in the United States previous to 1928?"

"No."

"Did you ever pay head tax?"

"No."

"Are you married?"

"Yes."

"What is your wife's maiden name and where was she born?"

"Mariya (recorded as Marie by court reporter) Slobodzin, born in my native town.

"When and where were you married?" "May 1925 or 26, in my native town."

"Was this your first marriage?"

"Yes."

"Have you any children?"

"One."

"What is your child's name and place of birth?"

"Daniel, born in New York City."

"Where is your wife at the present time?" "Poland."

"When did she leave for Poland?"

"In 1933."

Did she take the child with her?"

"Yes."

"When did she come to the United States?"

"Two weeks after I did, and in the same manner as I did."

"What is your wife's address in Poland at the present time?"

"My native town."

"Does your wife intend to return to the United States?"

"My wife went back because she came the same way as I did and was afraid to stay here."

"Have you any near relatives in the United States?"

"No."

"What is your father's name, place of birth, and present whereabouts?"

"Nyky, born in Kobylija (Kobyla) Poland, now deceased and buried in my native town."

"What is your mother's maiden name, place of birth, and present address?" "Czornij Paruka, born in my native town and now living there."

"Have you any other near relatives in your native land?"

"I have three brothers... Mike... John, and... William, living in my native town."

"What schools did you attend in your native town?"

"Public school for about six years in my native town."

"What is your religious faith?"

"Roman Catholic."

"What church did you attend in your native land?"

"The Catholic Church in my native town."

"Were you baptized there?"

"Yes, but I don't know the name of the church."

"What was the name and address of your last employer in your native country?"

"I worked on my own farm."

"What was your last address in your native country?"

"My native town."

"What date did you leave that address the last time?"

"About May 2, 1927."

"Where did you go from there?"

"To Canada."

"When did you arrive in Canada?"

"At Quebec, Canada, May 27,1927, on the S.S. Scotland, as a third-class passenger."

"Was your wife on the same ship?"

"No, she came one year later."

"Have you ever been arrested in the United States or any other country?"

"No."

"Have you ever been an inmate of any public hospital, or any other public institution supported by public funds?"

"No."

"Were you ever on home relief or on W.P.A. work?"

"No."

"What is your employment?"

"Window cleaner."

"Where are you employed?"

"Beaver House Window Cleaning Company, 24 Stone Street, New York City."

"How long have you been so employed?"

"Five years."

"What is your salary?"

"$41 a week."

"Have you any other source of income?"

"No."

"What money or property have you in the United

"I have $2,200 in the Chase National Bank." Sam presents his passbook, and the following is recorded: No. 475420, Chase National Bank, 11 Broad Street, New York City, showing deposits as of August 16, 1938, of $2200.61.

"Have you any other property in the United States?"

"Clothing and personal effects at my home address."

"Did you ever attempt to become a citizen of the United States?"

"No."

"Have you a passport, birth certificate, or any other evidence that would establish your nationality?"

"No."

"What have you to say in your own behalf as to why you should not be deported from the United States?"

"I like this country and I can make a living in this country. I didn't do anything wrong."

"I now advise you that under the Act of March 4, 1929, as amended, you will, if ordered be deported and thereafter enter or attempt to enter the United States, be guilty of a felony and upon conviction be liable to imprisonment of not more than two years or a fine of not more than

$1,000 or both such fine and imprisonment, unless you, following your departure from the United States in pursuance of an order of deportation, receive permission from the Secretary of Labor to apply for admission after one year from the date of such departure. Do you understand?"

"Yes, I understand."

Now the tick-tack-tick-tack sound had stopped. In its place were the echoing taps of his footsteps as he made his way down the stone steps of the public brick building. His lone footsteps seemed set apart from the world, as he himself felt.

He needed to begin to say good-bye to this country. He had failed.

He had not kept his promise to Mariya to make everything right. In fact, everything was very much not right. Like a man, he must face this.

His feet were on their own path, as though they knew Sam's mind was too preoccupied to follow for himself. They led him down West 6th Street and stopped at number 322. It was still a bit early in the day for his friend to be home from work, so he made himself comfortable on Mike Shegren's front stoop. The summer heat had warmed the steps, so he lowered himself cautiously.

Mike's wife took notice of him from her kitchen window, which was open, wide and unscreened in the hopes that the hot stagnant air in the apartment would find its way to the city street instead. She called out to him.

"Sam, what are you doing out there? Mike will be a while... but you can come in." Her accent was as thick as his own. She motioned as though she was about to head for the door, but he quickly stopped her.

"No, no I'll wait here, it's too hot to be inside, and besides you are busy making your dinner."

Sam settled in. He bowed his head and fixed his gaze on a wide crack in the sidewalk.

She could tell that all was not well, but she decided not to press him. Today, she knew he had gone to his hearing at Ellis Island. News, bad or good, he would want to share it with Mike first. So, after giving him a concerned look she turned back to her chores, hoping that Mike would be home soon.

Sam had befriended Mike just a month before, after the two had taken a strong, immediate liking to each other. He had not gone to search for other friends he'd known longer like Charles Biernak who also lived on West 6th Street or Stephen Lefko whom he had known since 1935.

No, it was Mike, his new friend, who he could trust to give the soundest advice. He was smarter, had greater vision and common sense. Hadn't he been smart enough to become an American citizen already?

Mike was two years older than Sam. In a way it made him the "older brother" of the two. Since they had met, they had shared many memories of their homeland. Though Mike was from Wolodymrci,

Poland and Sam was from Gorodnitsa, they were both from the Province of Galicia and it added to their initial bond and developing friendship.

It was close to six o'clock in the evening by the time Sam saw Mike walking down the paved street. As soon as Mike saw Sam notice him, and then lower his head downward, he knew Sam had come to share an unfavorable outcome of the hearing.

Sam choked out the words as though he could hold them in no longer. "I have ninety days".

Mike did not need this explained to him. He understood. His friend had been given ninety days to leave the country.

"I'm so sorry, my friend." It was the best that Mike could do as he shared his friend's regret. Mike's arm reached up and made its way around his friend's shoulder. There on West 6th street the two men embraced on this hot New York City evening and mourned a great loss together.

Sam had not yet told Mariya about his scheduled immigration hearings, nor that his deportation seemed inevitable. He simply could not bring himself to do so. No, not yet.

But his letters since spring had never-the-less carried sentiments of a depressed heart between the lines and Mariya was quick to pick up on them. In a moment of weakness, Mariya let a letter dated September 1938 bear her inner thoughts.

"Life," she told him "...was unfair! We should be together raising our son..." Sam silently blessed her for validating his own similar feelings, "...but, until that is possible, we will both need to be strong. Besides, Danyk and I are fine!" Her courage and brave words were medicine for a spirit weakened by his physical state and emotional turmoil. It was the best she could do. For Sam it would be good enough, as it had to be. One day would continue to lead to the next.

Hitler now wanted democratic Czechoslovakia!

European leaders gathered in Munich in the fall of 1938 hoping to avoid war at all cost by appeasing Hitler with what was to become known as the Munich Pact.

The agreement, reached without Czechoslovakian presence, participation or approval was decided by Italy's Benito Mussolini, France's Edouard Daladier, Britain's Neville Chamberlain and Hitler. The compromise or verdict was that Czechoslovakia was to be divided into three segments.

Hitler would get one-third of Czechoslovakia's land and population, while the rest would be divided up between Poland and Hungary, who also claimed to have rights to the area.

Czechoslovakian leaders, feeling abandoned by France's backing out of their agreement to defend them from Nazi Germany and in avid protest to their forthcoming fate, had refused to attend or witness the designs of their own doom. They had not been given any choices or say and their frustrating helplessness was captured in media headlines that couldn't help but embarrass the world. Who was the bully, anyway?

Neville would return to Britain claiming, "Peace with victory!" Churchill, more suspicious and distrustful of Hitler made a prediction, "Don't suppose this is the last of it!"

The rest of the world waited, hoping disaster had been avoided.

However, six months later, in March 1939, against his word...Hitler marched into what was left of Czechoslovakia... and took it.

Mike had not only become a trusted friend to Sam but a valued advisor. Quite a bit more Americanized and much less intimidated by the immigration services, he helped Sam connect with the International Migration Service and made sure Sam exhausted any and all opportunities to remain in America before giving up.

Sam had of course begun the process of securing a passport from the Polish Embassy in December of 1938 and booking passage home to the old country, should his efforts in the end be fruitless.

A month before, Sam had received official documentation from the Assistant Secretary of Labor and Chairman of the Board Review that his order of deportation would not be entered at this time. Its recommendation read:

"In view of the circumstances in this case, an order of deportation be not entered at this time, but alien be informed that he is required to depart from the United States, to any country of his choice, within 90 days after notification of decision, and to make arrangements with the local immigration office for verification of departure; that unless he does so depart an order of deportation will be entered and deportation effected, in which event he will not, under existing law, be eligible to apply for entry into the United States until after one year following the date of deportation, and then only if the Secretary of Labor has authorized him to apply for admission.

Departure in accordance with the foregoing will be sufficient to cancel the outstanding bond."

~

"Does this mean I must go... no hope to stay?" Sam reached across the dark mahogany desk to hand Miss Larned the official looking letter.

Mike was seated next to him. Both men respectfully held their hat in their hand. Sam could not help but to repeatedly turn his as though he did not expect to be staying long.

Miss Larned kindly reached across the desk's middle and gently smiled, not yet sure of what the letter would hold. Every day, vulnerable people entered her office at the International Migration Services looking for help. Each time she hoped she could offer some.

"I see that you have just received this; it's dated just a few days ago."

"Yes, I just got it; Mike said I should take it and show you. He says you'll know if I got to go or maybe stay."

Miss Larned smiled at his accent, which made his words seem difficult to get out. "Well... let's see..." she patiently reviewed its contents. Then, she reviewed it word by word to make sure that Sam, too, understood exactly what it said.

To clarify even further, his friend Mike, seated attentively by his side, would repeat the simplified English in Ukrainian, until Sam nodded, indicating his complete understanding.

"I do indeed believe there is a possibility that Mr. Szafranski could avoid deportation and even apply for citizenship." Miss Larned spoke cheerfully as she continued to review other forms and documents that she had requested Sam bring with him to the meeting.

At her announcement, both Sam and Mike straightened higher up in their chairs. Sam turned to his friend, gleaming tremendous gratitude for him having provided an avenue of hope.

Mike, in turn, took a relieved and sighful breath, for until Miss Larned had spoken these hopeful words, he was not sure if he had only given his friend false hope.

"The fact that he has been in the country for over twelve years, consistently maintained his own support and that of his own family, as well as a sizable bank account, should certainly support his case. You've also provided me with excellent references from various employers and respected members of the community. I also see that you have an American born son, Mr. Szafransky? Umm... I see he and your wife, they aren't with you; they are back in Poland?"

There was a bit of disappointment in her voice.

"Yes, they are waiting for me to send for them, after I make everything all right, then they come!" Sam ended with a huge, child-like smile.

Miss Larned could not help but return one. Then, she forced herself to be serious and brutally honest. "What of course, may work against you is that your family is not here with you. They've returned to Poland, and I assume they are established there? Also...." She could not help but be affected by the sad change in his expression.

"Mr. Szafranski, please, don't be discouraged. I need to be honest with you. There are no certainties here, but I do believe there is hope." Instantly, his face brightened again.

Miss Larned carefully and honestly reviewed what she saw as the reality and status of his situation.

"The most difficult point to overcome will be the fact that you were smuggled into the United States without inspection."

Sam felt compelled to explain himself. His pride would not allow him to sit silently while she perhaps thought the worst of him.

"At the time, I did not understand the seriousness of my actionsI had been told that many had done this before me... I was so new to being here, I was not sure of another way to go about it... and I needed a job quickly... my wife had just arrived from the old country."

"Mr. Szafranski, I can not condone your actions. The law is the law. And the law requiring inspection took effect four years before your arrival." Her soft voice did not carry the same harshness as the words she spoke.

"But in this country, every man may plead his case. We are a country built on the dreams of our immigrant forefathers, including mine. Your reasons may well be understood. I promise you, I'm going to do everything possible to make sure your case is adequately presented and fairly judged. But again ...there are no certainties."

Sam understood clearly where he stood and nodded his acceptance of her every word.

Then, his lips eased at the corners into a slight smile and his eyes narrowed in respectful regard. He was on a rocky edge but he could trust the hands that were going to steady and guide him. A sense of calm direction washed over him as she continued.

"Ultimately, you will need to leave the country and apply for pre-examination before returning. It isn't a sure thing, but there have been many such cases before the Bureau of Immigration and many success stories. You will also need to keep accurate records and be responsive to any requests made by the Department of Immigration. There may be many references to the word 'deportation' in their communication with you as we apply for a voluntary departure and a pre-examination appointment, but you needn't panic, at least not yet.

Part of this process will involve one department notifying and updating another.

Sometimes there is a delay or things overlap. You should expect notification of deportation extensions as the process is played out."

Sam had seemed so alert, so attentive to what she was saying that her momentum seemed naturally to speed up. Then, she would catch herself, slow down and make sure that he had been able to grasp and understand it all.

He had. He would need to follow-up and do his part as they proceeded. In the end, a deportation might still be unavoidable, but for at least now, there was hope. Either way, he was one day closer to being with his family again.

The world held their breath anticipating Hitler's next move. Poland knew it was next.

Hitler was interested in the Polish city, Danzig, and a strip of land called the Polish Corridor, which he would use to build German highways, railroads and a new route to the sea.

World War I was still a fresh memory. Europe's great powers continued to measure their own vulnerability and scrambled to make decisions about what their own involvement would be and under what conditions, it would occur.

Would they enter only to rescue themselves after direct attack or, as the defender of an aligned neighboring nation.

America in a period of isolationism was watching too. Though an ocean away, the media and life-like photography made it seem that trouble was at their doorstep, as well.

Was another world war inevitable?

On April 4, 1939 another notification arrived for Sam from the Department of Immigration.

He had not yet gotten a passport from the Polish Embassy and was not sure how he should respond to the notification of deportation. He would take it to 122 West 22nd Street the following day and make his way up to Miss Larned's office at the International Migration Services.

Miss Larned assured him that she would notify the Department of Immigration that he was still waiting for a response from the Polish authorities. He left feeling confident that he had done what he needed to do. He did not care if the $500 bond mentioned in the letter would be returned to him, only that he had been sure to handle the situation properly and that the authorities realized it was the Polish Consulate that was delaying and not Sam's unresponsiveness.

It was a matter of self-pride, not only a matter of keeping his reputation for responsibility untarnished, which, of course, would also help him gain citizenship, that mattered to him.

The correspondence he received dated July 7, 1939 from the United States Department of Labor, Immigration and Naturalization Services was most probably in response to the communication Miss Larned had sent them concerning no response for a passport from the Polish consulate. He was given an extended date of departure to August 30, 1939. It did not seem that Sam's passport was a priority to the Polish government at this time.

Staying on his course, Hitler was overwhelming Europe. On August 24, 1939, Germany and the Soviet Union had signed a Nonaggression Pact agreeing that neither would attack the other.

Stalin was smart enough to know that soon he would be Hitler's target, as well. He wanted time to prepare; the pact gave him time to stall so that he could build his own military forces.

Secretly, both Hitler and Stalin were planning to invade several other countries.

Particularly on Stalin's list were Poland, Estonia, Latvia, Lithuania and Romania. They had all once been part of Russia but had been given up in the treaty with Germany in 1918. Germany, defeated in WWI, had given up the territories and they were now independent.

Each felt, due to prior holding and loss, that they had a right and claim to these areas. They would work together and then divide control. The world of course was distrustful of the pair, but at the time they knew nothing of these secret plans.

Sam, however, was even more suspicious. He was familiar with the history of his homeland and the constant turnover of governments. Hitler, he was only beginning to know, but Stalin had been his neighbor for many years.

He was a brutal bully who aggressively sought what was his and even more aggressively sought what was not his. He did not conquer armies; he took over people's souls, working them to death like horses on land they could not claim as their own because he had taken it from them. He took their dignity, their self-esteem and their identity and then told them who they were and what they would do. He policed them relentlessly until they were mindless and useless even to themselves. He accepted nothing less than total surrender.

The outside world sometimes accepted his propaganda, but Sam had heard too many stories.

The people of his rural, somewhat backward, village and the surrounding areas had no reason to lie. They had not imagined the moans of starvation and cries from grown men. Stalin was smart enough not to underestimate the illiterate county folk. He took every precaution to contain the stories of harsh Soviet life.

But news traveled. Stories were told and carried as they had been for hundreds of years in the backward rural area he had come from - by word of mouth. This was why Stalin had always felt it was his most vulnerable border. Where there were unharnessed peasants, news traveled!

The community that surrounded Sam wished that they too could be in as much denial as America and much of Northern Europe were permitting themselves to be. However, for them the next world war was too easily foreseen. Many had lived through the realities of the last one. They had not just sent their sons across an ocean to fight a distant war; they had watched them die in their own front yards.

This foresight left the immigrant community charged. Sam could sense the energy mounting. What, however, was he to do about it?

On September 1, 1939 German tanks began their attack. A German battleship entered Danzig's harbor and began twelve hours of non-stop bombing until the Germans had overpowered Danzig. Warsaw was to be next. Homes, schools and hospitals were all left in ruin. Few buildings would be spared. Poland would be taken!

On September 3, 1939 Neville Chamberlain sent Hitler an ultimatum. "Withdraw or Great Britain goes to war".

By 11:30 am. Britain declared war. By 5:00 p.m. France followed.

World War II had begun!

It was only a matter of time before America would be at war, too. How much of Europe would still be standing by the time they did?

Sam read and listened to the news with outward calm. It had been expected.

Inside his heart a knife twisted. With each report it twisted more deeply, not only bleeding his emotions but also causing physical pain. Bit by bit his last reservoir of hope was carved out of him. It being gone, left him breathless and numb. One panic attack led directly into the next.

As each day passed it was as though he sat on the edge of a crevice and waited to be pushed off. Events were now out of his control. If before in life he had felt helpless, what word in English or Ukrainian or Polish or any language on God's green earth could describe how he felt now? There was none.

Yet, when he wasn't oblivious to anyone but himself, he could see the same emotion on the faces of his neighbors and friends, even total strangers who too had loved ones far away from them and in mortal danger. How could such a severe emotion not have a name? Was it because such devastation was felt by so few in life? He hoped so, for he didn't wish it on any creature that lived.

Media reports were that Poland was in total and utter devastation. Hospitals, schools, churches and homes were now mere holes in the ground. Hundreds of thousands were now homeless and astounding numbers of children had been left orphaned with nowhere to go.

Of course, Sam continued to write Mariya many letters, but not unexpectedly, nothing was heard back. Each day he looked to see if some communication had arrived. Each day, nothing came. He continued without question to send envelopes, even with money, in the hope that she might receive them or even just one. What were she and Danyk doing without his support? Terrible thoughts ran through his mind. He reminded himself of his wife's cheerful optimism and tried to maintain hope, as he knew she would want him to do. Maybe he would hear soon.

Sadly, he did not. He began to realize it was too late. Communication was cut off. Each day he went through the motions of living. He continued to save money because, holding on to his wife's optimism, he wanted to believe they would be reunited and would need the money to begin a good life together.

It was difficult to sleep, though his busy days left him exhausted. Soon, dark circles fell under his eyes.

Where was his wife? Where was his son?

Were they still in their village? Did they have a bed to sleep in? Did they have food?

He couldn't eat for the guilt of knowing those who depended on him might be going hungry. What had become of them? It was so unbearable; he feared going mad.

Sam was a quiet, reserved man and as difficult as it was to talk to anyone about his fears for his family, it seemed too much to bear to keep those feelings inside himself. At times, he shared his darkest thoughts with complete strangers willing to listen. This was so unlike his character, but he felt a deep overpowering need to express himself, and somehow it felt safest to let those who knew him least see how vulnerable he was.

On the front stoop to his apartment building, on the corner of the outdoor fruit market, hanging laundry outside windows, people talked. Using low monotone voices and extended arms, eyes met in shared understanding...you too?

While the rest of Americans feared involvement in a possible war, European immigrants feared their non-involvement. They were already counting casualties.

For Sam, and a good portion of the world, everything had been turned upside down. He lost track of events; they all seemed merged together. It was difficult to keep details straight.

His once reliable memory failed him often. He couldn't keep track of his keys, he forgot people's names, and he would not notice that his shirt was only half buttoned or that he was wearing mismatched socks.

He only lived for...news. News of his family. News of his village. News of Poland.

News of anything that might offer hope. Then one day he received a letter from Mariya.

~

Immediately the handwriting on the envelope caught his eye. Instantly, the pace of the world which had seemed out of control, now moved in slow motion.

His fingers seemed clumsy and arthritic. They could not move fast enough, nor were they even strong enough to tear open the envelope. Should he hesitate and savor the moment of finally getting word... or perhaps delay the bad news it might hold? Or should he hurry and read from Mariya the contents before he woke from this dream. He did a bit of each as his fingers trembled, fumbled and searched.

Finally, the letter was opened and within a few lines he realized what a mixed blessing it was. She had assured him that they were fine but struggling. It seemed his monthly allowances were not making their way to her. They could manage for a while but could he send more quickly.

Her brother Marion had been helpful to her but was now going into the Polish army. She did not say if he had gone by choice or not. He just assumed it was not by choice, as a Polish peasant of Ukrainian descent was not generally given choices, nor anxious to show Polish national pride.

Sam had now been away from Poland for twelve years. The Poland he had left repressed Ukrainians in all ways and had produced generations more loyal to their Ukrainian heritage than their Polish citizenship.

Though he recognized the threat of war, he could not have been expected to understand how its daily cloud could stir and tug at a young Ukrainian man's loyalties to unite with his fellow Poles in creating a strong, united front against the Germans and possibly their country's only chance of defeating the Germans.

Mariya also indicated that she read the concern he had for Danyk and herself between the lines of his last letter. He should not be concerned, she told him. Had he forgotten what his wife was made of? She was strong and smart, she reminded him, sometimes too much for her own good. That was something of which he had always teased her.

She reminded him to be strong as well, and though life was not always fair, in the end they would be together and happy. It would all be worth it. She missed him terribly and asked if anything had come about in terms of "making things right."

For a moment, she was with him.

He could smell her hair and see her eyes.

He felt at peace and relief, so unfamiliar to him, washed through his body and soul.

Then... he noticed the date.

It had been written well before the invasion of Poland.

He knew no more about the state of his family than before he had read the letter.

Chapter 9

War Arrives

It seemed to take longer and longer for mail to arrive. Mariya had last heard from her brother, Paul, in France in July. He had expressed concern for Poland and how it and his family there might fare in a possible war. He hadn't wanted to frighten her, just urge her to prepare.

Sam's last letter had arrived shortly after that, but ... nothing else had arrived since. The mail system in Poland had never been as strictly monitored as it was in America but each day its reliability grew worse. Mariya did not know if it was mismanagement, thievery or difficulty with transport that delayed it or more recently, caused it never to arrive.

She worried how she, Danyk and her mother could survive until the next allotment of monies that Sam, until this point, had faithfully sent, arrived. If even one letter could make its way through, the $35 to $50 he usually sent would go a long way.

She economized as well as she could and had grown exceedingly careful with their supplies. She held onto her hope that sooner or later a letter would make its way through the turbulence that surrounded Poland.

She was not the only one disturbed by the subtle tension that one could not hold or touch, but that seemed to fill the air as each day the war became less of a shadowed threat and more of a very real and dangerous intruder.

It was odd to see the effect it had on the temperament of the people she had known since birth who surrounded her. The one thing she had thought she could be sure about was that they were as unchanging as the land was fertile.

Their village had a small population of two to three hundred people who farmed the land. A few occasionally made their way to the larger markets to sell their goods. However, wealth did not wax and wane here as it could in America. A farmer expected to have sons who would farm the land after him. He did not have grand expectations but rather lived a very simple life and somehow always found joy and contentment in the day-to-day events that he shared with neighbors and friends who were bonded together by a common Ukrainian heritage.

The stillness of their lives was something one could depend on and take for granted. It was not something to be given much thought.

But now, neighbors seemed to withdraw from one another, too preoccupied preparing for a war they knew was soon to come. It was somewhat like the quiet before a storm - the noiselessness deafening, the stillness pulsating and disturbing.

The only neighbor that had not seemed to forget that she and her small family existed was Kupetsky Alexa. He and his wife were in their early fifties and childless.

He brought news to Mariya in the same manner that he received it...by word of mouth. They had little access to newspapers or radios but he was one of the few who had contact with those outside their immediate area.

Once a month he would bring his goods to the larger market and receive word from more worldly merchants who listened carefully to reports over the British Broadcasting Corporation.

Many of these worldly merchants were Jews and she had at first dismissed his reports, certain he was exaggerating or incorporating an overreaction by others, who quite rightly so, had much to fear. But each time, his reports grew more graphic and detailed as they cataloged the Nazis' victories. Each time, his voice grew weaker and more apathetic, reflecting the helplessness that not only he, but also other Poles felt as well, as the war seemed to be circling and squeezing in around them.

They were to meet this enemy alone it seemed, as the rest of the world turned their back.

Did they not understand that the Poles could not resist Hitler's armies without their help? Of course they knew, just as they had known Austria and Czechoslovakia couldn't either.

This knowledge was shadowed in Szymon's letters. Mariya, who knew him so well, had easily detected his unease. Why had she ignored the warning tone of his letters and dismissed his concerns? Still, what could she have done? Was she not as powerless as any other Pole, even more so as one of Ukrainian descent, to avoid the coming events? Could she have done something to help her family avoid being caught in the middle of it?

If her mother or especially Danyk were in earshot, she would change the subject quickly. Why did they need to hear such news if there was nothing that either of them could possibly do about it anyway? She would do the worrying for all of them. For as long as possible, she would protect them. It was her nature.

Kupetsky's industrious travels to various cities and industrial regions made him a sought- out courier of outside news. Though he was a simple trader, he did business with enterprising Jews whose families were denied property as well as political, cultural and economic opportunities at the turn of the century when under Russian rule. Now, clustered in urban Polish areas they were utilizing their skills, business sense and savvy developed over time due to historical necessity, to flourish in the age of modern industrialization. They, of course, had the greatest reason to stay alert and informed. It was no secret how Hitler felt about the Jews.

It was not always the news itself that alarmed Kupetsky most, though it was always grave. It was the unspoken gravity given it by the Jew who shared it.

Like the rest of Poland that seemed too still and quiet as the war approached, the news was cast in hushed tones. It was sensitive information and needed to be conveyed with decorum and respect for a fellow Jew who might overhear and be caught off-guard. The community's nervousness and fear alone sketched an ugly picture of what was to come.

How had Poland come to such a point?

First, Hitler had taken Austria, and the world had done nothing. Then, he had negotiated a take-over of a third of democratic Czechoslovakia with other world powers sitting at his side. Finally, he had simply taken all of it.

The reports had come steadily, relentlessly, and endlessly. Each time, the world acted surprised, even though it was known that they were not!

Now, the world knew what the Poles had suspected and feared with every Nazi advance... their turn was coming; it was inevitable.

Patiently, the Poles waited, using the time to display and bolster national pride with patriotic signs of "STRONG, UNITED, READY!" As well, they recruited an inadequate yet courageous army which was to include Mariya's brother, Marion.

Under any other circumstance he would not have been so patriotically enthusiastic. He was an energetic, fearless, strapping Ukrainian youth who had grown up under Polish repression. Still, he had retained a light-hearted boyishness that captured Mariya's and her mother's heart, as well as his new wife's ...whom he would hate to leave to go fight a war!

However, the uncertainty of the future made many Polish citizens rethink their priorities and stir national loyalties.

Joining the army seemed to empower Marion as well as others, at least outwardly. She knew him well enough to detect a nervous undercurrent that he seemed determined not to show, much like herself, she supposed. Though he had been a great help when she first returned to Poland, she knew his duties and attention needed to be laid elsewhere for now. Much would simply be left to her. Poland would not be given up so easily.

Nervous energy now interrupted the stillness and vibrated through their daily activities.

People hurried through their chores not even sure as to why they were rushing.

It helped though to engage in familiar, day-to-day activities during these days and months of waiting and wondering when and where they would finally be struck. Some, of course, remained in denial. Perhaps they were just brave, smiling through their days, counting their blessings and trying to continue on with life as it had always been, until it was no longer!

Mariya was one so brave or as she thought in her weaker moments, one so foolish. As best as she could she carried on with her day. She tried to remain cheerful, anxious to hide her growing fears from Danyk and her mother.

Her mother, with some of her earlier energy and vigor restored, tried as best as she could to help with the chores, but she would soon tire easily. Mariya would feel guilty accepting her help, fearing it was too much for her. At times though, she did not know what else to do. She could no longer hire help to tend the farm.

Her brother Marion, who would always try to lend a generous hand, was off preparing for war. With fall approaching, the last harvest would have to be made. Now, more than ever they needed the yield and... they would have to do it alone. It might be all they would have to sustain them through the cold winter.

Danyk, too, wanted to help. Even at his young age he was keenly aware that his mother did not have a man to help her as the other women did. Too, he knew he was a boy without a father, at least in his day-to-day life. That meant more was to be expected of him.

No one had ever told him this. His mother and grandmother never suggested it. It was just a fact that he alone had come to terms with. Because it had never been any other way... he simply accepted it. His mother too, had come to accept it, though with a shadow of guilt. She knew a child should not have to work so hard, especially one not yet eight years old.

Still, she was always grateful for his help and easygoing acceptance. How proud his father in America would be of him!

This year she had begun sending Danyk to school, but without the money she was accustomed to receiving from Szymon, she was not sure how long he would be able to attend. Books could be borrowed from helpful neighbors but as he was so helpful to her on the farm and possibly the only other help she would be getting, she might need to make his schooling wait. It would be a terrible shame.

Danyk was a strong, eager student and well-liked by the other students. She had worried about his adjustment. After all, his life revolved around her, his grandmother and the farm animals that he cared for. There were not many other children around for him to share his time with and no father for him to model himself after, though Marion and Sam's brothers did their best to fill that role.

As Danyk grew and his world expanded, there seemed to be more and more her son was denied. Once she had thought he would live a comfortable life in America. When that was not possible, she had at least thought he would live a life of far more privilege than she had ever known here, in the village where she had grown up. But he had lived his young life so far without a father's emotional comfort and as the approaching effects of war made themselves known, perhaps without the benefits of his father's financial support as well.

As it would affect any mother, it hurt for her to see her son receive the least of all the children in the village. Outwardly, at least, it did not seem to affect Danyk similarly.

If his mother was happy, then Danyk was also. Especially for this reason, she knew she would maintain her composure and remain strong for her son. Imminent war had snuck up on her!

Busy raising her son as a lone parent, nursing her mother back to health and managing a one-acre farm as best as she could had distracted her. Her own eternal optimism and need to deny any threat that loomed over her vulnerable family may also have played a part, but now war was on her doorstep. How could this have happened? Why was she not more prepared?

But, looking back, what else could she have done?

Over and over again, she would torture herself with this question, sometimes out loud.

What else could she have done?

If only Szymon were with her, then she could bear it. But he was not; she was alone, at least in terms of being the head of this small household.

That emptiness left a vast hollowness that ached inside her with a rebounding echo. At times she covered her ears to cease the sound and beat of it, but still it followed her through her day and kept her awake at night. Had she made the wrong choices? Had there been solutions she had overlooked?

When she did sleep, she would dream she was back in America, living in Manhattan on First Avenue with her husband. Even as she slept, she would smile reliving what had been a most wondrous and magical time. In America she had been a young wife with a strong handsome husband in whose arms she had felt a wonderful sense of being protected. She knew that at one time, it had been a reality, but now... it seemed more like a fantasy that she had imagined. So far away was that life now, that she feared if she did not keep it alive in her heart and mind that it might never exist again. So, she clung to it.

When she was not preoccupied with thoughts of war, she daydreamed about what had been. Many private thoughts she kept to herself, guarding them behind loving smiles that she showered upon her son, but there were those that she shared with Danyk, hoping that at least in a small way she could give him a glimpse of a reality so pleasant, that it seemed a fantasy.

Childhood should be filled with pleasant, comforting thoughts, she reasoned. So instead of fairy tales that were imagined she colored her son a real world, one that really did exist, she promised...across the ocean where his father lived. What had been her happiness and could someday be his, really did exist, in America.

This was encouraging news to a little boy whose entire world was a one-acre potato farm and the company of two older women. Her stories were her greatest gift to him, for in them he found a hope that he could carefully tuck away within himself. He would listen for hours to her every word as though they painted beautiful master-pieces for his eyes alone to see... and the images he held gave him the seeds of hope and strength he would need later.

One day, the hope within him... would be the arms that carried him and be his greatest strength,

Finally, the expected happened. On September 1, 1939 German tanks crossed the Polish border and their battleships entered Danzig's harbor. After twelve hours of non-stop bombing, the people of Danzig surrendered.

Then, on September 2nd, Hitler ordered air raids on Warsaw. Hitler, perhaps angry that Poland had been the first country to offer military resistance, spared little. Homes, schools, hospitals were left in crumbled ruins.

They were attacked from the north, west and south covering a front of 995 miles.

By day's end, insult would be added to injury. They would be attacked from the east by their secretive neighbor...the Soviet Union!

On the one hand, Poland was paralyzed. On the other hand, it was in a mad fury as everyone dashed about to reposition themselves according to their status. Polish soldiers still in Polish army trucks drove back and forth over the countryside, not really heading in any detectable direction. There was talk that many were headed to France to continue fighting for Poland in the Resistance.

Mariya prayed that one of those soldiers would be her brother, Marion. Did he live?

Was he rushing to France to fight again for Poland or was he lying hurt somewhere or worse, dead in Poland's rubble. Unknown. Unclaimed. She and her mother could not even speak aloud their fears. They preferred denial to considering any of these real possibilities.

Jews, well aware of Hitler's beliefs that everyone, particularly the Jews and the Gypsies, were inferior to the Aryan race, had packed their families and were headed to the Romanian border, many in packed cars, some in horse-drawn wagons filled with their belongings.

Desperation was clearly printed on their faces. Even the youngest seemed to understand their perilous situation and sat grimly and silently. The local Jews were poorer and fewer in number than those coming from the city. Often, they did not have the advantage of transportation. They walked carrying their baggage and children. Though they knew their future was uncertain, they also knew that under the Nazi regime, it did not exist at all.

It was little satisfaction to learn that by 5:00 p.m. that day, Great Britain and France had declared war, as well. For Poland though, it was too late. Their outnumbered and ill-equipped army had fought bravely, even heroically. However, their efforts had not succeeded and their defeat and predicament was clearly seen on the faces of every citizen.

Everyone appeared lost, even those who had not dared to take a step from their home. The Germans did not bother with Mariya's small village right away, it seemed.

First, they would secure the larger cities, and then, bit-by-bit they would go out in force to notify the people that a Nazi government was now in charge. The people, numb with fear, knew what was coming. Many of the older people had survived WWI. They urged everyone to hide what they could, especially the grains and staples that would be basic to their survival.

"Think, what do you need to survive?" they were told. "Hide food!"

A large population of Poland did not worry about what to hide because they had not been left with anything to secure. Their homes were gone! Their friends and neighbors lay dead on what had been the streets of Poland. Their children searched in vain for parents they were never to find. Winter was coming. Many cold and brutal days lay ahead for the Polish people. It would be especially hard for the parentless children.

The word spread quickly. The Germans would arrive soon. It was most surprising when the victorious army that did arrive ... was not the Germans.

It was the Russians.

Chapter 10

America, My Homeland!

Their arrival on September 17, 1939 fulfilled an earlier agreement between Hitler and Stalin. If Stalin did not interfere when Hitler invaded Poland on the west, the Soviet Union would be given the eastern half.

The Soviet Union could also use the opportunity to seize a buffer area between itself and a Germany they did not trust.

The Village of Gorodnitsa (Horonitza according to certain documents), Province of Galicia had once been part of Austria-Hungary, then a part of Poland. It was now part of the Soviet Union. By early October all resistance had been extinguished.

However, the Russian army sent to indoctrinate the area into the Soviet system did not appear to be the victorious army that one might have expected. Even to a poor Ukrainian farmer the Russian soldier looked deprived. He was too thin, dirty and most obvious ... smelly. It was difficult not to turn away from one of them and chance being thought disrespectful.

There was uncertainty as to how the people should respond. Were they there to liberate the Poles from the Germans? Should some small degree of hope remain? Or were they the enemy? Most of the villagers intuitively and cautiously kept their heads modestly down in surrender. As the Soviets approached, a feeling of helplessness and dread weighed heavily in the air and the shoulders of the proudest of men began to sink.

Danyk was too young, too inquisitive yet to understand that it was best not to attract the attention of the enemy. He could not help but to peer upward, though he shielded himself behind his mother's skirts. He saw a startling contradiction from the image he had conjured. There were no proud erect soldiers marching by.

Rather, they appeared to be a beaten people disguised in uniforms. Even the youngest Soviets were hunched over, appearing to exert effort with each step they took in their approach. Literally, they were dragging themselves down the dirt road. They looked more like a pack of hungry, desperate dogs, nervously surveying the countryside with glazed and bloodshot eyes for a prize with which they might sneak off.

It would not take long for the Polish and Ukrainian people to get to know their enemy, who for the next two years would become an everyday sight. The Soviet soldier was indeed an odd-phenomena for he had long been hardened by the upheavals of civil war and purges in his own country through the 1920's and 1930's, as well as by Stalin's iron rule. He did not fight because of national pride; he fought for mere survival, though the media and propaganda throughout the Soviet Union would do a fair job of convincing an outsider otherwise.

The Soviet soldier had already withstood the cruelest of life's hardships and losses. He had no home or possessions to call his own for they had long been taken over by the state.

Dignity, pride and freewill were not elements of a way of life known to him. Stalin had taken them all away. Hope was already gone for him. It did not matter if the war was won or lost. His life would not change.

If he obeyed all orders and did not displease his superiors, he would return to Stalin's Russia and be a prisoner of his own country once again. If even a small degree of disloyalty was suspected, it would mean his death or that of his family members. It was a way of life living under Stalin.

So, if now he could fill his stomach, his pockets or his empty existence with the bounty of his pillages, so be it. He, with no sympathy for those now devastated too, would be remembered as the cruelest of captors, even when compared with the Germans who were so greatly feared by the world. However, during this first two-year occupation by the Soviets, their furious threshold for inflicting cruelty would not be completely displayed or yet fully matured. That would come later after the savagery of war had left their own country in such utter, pitiful devastation, almost beyond man's imagination. For now, the Soviet soldier would be restrained. He would be kept somewhat in check and see himself as the "liberator", not the "conqueror".

First, Stalin would need to be served, as his campaign to take over the minds and will of the Polish people would begin.

Poland would have much to fear from the Soviet soldier once his rope was loosened. He would be angry at a world that had not shown him any mercy. He would deny any compassion to these neighboring villagers, who had sat by a few kilometers away, as Stalin harnessed his own people like animals.

Much would be saved for later.

All this could be foretold and seen in the eyes of one Soviet soldier who happened to look young Danyk's way. For each, it was only a moment's notice but it was enough for Danyk to capture his impression and commit it to memory.

Though Danyk was a mere eight years old and knew nothing of the outside world, he had an innate sense of who it was wise to trust that would serve him well in later years. In the eyes of this Soviet soldier, he saw a bitter enemy.

It was a sight that burned his eyes from a mere glimpse and he was not anxious to look again.

Mariya sensed her son's curiosity had turned to fear and protectively pushed him further behind her, as though to say, "Don't look, don't look!"

He obeyed her silent command and as the soldiers stumbled into their village, he buried his face in the back of her apron strings. But the memory of the soldier was carved in his mind.

Over and over again, he recalled the impression. Each time he restudied it, he noticed more and the lines, that had at first been blurred by his fear, were now crisply drawn.

What had, at first appeared to be red blotches of the soldier's lapel grew tips and formed a star. The hat, at first not impressive, now peaked to a point. The image was now more detailed, but by far not yet complete.

It would evolve and turn as though it had a life of its own. Unfortunately, never would Danyk quite come to terms with it. He would simply learn to live with it.

The war had now come to them...but this was only the beginning. For the next two years, the Russians would be an everyday sight. The pointed hats and starred lapels would become commonplace, yet remain uncommonly provoking.

For the most part, at least in the beginning of the occupation, Mariya's village continued on with life as usual, although supplies were limited and available sporadically. One had to be patient. But they, for the most part, were poor self-sufficient farmers, not "money-making capitalists" who at this point had the greatest to fear from the Russians.

As well, their area had not seen or felt the physical devastation and bombardment suffered by other areas of war-torn Poland. Their homes were still intact while much of Poland was now homeless or orphaned.

The Soviets claimed they were saving the Poles and freeing them from "capitalist oppression." With arrogant politeness they took over businesses, forcing owners into lesser positions. Those that protested mysteriously disappeared. The people were left to wonder. Though certain courtesies and consideration might be given and a pretense of freewill permitted, one knew not to question a direction given by a Soviet soldier.

The Soviets began to confiscate the property and land of the "royals" and redistributed it to the poor. This of course, created the intended confusion and the poorest of the poor felt uncertainty as to where his loyalties should lie. For generations the elite of Poland had repressed the poor working class, particularly the Ukrainians. Their customs had been restricted; their language barred from schools.

The Soviets were there to convert the Poles, brainwash them so to speak, and indoctrinate them into the Soviet system. Masterful servants of Stalin, whether willing or not, set about to manipulate and build the foundation for winning loyalty in the minds and hearts of the peasants.

This time period was to be used for relentless propaganda. As human nature would have it, certain Poles befriended the Soviets even earning positions of power and authority. One began to realize that not every neighbor could be trusted. One needed to be careful especially because most Ukrainians remained strong anti-Communists and this knowledge in the wrong hands could mean deportation.

Word was spreading that to even express an opposing idea to the Soviet doctrine would mean being sent to a work camp in Siberia, not only for oneself, but one's entire family as well. The discipline and consequences seemed so harsh and ridiculous that one resisted believing it. However, as the lists of missing persons began to mount, one dared not test it.

Schools, of course, were taken over by the Soviets who believed in starting the indoctrination early.

Mariya, who had started Danyk's education the year before, did not send him partly because she did not want him exposed to the propaganda of the Soviets who bombarded the children with the "evils" of capitalism, pictures of Stalin in fatherly poses and stories of heroism and loyalty to the motherland, Russia.

She had shared many wonderful stories with Danyk about her life in America shared with his father, and she knew she did not have to worry that the distorted realities would influence him. Danyk had his own conjured realties which she had helped instill in him early on and she knew he would hold on to them with all his might, no matter what. Of this, she was certain! But she saw no reason to add the stress of dealing with conflicting values that this would add to her household and in particular, to her young son's daily life. Living with war was enough.

Mostly, however, she simply did not want him to be separated from her when she did not know what to expect from day to day. It broke her heart to interrupt his schooling, not only for his education's sake, but because he had begun to meet and play with other children. With no brothers or sisters, she knew how important it was for him to be with his peers. He had begun to make friends... Bogdan Dushka ...Vlad Kolysnyk ...Volodymyr Tyholiz.

Too many frightening and unpredictable events seemed to become everyday occurrences. Mr. Brigda, who had served as the village teacher for many years, no longer came to the small village schoolhouse each day. His presence was obviously missing by the students, but never discussed. It was understood that he was a Polish royal and had been dismissed as a part of the Soviet campaign. It was rumored when he was nowhere to be found that he had been "relocated" by Soviet dictate and taken during one of the night marches that passed occasionally and seemed to be increasing in frequency.

The marches could be heard but not seen due to the curfew that had been imposed. One could only wonder or surmise that those being marched, even past the remotest of towns on the way to the trains, were not willing travelers.

The Soviet voices were curt, commanding and ordering. Though muffled and distant at night, their voices were not disguised with polite falsehood as they were in the village during daylight. Danyk would usually sleep through the marches, but at times Mariya's mother would join her in her wakefulness brought on by the disturbing voices and sounds. Together, they would sit in the darkness and listen.

Occasionally, a distant angry or pleading voice would crack through the air. It would echo and bounce off the surrounding stillness like a firecracker. It made one's heart stop and breath hold. Neither she nor her mother dared to speak. It might have woken Danyk and moreover... there would have been no purpose to it. Both knew terrible things were happening to their neighbors. As well, both knew there was nothing they could do about it.

Mariya and her mother would need to turn their full attention to survival, they knew.

~

Now, with no hope of support or even word coming from Sam, the world at war and their resources very limited, they needed to stay and work together.

If she were asked why her son did not attend the school, provided free by the state she would explain that he was needed at home. It seemed reasonable, as she was a woman alone with an elderly mother and a young son to provide for. But she hoped there would not be a need to explain too often. She did not like to highlight that she was a woman alone.

Between the three of them, they could at least do the work of one strong man. She was determined! As for Danyk's lessons, they would now be given by her in their one room house at day's end when their work was finished but before dusk so they would not waste fuel for light.

After all, her son would need to be prepared for his life after the war, when the world was once again sane and she could rest easy in the arms of her husband.

It was Mariya's full intention to survive the war.

During the second year of occupation, things began to change.

The Soviets, who had so far been crude but rather tame, seemed to break from their leash.

The arrests increased. Even the village of Gorodnitsa (Horonitza), far removed from the mainstream of Polish life, could

119

not escape witnessing the deportation of one to two million Poles to Siberia, the Soviet Arctic, Kazakhstan and work camps.

Down the dirt paths and through the wooded areas they were marched on their way to the freight trains for deportation. There, many women and children whose only crime would be they were the family of wealthy businessmen, would be herded into cars, even during the dead of winter, with inadequate clothing, many barefoot, to travel in unheated freight cars for days and weeks to get to the work camps in Siberia.

The tension had increased and now Danyk too, unable to sleep, sat in the dark with his mother and grandmother listening to the endless distant parade. Screams, sobs of pitiful misery echoed or were recalled when one tried to sleep. There was no mother's comfort that was adequate enough to give her young son a moment of peace. She could not shield him. There was no sense of security for anyone, no moment of the day or place where one could hide from the realities of life in war-torn Poland.

Old women and children were now as vulnerable to deportation or death as healthy strong men, who were carted away each day and forced to be soldiers or laborers.

By the winter of 1940 all the land that had been given to the peasants to gain their loyalties had now been taken back. Instead, the Soviets began to form government farms. The people were forced to work for the state. They received no payment in return. For the Soviet soldier, it was just more of what he had had back in Russia. It was what was expected when living in Stalin's Russia.

All property and goods had to be reported to the Soviet government. Goods that were hidden and not reported were forbidden. If they were found, harsh punishments or even death occurred, seemingly on the whim of the officer in charge.

It was no longer just enterprising capitalists or political resistors that were being arrested. More and more peasants were being sent to Siberia. Some, perhaps many, since there was no real way to keep track, were sent simply because they were "suspected" of some offense. There were never any real substantiated reasons. People just began to disappear from the streets or be seized from their homes at night and never heard from again. Consistent contact with anyone was difficult. Too many people had been displaced. The Soviets wanted to limit organized rebellion, no matter how small.

One night, the Soviet soldiers came to Sam's mother's house. They indicated that they were recruiting Soviet soldiers and they wanted Sam's brother, nineteen-year-old Vasil, to enlist. Of course, he did not want to go. Knowing it was going to be fruitless, he still could not help himself from protesting. They removed him forcibly. Due to the curfew, Mariya would not find out until the following day.

Mariya was beginning to count her family's casualties. She, her mother and her sister-in- law had not yet heard from her brother Marion. Had the Germans killed him during the original invasion or was he hiding in a distant village? Perhaps he had made it to France to continue fighting in the resistance.

She hoped.

She prayed for him.

Now, she would pray for Vasil, as well. There was little else to do.

Mykhailo, Sam's brother, had managed to avoid deportation or being forced into the Soviet Army by living in the great forests and Carpathian Mountains with other young Ukrainians where the terrain was difficult to navigate and they were less accessible. These smaller bands would eventually unite to become the Ukrainian Insurgent Army. She did not know how he managed there, nor would have thought to ask. For everyone's sake it was best not to know too much about someone else's business.

For a time, Mariya, her mother and Danyk had managed to keep the war from being more than a major inconvenience. There was of course, frequent fear and constant hunger. Meat was rarely available and if it was, the Soviets were quick to find it for themselves. Food in general was scarce but they were not starving, not yet. They commonly sipped beetroot or tomato soup. One tomato could be stretched to feed the entire family.

Long gone were the days of their privileged peasant diet of home-grown cucumbers, apples and cherries. They certainly lacked for luxury, even at times for what was necessary, but they had to a good extent avoided the raw brutality and violence of war. By 1940, this could no longer be so.

The Soviets had initiated mass execution of Polish citizens. The underground which had quickly formed a network of collaboration to establish anti-Soviet propaganda gave rough estimates of 28,000 Polish citizens murdered.

The population was outraged... and terrified!

Coming to realize and accept this was against Mariya's basic nature. She needed to admit defeat, which was a form of negative thinking that she, under almost any other circumstance, would not have permitted herself. But it was so, and she needed to come to terms with it so she could fully prepare to protect her family. She needed to move quickly and think clearly. Her decisions and actions had to be reasonable and appropriate to the situation.

Her weariness from her daily chores, and even more so, the stress of war, were already slowing her thinking processes. Too, she missed having contact with Sam, who though far away had always remained her life's partner. She had not heard from him in over a year.

Denying reality because it was too painful to face must not be another factor in impairing her ability to protect her family. While her mind mentally prepared itself, her body took over. Somewhat like a self-defense mechanism it allowed her to go through the necessary motions that her mind was not yet prepared to endure.

Late one morning, an elderly widow, that Mariya had known all her life, had been shot for hiding wheat. She had not reported it as was mandated and had taken a huge risk.

Mariya understood the desperation to keep just a bit of wheat crop to feed her family, for she had done the same.

Behind the house, a few feet into the surrounding forest she had carefully dug a small hole, placed a ten-pound burlap bag filled with grain into it and then covered it with loose soil and dried leaves. She had pounded the earth over it so as to make it appear untouched and dusted her footprints away with a leafy branch. No one would ever suspect she thought. She had proudly patted herself on the back for her thoroughness and cunning.

She and Danyk had been working the field when the shot rang out over the clearing that she shared with her neighbor. Instinctively she ran to her son and covered his ears. She did not want him to hear the wailing of the woman's daughter that followed or worse yet her silence, after she too was shot. She was not sure then why the woman and her daughter had been shot, she only suspected. Later, when men of the village went to investigate, they found the two dead women and the empty hole where she had been hiding her grain.

It had been such an unjust killing...but then they all were. The woman only wanted to feed her family. It made no sense.

Neighbors, entire families were being shipped off to Siberia. First it had been the Bortniks, then the Smakovuses. These were people she had been held by as a baby, greeted each day on her way to the village schoolhouse or cooked for during illness or periods of mourning.

It was lunacy!

And lunacy was all about her. It made her so tired. So very, very tired. She knew it was affecting her thinking. She needed to stay focused, to concentrate on what needed to be done next. If only she could sleep for a few hours, not even through the night, as that would be too much to ask.

It was best just to put one foot in front of the other.

Keep going.

Don't think too much. But she was overcome with self-doubt about her decisions.

Dare she go to the forest that night and empty the hole?

What if the Soviets should find it first? What if she were caught for being out after curfew? What if they caught her with the wheat?

What if she was killed, too?

Would they kill her mother and Danyk too?

Or what would Danyk and her mother do if they had to survive without her? She had images of her son orphaned as a good part of Poland had already been, staggering over the carcasses of destroyed buildings begging for food or a warm place to sleep.

It was just before dusk when word came. A ten-year-old boy who seemed to have the talent, the energy and the nerve to slip by the Soviet soldiers undetected through the forest delivered it. The Soviet soldiers were coming to search. Mariya's farm would be next!

She knew the Soviet who would come to search her home would not resemble the earlier Soviet who might have used polite diplomacy and propaganda. The Soviet who pretended to follow some set of rules was long gone. Victims were chosen at random now. Justification was never given. None was any longer expected.

Each time the Soviets searched the ordeal was more vicious than the last.

They looked for anything that might indicate involvement in the mounting resistance movement, especially if there had been recent activity such as use of explosives or weapons stolen.

Fuels, grains and ready-made foods were of course taken right away. Then, tools, blankets, candles, shoes, glass jars, baskets, cooking pots and utensils...anything. A most prized discovery for a Soviet soldier might be a clock or wristwatch as none had been produced in the Soviet Union since 1919.

The Soviets, used to being secretive and hiding things, were artful in their searches. Each time they took more and left less. What or how much would her family be left with this time?

Would it be enough to see them through?

Should I have done something differently?

Could I have sent Danyk back to his father in America, somehow?

Tiredness and self-doubt seemed to consume her and for the first time she felt too battle weary to ward them off.

This time someone else seemed to take possession of Mariya's body as she went through the motions of preparing for another search by the Soviets.

Her son watched her from a darkened corner and heard her as she spoke aloud the words that usually only echoed in her mind.

They frightened him.

His mother was always in control and careful to maintain a protective yet light spirit, especially in front of her young son. Now she seemed blank, expressionless, though he himself would not have been able to find quite the words to describe her. It had not been like anything he had ever observed before.

He felt small against the terror of so much but never before had he felt the horror of such aloneness. As his mother's spirit seemed to drift away from him, out of reach, he felt something very unfamiliar... abandonment.

For so long Danyk had grown up without a father. He had left America when he was two, but had managed to hold a vague image of him in his mind. He had seen the picture of him that his mother kept and looked at it often. It helped him keep the image from disappearing.

As well, her stories and descriptions sharpened the fading lines, and at times he thought he could see his father so clearly that should he reach out he would be able to touch him! He needed his father now as he felt his mother's attention stray away from him.

A year of schooling and his mother's tutoring had helped Danyk learn how to read. This had given him some access to his father as he could then read the letters his father had sent to his mother over the years. By doing so he was able to establish a stronger connection to the man whose image had faded and focused over time.

Especially now, when his mother was so unusually distracted, he needed his father's words to sustain the grains of hope that his mother had planted in him. So, he came to know them in the way they were available to him. He read them. Over and over again, he found answers to his questions and came to know and love even more his father and the wondrous place his mother often talked about... America!

The two intermingled.

There could not be one without the other. He painfully longed to know them both and through the words of his parents, he did. From the written words of his father's letters to the spoken words of his mother's shared daydreams, he knew his father to be a hard-working, loving, devoted family man and America to be the land at the end of the rainbow where one met their heart's desire. It was a place that served one well...and one was well honored to serve it.

One day, he was certain he would.

He did, however, begin to understand by the difference of what his mother related to him in her stories of America and what was happening in his day-to-day life in war-torn Poland, that now would not be the best time to announce it to all... or even anyone he knew. It was a dream not to be shared passed his family. Even then, only in assured privacy.

In place of his father's loving embrace, he would hold the promise of dreams and realities in America like a child's security blanket, close to his heart. It would protect him, keep him secure and in return he would give it unconditional love and loyalty.

First given as a child, it would have the enduring strength of innocence and create a bond like any other established during childhood that he would have no willful way of breaking. His adoration, love and loyalty to a country he had never actually seen would forever be a part of him that he could not deny. Hope and his belief in America would be the arms of this mountain of emotions turned rock hard, that would keep him standing against all enemies and would carry him, small, humble yet uplifted in a world that was now torn by war and chaos. Even so young or perhaps because he was so young, he would know from where to draw strength.

From his darkened corner, as he watched a growing unfamiliar weakness overtake his mother and felt her drift away from him, he turned to the sweet embrace of hope and promise and wielded it like King Arthur's sword.

"Maybe, we go to my father now, in America? He will take care of us."

When Mariya turned to him, she was a defeated woman using the last of her strength merely to stand but, as soon as she beheld the luminous blue eyes of her little son trying so desperately to be brave, all her natural protective instincts returned and she immediately took the reserve of strength her meditative state had returned to her and regained the pose of a determined woman.

Her choice to remain courageous had been made. Instantaneously, she was his mother again.

She gathered all her calm, as much as she could, and reached out to him to reassure him.

She had not meant to frighten him, only clear her mind so she could fight this enemy cunningly; she struggled to reassure herself.

He had done well, he thought. Reminding his mother, about his father and America had soothed her, as it did him. It was good to remember him.

But as Mariya's reasonable state returned, she realized there was not much time for remembering and reassuring. They needed to prepare. It was time to face the enemy and they would be ready.

They hid what they could not do without. It was only the barest amount of food, but if they were caught it would mean their certain death! For now, the ten-pound sack of grain would remain a part of the forest's floor. Mariya would have to trust that her own instincts had been good enough and that she had hid it well.

It would not be the last time she would need to call upon her own courage and bravery to take herself and her family through this war. But it would be the last and only time she would allow her son to question if she were up to the test.

Danyk keenly followed his mother's brave footsteps. It was a dance they would perfect. He had handled himself well during the searches once again and his mother marveled.

Danyk had learned to keep his head down and stay out of the soldiers' way. He answered questions politely but briskly without emotion. He had learned to detach himself and never offered information or a reason for the soldiers to look again or more intensely.

What he did best was present himself as a child confused by war. His guise of insignificance gave Mariya, her greatest sense of mother's pride. For she knew he was anything but insignificant and that the mask he was so adept at putting on and off might well be one more reason they would be able to survive the war.

Perhaps, he was old enough to know a secret. She decided she would tell him soon. It would not do for the secret to die with her, should that be her inevitable fate.

Danyk had to know.

Chapter 11

Marion at War

It was never Marion's ambition to be a Polish soldier. In all ways he was Ukrainian. But it was a desperate time and better to be repressed by Polish politics than to be under a Nazi dictatorship.

So... here he found himself, perhaps preparing to die for a country that had denied him and his family his entire life.

He dared not move. The enemy was so close that he could smell their sweat. That was just before his lungs filled with the dust their moving trucks, jeeps, tanks and marching men caused to stir and bellow out into the air like smoke.

He struggled not to move, nor to gasp for oxygen. He kept his head as far down to the ground as possible. One ear dug into the earth while his nostril hid against his coarse jacket sleeve hoping to filter out as much debris as possible. Still, it managed to find its way to his tongue and mix with saliva to make a gummy paste he longed to spit out.

He began to feel dizzy and nauseous from...fear, he supposed, but he also knew he needed air. He wasn't sure if he was forgetting to breathe or just afraid that the expanse of his chest would be noticed if he did.

Breathe, he thought.

Breathe, slowly but... breathe!

No, don't gag! Don't cough! It took all of his will to do so, as his body rejected the cloudy air, mixed with fine dry dirt and warm car exhaust.

His chest began to rise and fall with its own exertion and he hoped the dead branches covering him were not keeping time, rising and falling obviously, along with what felt like his gasping, panting lungs. His heart labored, seemingly thumping the ground that lay directly beneath his flattened body.

Could his pounding heart pump any harder? Any louder?

It seemed to echo through him and pulsate in a vein that ran down the left side of his throat. The pressure of blood rushing added to the tightening of his throat.

Don't gag! Don't gasp! Don't choke! DON'T MOVE!!!

It all caused a terrible racket in his buried ear that received every vibration of the Nazi advance and his own panic in amplification.

Could the Germans hear it as well? Shhh!!!

Quiet, be still, breathe slowly!

He could detect his own movements, which meant if a German was alert or observant enough, so could he. It was too late to reposition himself. The Germans were too intimately close; they were just upon him!

He'd been hiding in the woods, part of the great ancient forest that had always surrounded his homeland, all afternoon. Lying under a fallen tree and its branches he had watched the commotion and chaos of Poland's demise. Germans were everywhere. Civilians too, but these were the harmless ones, orphaned, hurt, aimlessly lost and bewildered. For the moment they were being overlooked by the Germans, who were disciplined and intent on completing their mission as they rushed by to finish business.

He had no real immediate plan... except to stay alive ...

He was not sure he wanted to live and endure Poland as it now was...empty. Selfishly, which was not his usual nature, he prayed that the fighting and destruction had been mostly west and that further east, where his family was, had not been destroyed.

Poland was a skeleton of its former self. Homes, churches, hospitals and government buildings had all been destroyed. They had crumbled like broken shells. Gaping holes in the ground exposed opened cellars and pockmarked the landscape. Thousands had died! Their lifeless bodies covered the once beautiful countryside, transforming it into the largest gravesite one can imagine.

This did not exclude women and children. The site of mass death and gore was so ghastly that it seemed to stun and absorb even the German soldiers, who passed by and were not aware of his close observance.

They had fought hard and honorably, desperately trying to protect their homes and families from Hitler's invading armies, even though they knew almost immediately and with certainty that in the end they would be defeated.

Their small, ill-equipped army was simply no match for Hitler's polished, well-trained troops and developed weaponry. But they had not given up easily. When ammunition was spent, they continued to fight using any means possible. Joined by the civilian population, including women, they used shovels, hunting rifles and butcher knives. They even threw stones until it was impossible to go any further. Until they were dead... or captured... or hiding as Marion was now.

Fear was wrapping its arms around this big strapping Ukrainian like it never had before.

Farm work had taken the body he had been given by nature and made it firm, muscular... Herculean even, but little good it did him now, except make him easier to detect.

He had always been a gentle lamb in a giant's body, considered soft-spoken, approachable, calm and soothing. Never before had he been given to fighting or harming another living creature. Even the slaughter of livestock had left him unsettled but today he had found a part of himself that he had not known existed. Where had it come from... the part of him that could kill? Did he even know who he was?

Nothing to do but wait. Just stay alert. Live if I can. My family will need me.

Adrenaline ruled.

The unit had almost finished passing. More would come of course, but in-between he would be able to reposition himself and make his hiding spot more secure.

Then, after dark he would make his way up north and over east.

It was the hope that the Polish soldiers who had not been killed or captured could regroup and continue their efforts in some way. Exactly how that was to be done had not been completely figured out. The Polish army was in tatters but perhaps the surviving soldiers could join a foreign army or organize an underground. These were short-sighted, inadequate plans but it was the best they could do since they had not expected to be overtaken so swiftly.

This region of Poland had taken the most severe beating. For now, his own Ukrainian village had been spared the degree of the devastation that surrounded him. But there was no way for him to know that. He was deeply worried about his family.

Marion's praying was continuous even as he tried to keep his mind working and alert.

God, are you there? Is this the end of the world? It felt as though it was.

He might have gone undetected but for two German soldiers who'd turned from the road to relieve themselves. They caught a glimpse of pink human flesh against brown leaves and jumped back. Startled and surprised, they awkwardly readied their weapons. They were not fully used to fighting a war yet, either.

The barrels of their guns now aimed nervously at Marion's head, telling him to stand.

Instinctively, he stood. His body moved the dead branch with its decaying leaves out of the way as he simultaneously folded his hands behind his head. Just like that, he was out in the open for all the German army to see.

Then he bent forward, anticipating it all to end, at any moment.

They have already killed most of Poland; why would they not kill me?

He could have gone for his own gun. He could have continued to fight but he didn't.

Marion wasn't at all sure why and later he would reflect on it.

Have I surrendered to my death? A hero's death? A coward's? Or, do I just want to live? Regardless? Because?

One of the German soldier's guns swung and he put his hands higher in the air. Then, it swung again and he realized it was pointing toward the direction of the road. He followed its lead and suddenly, he too was part of a parade marching and keeping step. His boots were sinking into the dirt creating clouds, just as hundreds of Germans had done before him all afternoon. It was all somewhat unreal. A dream? A nightmare?

His breathing continued to labor and his heart continued to race, not yet adjusted to war or captivity or exposure. All the while his hands bounced in the air marking his status as prisoner. When, after a distance, his hands began to go numb, he looked to the soldier whose gun was pointed at his head. Marion used a soft grunt and cautious, beseeching eyes to communicate his request to lower his hands to his head. The soldier seemed to answer when Marion did so and was not shot.

They marched an hour more and then came upon trucks loaded with Polish prisoners captured earlier in the day.

At gun -point he was ordered to get into the back of the truck, which he did, still with his hands on his head. When the truck began to move, he tried to lower his hands to scratch his nose, but it was nearly impossible, as the captives had been very closely packed in.

Hours later, he and the other prisoners were directed off the truck. After being cramped, hungry, exhausted and smothered he felt immediate relief at his first intake of fresh air. A collective sigh could be heard as each soldier rushed in a lungful of much-needed oxygen.

Officers were quickly isolated for interrogation...but not seen again.

No one knew quite what to expect. They were all weary after a full week of combat and a day in captivity. Many had not slept for days.

Once again, they were ordered up at gunpoint and told to march. They did so until just before dark. That night they slept on the bare ground and were grateful to do so. Many tossed and turned; it was not a restful sleep, just a much needed one. There was not much speaking. They were defeated, what more could be said. What they had known and loved was no more. It had all been destroyed, right before their eyes. They had been powerless, help-less, useless.

Morale could not have been lower.

Marion was now one of 400,000 Polish soldiers captured in 1939 by Germans at the beginning of the war. Until February 1940, the Germans gave ICRC a list of the Polish prisoners they held in captiv-ity. Thereafter, the reports were discontinued. Marion hoped his family knew that he lived but he doubted that any real effort would have been made to get such notification to his small Polish village of Ukrainian peasants. Instead, he focused on his own survival. He was not unlike the rest of what was left of Poland. But that did not ease his conscience or protect his self-image as protector of his family and people.

The next day they were loaded onto trains, not knowing their destination. They couldn't ask their captors as the Germans only spoke German and Polish soldiers only spoke Polish or Ukrainian. The Germans were not yet used to being their captors, just as the Poles were not yet used to being prisoners. Everyone was very nervous, jumpy and cautious in interacting with the other.

They were no more comfortable on the trains than they had been on the truck, however, this time the journey was longer. The only thing Marion could tell was that they were headed north.

"Germany?" he wondered, as did the others.

When the train stopped, they were given water, a loaf of bread and a bag of dehydrated vegetables, a food Marion had never seen before, to split between seven men. Until this time the shock of their circumstances had kept everyone very subdued and much to their own thoughts... but now, an exchange was needed to divide the food up fairly.

When the guards pulled back their direct attention for the first time since captivity, the men began to share their names, identities, and the names of their villages. Slowly they began to speak... of their families, their capture, their fears for Poland's condition... and to question what might be next to endure.

Satner Powell was Ukrainian also. He too, had been a farmer but his build was far slighter and less impressive than Marion's. He had joined the Polish army, not for Polish pride and loyalty but just as Marian had, to protect his Ukrainian family and neighbors from war.

They had both chosen the same rock upon which to lean when their first conversation occurred. Shyly, soon after they had introduced each other, Satner pulled a photo of his wife and young son from his pocket. It seemed new and unweathered except for the wrinkle where it had been folded to fit in his pocket. His hands shook slightly as he propped the treasured memento in front of Marion who politely wiped his dirty hands on his sleeve first, then nodded respectfully as he reached for the photo. Marion continued to nod as he admired it.

"Handsome family! You are a proud father!" His enthusiasm was dulled by his exhaustion, but sincere never-the-less.

"Yes, the soldier smiled, then quickly grimaced as he remembered where they were and their circumstances.

Marion could see the soldier's withdrawal and his mind working. "It is good to remember why we fight."

The soldier nodded back and Marion realized his understanding was greatly appreciated.

As dead as Marion was feeling on the inside, he could not help but to continue to show his humanness.

"Poland?" the soldier began, and then could not finish; he did not need to.

"...may never recover, my friend?" Marion assertively finished his thought for him. "Perhaps? God forgive me, but I fear more for my family right now, than Poland." For this, Marion was not ashamed, though it seemed that with each passing moment there was more and more he regretted.

"None of us knows what to think of our families... I think it will be a long time before we know." It was mournful, the way he spoke. It would have been senseless to speak otherwise.

"Communication was not good in Poland before the war. Now it will not exist at all."

"How will the people survive? They are devastated. There will be no help from the outside." Satner looked at Marion, feeling foolish. "I state the obvious, I am sorry."

"We are all thinking this," Marion confirmed with resignation. "We may not say it, but we are all thinking it."

"My son is so young. This is not a world I meant to bring him into." Satner's head shook in sorrow and apology for again saying what need not be said.

There was silence again for a long time and Marion mistakenly thought his new friend was asleep.

"Do you have a wife?" the soldier whispered through the dark. Marion wondered how he had known that he too was still awake or had he just taken the chance.

"Yes, I have a fine wife." He spoke thoughtfully. "I waited too long to marry her. I should have done it much sooner. So much time wasted. I frustrated my sister, Mariya terribly." At another time and place he would have smiled slightly with amusement as he spoke of his sister and his brotherly mischief.

Now, he just embraced the comfort he felt remembering her. "She feared I would never marry. Women always think you are better off married... and perhaps they are right. I am very happy," he admitted realizing as he spoke that perhaps he should have used the past tense.

"Children?"

"A beautiful daughter... my Anna. My wife, Anastasia and I would like a large family, but now...".

It all was a question mark now. "We will see. I hope one day it is possible. If the war ends... if life can be lived again? If?" He was satisfied to leave his questions hanging in the air.

Again, a long silence followed and the two men returned to their own similar thoughts.

Will there be a future? Is the world at its end?

Should he just give up? Or should he be brave, prepare to go on? Was there a right answer, regardless of what the outcome would be?

Was there a right answer for him, but a different one for Poland? For his family?

Captivity gave one such a sense of powerlessness, a loss of control. Marion was so tired, and hungry, and his mind was filled with worry for his family.

Before morning's first light, he had made at least one decision.

Brave men would be needed to see the war ended. He knew he would at least try to be one of them. Mentally, he made a 'To Do List'. On the top was – SURVIVE!

Hours later they were back on the train. The next stop was a factory. The third floor was empty except for the straw that covered the floor.

It would be their bed. There, they were given weak hot tea and more rations but told by a guard who spoke broken Polish that it would need to last them the rest of the trip. However, they were not told how long the duration of the trip would be.

Some men being ravenous could not avoid the temptation and ate their rations all at once.

Others, more cautious and willful like Marion, rationed their food carefully.

At times over the long journey, bickering would break out between the prisoners when one suspected the other of stealing rations, which did occur. It was shocking to realize that under such circumstances your ally could also become your enemy. Soon, prisoners began to cradle or sleep over their possessions protectively, guarding what little they could still claim as their own. It was to become a way of life in prison.

Finally, the exhaustive trip appeared to be over when they reached a camp one and a half kilometers west of Hammerstein, Germany. It was on the east side of a highway leading to that city. Most had already decided they were in Germany by the richness of their surroundings. The livestock appeared well fed and citizenry rosy with good health. They had long since passed the fields of dead bodies and stench of mass death. Here modern buildings, paved roads and well-tended farms glorified the scenery.

Mothers smiled as they wheeled babies in carriages, elderly men conversed on street corners without a care in the world and young boys ran or raced bicycles alongside the convoy of trucks transporting prisoners, cheering and hollering victory for as long as they could. The Poland they had left could not be any greater contradiction to the Germany that had swallowed them up whole. The only ugliness to be found were the propaganda banners that seemed to line every street and highway. Otherwise, Germany sparkled; it glittered superiority.

The camp however, portrayed Germany's darker side, surrounded by two barbed wire fences and additional fencing that marked compounds and sub-compounds. Later in the war they would be filled to the breaking point with various nationalities- French, Serbs, Belgians, British, Russians and Americans. For now, the Poles were to be indoctrinated.

The barracks were fifteen by sixty-yard structures divided by center washrooms each having twenty taps. The Hammerstein installation was headquarters for work detachments in the region and seldom housed more than one fifth of the POW's for which it took credit. But on and off it would serve as home for the prisoners between work details. It was known as Stalag IIB.

First, everyone was registered and interrogated. Then they were stripped, deloused, showered and shaved, processed and given a POW card that had their photo on it. Satner was visibly disappointed when his POW photo replaced the one of his family which to this point he had managed to keep safely tucked in his pants pocket. He had thought to request his own pants back, but Marion had talked him out of it. The guards were jumpy, very alert and he didn't want his friend being made into an example. That was never pleasant. Better to know a certain guard's temperament before making a request.

Fortunately, these clothes were later returned to them with KG painted on the back legs and two diamond-shaped patches were sewn on the back of their jacket and left trouser leg.

The camp was divided into nine Kommando Companies or work companies which were then subdivided. Three days after he arrived, Marion was transported with twenty-nine other men to a potato farm six kilometers from Stolp. There they would be expected to labor for Germany under the inspection and eye of German soldiers and their guard dogs.

Each day, Marion was awoken at six a.m. and was given breakfast until six-thirty a.m.

On good days it consisted of potato soup, bread and hot water for coffee. Then, he and the other men began their daily ritual. They washed their spoons and enamel bowls, cleaned their "barracks" which was a large section of a brick-floored barn shared with pigs, cows and horses, as well as grain in nearby sections, and then shaved and washed themselves in large wash pans of cold water. Nearby was a three-seater latrine, which everyone visited before being transported to the potato fields in horse-drawn wagons. Nervous farmhands watched their every move and thought nothing of aiming guns at prisoners' heads.

Often Marion worried that he would have his head blown off simply because a farmer had sneezed or lost his footing. Marion had always been a mild-manner man generally, but still he took care not to aggravate the German farmhands or guards. His size already worked against him as his towering form, for all its gentleness, made him an intimidating figure. He often stooped or bent his huge frame forward and hung his head to be less noticeable which left his back and neck sore by day's end if farm work did not.

By eleven-thirty a.m. the men were marched back to the farm house for a noon meal, generally a German vegetable soup. Then they boarded the wagons once more for the last of their work detail that day. The farmer generally provided the evening meal which would consist of soup, potatoes and gravy. After dinner, they were permitted to sit outdoors in a fenced-in area, approximately thirty by eight feet until eight-thirty p.m. Then they were locked up in their section for the night.

Each day was like the next... at least for them. Any change in activity was exciting and as the years passed and more countries joined the war, more POWs of different nationalities joined the mix. Marion didn't wish harm on anyone but as he saw more and more nationalities represented, he grew more and more hopeful. It was not just Poland and Czechoslovakia against the Germans. There were the French, the Englishmen, and later the Russians, Italians and Americans, too.

It was the world against Germany! Surely, their unity would break the Nazis eventually.

When a work detail was over, they would at times return to the barracks at the main camp until their kommando was reassigned. A favorite pastime, after many nationalities had joined the camp, was to go to the intersecting fence of all the divisions and trade. The dialogue was interesting, a mixture of signs and signals, facial expressions and hand movements.

Humans can be fascinating as they overcome language barriers when the need is great.

Getting food of course was always a top trade but one could get interesting exchanges especially from Americans who were considered the quickest to trade pens, pencils, rings and wristwatches of great value for bread, potatoes or a smoke.

If you traded for food, it was best to eat it right away, out of the sight of others who were for the most part so preoccupied with food that little else was the topic of conversation.

Those that fared the worst were the Soviets.

It was not an easy sight to see their suffering. In 1941, when Hitler betrayed his earlier agreement with Stalin, many Soviets were captured from the Soviet-occupied area of Poland.

Entire divisions surrendered and German Kommandos were simply not prepared. Soviet prisoners, many of whom were not even Soviet but Polish citizens forced into the Soviet army as human shields, would be surrounded by barbed-wire and little else, forced to construct their own shelters from little.

Not provided regular aid from the International Red Cross or YMCA as all other nationalities were, they were forced to provide for themselves. Of course, they could not, and startling numbers died of exposure, dehydration, disease or starvation.

Stalin had not signed a signatory of the Geneva Convention and wouldn't until 1949.

Therefore, the Germans felt no obligation to meet the standards of the Conventions, knowing full well that the German POWs were being treated likewise by the Soviet Union.

It made one grateful for the little he had... and it was little. So much depended on luck, being the right nationality, getting on the right work detail, being at the right place at the right time... if one could consider being in a German Kommando camp during WWII, good luck.

Other than praying that his luck would hold out, scrounging for food and staying warm, Marion's greatest preoccupation was his thoughts of his family.

Chapter 12

Sam's Efforts

S am had come to terms with returning to Poland before the war broke out. At the very least, he realized he would need to leave the United States in order to reenter legally with pre-examination and proper documentation.

If, in the end, America did not want him, it would hurt, but it would be necessary to accept the decision. A man did what was necessary.

Here in America, he had become a father. Yet, he had no son. Danyk was growing up without him in his long-ago homeland, where his wife too, was waiting for him. At least he prayed this was so. America would always be a part of him, but perhaps, he would not be a part of America. He would need to focus on his greatest blessing - his family, to give him back the equilibrium he would need to go on.

In truth, he longed with a pained heart to see his family and know that they were well and safe. That it would be America, not him, that had made the decision relieved him of the enormous responsibility he would have had to shoulder, had the decision been his alone to make. Yes, he had come to terms with the possibility of returning to Poland, if that was what destiny had chosen for him and his family.

However, Poland had not come to terms with taking him back. It had been undecided or too busy attending to mounting aggression that loomed just outside its borders. Poland was the caged rabbit and Hitler's forces were the attack dogs pacing for another taste of easy prey. Sam had been a safe rabbit and the least of its citizens requiring attention.

Of course, after war broke out, he was considered even less than that.

On February 11, 1938 the Board of Review for the U.S. Immigration Services made a recommendation regarding Sam's case. However, they made the recommendation with somewhat of a blind eye as to what was happening in Europe and how it was affecting commercial travel abroad. They did not require deportation, but were requiring that he voluntarily leave for Poland within 90 days. A later extension was issued to him, giving him until August 30, 1939 to leave.

This was part of the complicated paper process about which Miss Larned foretold.

Though he drew comfort from the preparation her counsel had given him, the total uncertainty of his life's direction made him feel jittery and nervous each time he opened an envelope from the Immigration Department and saw the tentativeness of his life in black and white.

After the invasion of Poland, Sam was granted a series of extensions of notably greater length giving him to August 1, 1940.

It was noted on Sam's immigration records that he was still awaiting a passport and, "...that this is a Polish case." In truth, Poland had enough Polish citizens already in Poland to worry about.

Issuing passports for Americanized Ukrainians returning due to an intention of deportation by the United States government was not on their official priority list, especially because the Polish embassy's staffing had been reduced to one.

This lone official spent his day telling people that were requesting passports to, "come back after the war." Repeated requests for the issuance of Sam's passport were repeatedly denied.

Indirectly, his files were allowed to reflect the extenuating circumstances of his predicament. That being, Sam's country was at war...and perhaps no longer even existed!

No one seemed to know quite what to do with him or the thousands of others that were in similar situations. Even Sam was not sure what to make of himself.

The vessel with Gdynia American Lines on which he had tried to book passage would be holding his ticket for a year. If they still could not transport him to Europe, within this period they would return his money.

Though he made his way to work each day, waiting became the main activity of his day.

He waited for word of his family. He waited for word from the Immigration Department.

For Sam, the world had stopped. He could not go forward, he could not go backward emotionally or literally. He had "made his bed," he thought.

On April 8, 1940 at a United States Immigration Hearing, he did his best to explain the irony of his situation and the difficulties he had faced to follow the orders of the United States government. He was a man worn thin. His rigorous work schedule, his neglected health and his constant worrying about his family, whom he'd not heard from in over a year had weakened him and his voice reflected his weariness. He no longer looked like the proud man Mariya had left in 1933.

"What arrangements have you made to leave the country?" he was asked by an intimidating voice.

His response was in broken English. He spoke slowly and clearly, giving proper respect and wanting very much to be understood. "I went to...Polish Consul...nothing they can do until war over...they only watch the place. I bought ticket with Gdynia American Line and they promise to put me on ship- Batery, then... they couldn't, they held my ticket for one year they say, at which time they return my money. Polish consulate say as long as war lasts they can't do anything to give me passport."

U. S. Immigration officers were aware that the Polish Embassy existed in name only.

Concern for their citizens who were safely tucked away in America was of little importance when their country was in devastation. Anyone of importance or authority had been called to deal with much more urgent matters.

Without a second thought, he was believed and dismissed. However, this did not nullify the formal procedure that was mandated to be followed. Regularly, he would be notified by the U.S. Department of Immigration that he was expected to leave the country. The paper documents began to mount, and Sam's file thickened. At one point, they finally referred to it as "deportation".

He was called in at varying intervals to report and retell his situation at formal hearings. There was a certain redundancy to it all and the presiding inspector exuded a certain boredom as he blandly delivered the interrogation. Each time, Sam listened nervously and intently to the questions that had all been asked of him numerous times before. Each time he answered them directly and honestly.

Such was the case on October 29, 1940. This time the presiding inspector, Mr. T.R. King asked new questions.

"Do you know if your wife and child are now alive?"

Of course, they must be alive!

They are my life, my reason for living!

They are the reason I get up each day, work and save... and try to become an American citizen.

"I do not know. I have had no answer to my letters."

"When was the last time you attempted to get in touch with your wife?"

"About three or four months ago. I sent her a telegram but...." Sam's voice weakened with a touch of apathy, realizing he was spilling his guts to an inspection officer who would probably be going home to eat dinner with his family and play with his children after. " ...but ...I have not heard from her."

"Then, you haven't heard from your wife for over a year, is that right?" Simply... "Yes."

His utter misery was apparent, and even those who did their best to remain detached felt for him. It was clear from his tone that he suspected she could be dead.

"Have you heard from her or of her through any other person?"

Please, do not make me acknowledge this fact.

"No."

"When your wife left the U.S., was she in possession of a re-entry permit?" "No."

"Was her intention to return to the U.S.?" "Yes."

Still, the proceeding continued, so the Department could be fully updated on his circumstances and review his proof of good character and standing.

"Have you been arrested at any time since you were at this station?" "No."

"Are you in possession of a certificate from the police of the various localities in which you have resided for the past five years?"

"Yes. "Sam lifted the documents he had been holding tightly in front of him. For a moment he shifted papers from front to back and then pulled with slightly shaking fingers the papers he believed were required. He offered the papers to the clerk.

"Have you any other evidence you wish to submit as to your good moral character? "Yes." Sam went back to the remaining pile of documents and quickly found the letter from the Beaver House and

Window Cleaning Company, Inc. attesting to his good work ethic and fine Christian character.

Miss Berman, the secretarial clerk who had been seated nearby, reached for the second document, attached it to the Police report, labeled the documents Exhibit 1 and then handed them to the inspection officer.

"Are you still working?"

"Yes." His voice was quiet, yet clear. "I work for Beaver Cleaning House and Window Cleaning Co. Inc. for seven years. I make $42 a week.

Again, he was asked the relentless question. "How much time do you need to leave?"

Patiently, he answered truthfully. "I can not leave on account of war. I would like to stay here."

Once again, he was sent on his way.

While Sam tried desperately to resolve his lack of citizenship and waited impatiently for any word of his family, his now nine-year-old son was being asked to come to terms with what was his own birthright.

Chapter 13

I'm An American!

It was frustrating but also comforting for Mariya to think that at least Sam was safe, far from harm's way, constructing a life, not consumed with its destruction as she was, here in her homeland. She needed to assure herself that her son, too, would have a chance for a future, hopefully one shared with his father, surrounded by all the opportunities in America.

For so long, she had not told Danyk about his American citizenship for his own safety. Now, she must tell him for the very same reason.

In the spring of 1940 in Katyn near Smolensk in Belarus, the Soviets had shot and killed an estimated 20,000 to 28,000 Polish prisoners, including 5,000 senior army officers. Mass graves would not be officially discovered until the Germans uncovered them in 1943, but it did not take an official report for the common Polish citizens to understand the uncertainty of their day-to-day existence.

They were living in "uncertainty" as no nightmare could have dreamed up for them. Each day, family members disappeared. They worked exhaustive hours only to have the products of their labor carted away for the benefit of those in power but not for the children they had left at home hungry and neglected. Their homes, if still standing, could be invaded or confiscated at a moment's notice. There was no resource left to them untouched, not their crops, not their livestock, not their water supply. Their continued existence, if they managed to survive, was controlled by the whim of the local senior officer.

It was a nightmare of nightmares and there seemed to be no end in sight. Hitler, his authority a stone's throw away from their front door, was establishing death camps for over 3 million Jews, most of them Polish. Any gentile, who was alert and savvy enough to comprehend what was happening and dared to protest, was taken away as well.

The living seemed to walk on threads of hope, or lack of, as they watched the world around them stripped bare, mutilated or destroyed. People trembled through their day and in the silence of their own consciousness, they questioned God, themselves and each other. Nothing seemed sacred anymore.

There had been too many close calls to be certain she would live through the war, Mariya realized. It was an impossibly difficult fact to bear but it needed to be dealt with. Danyk might be left to survive on his own.

It had already happened to thousands of Polish children, left orphaned to fend for themselves. If it happened to Danyk, he had to know.

He had proven to be her brave little man so many times. He knew how to remain quiet and not provoke suspicion. He was quick-witted and observant but still he was only nine years old. She would need to impress upon him the importance of secrecy. Her words would need to be strong. She had to make him understand as though he were a man. It was so much to ask of one so young, but time and again she had required much of him and received much back. He had never once failed her.

She sat down on one of the two chairs they owned and waved her hand for Danyk to come close. She swung her left arm over his shoulder to draw him that much closer and then put her right pointer finger up to her mouth to let him know they were to proceed quietly. Secretly.

He looked around to find his grandmother where he had seen her but a moment ago. She was sleeping soundly on a pile of hay in the corner of their mud brick house. He wondered why his mother wanted them to talk so quietly. Not much would wake her when she slept so soundly. Lately, she had been so exhausted that not even the night marches to the trains had woken her. But he was an obedient son, and he gave Mariya his absolute attention without question.

For a pensive moment she sat, realizing she was about to take the last of her son's innocence away, for with what she was about to tell him would come tremendous responsibility and with-it full comprehension - fear.

In truth, he would fully need to understand his own vulnerability. In his short years, he had seen terrible brutality acted out upon others. He had seen the marches of people being sent away, never to return. He would have full knowledge of the dangers of which she would speak.

One last minute of her son's innocence.

She wanted to memorize it. She looked at him, committing to memory the questioning blue of his eyes, the gentle sweep of his chin, and the plumb curve of his childish lips.

Then, she began.

"You know, I like to tell you about your father in America..."

"Are you going to tell me another story?"

"No Danyk, don't interrupt, please. Listen carefully. I want you to remember everything I'm saying, everything. To do that you will need to be very quiet and listen." She nodded, questioning his understanding.

She did not have to caution him again. She spoke. He listened.

As others remember important occasions in their lives... a birth...a marriage...a death, he would remember this.

He was an American citizen. America was not just the wondrous place in which his father lived; it was his country, too. He had been born there. It belonged to him. Though some might try to deny him, it was his right to go there if he wished. Someday, his mother had promised him, he would go there! The hope that it would one day happen was almost as good as the occurrence itself. Hope was a very strong medicine, especially for a little boy surrounded by death and misery.

"Danyk, you must not speak of this or tell anyone. The Soviet's will be threatened by your American citizenship. In a way, it will question their authority over you, just like a student who questions a teacher. They will not like it. They will punish you. For now, it is our secret. Keep it only in your heart, never let it out. It is more valuable than I can ever tell you, it is almost like a magical power that you must use only at the right time - or you will lose it forever. Do you understand?"

He stared up at her in amazement. He was not totally sure what "citizenship" meant.

But he knew this was something outrageously wonderful! It was something to take note of. In the drabness of war, its mystery gave him a reason to feel special and allowed him to feel the touch of hope like a hand on his shoulder.

From that day forward, Danyk did not speak of the secret his mother had told him. But he thought of it several times a day, every day.

It served as a shield to protect him if the war came too close or his mother was too far away. If he was hungry, it helped fill his stomach or at least distract him for a bit. If he was lonely, it entertained him. If he was sad, it was a reason to smile. It gave him a reason to feel he had worth in a world that seemed determined to value him less than spit.

From that moment onward, he would not be a sad, frightened child of war. For now, and forever, he was a proud American. Nothing or anyone could change that.

~

Danyk wondered if Uncle Mykhailo knew his secret.

He dared not even ask his mother; he had promised not to mention it again and he wanted her to trust him. It took all of his control to only smile but not share any of this with Uncle Mykhailo when he appeared out of the forest.

Danyk and his family never knew when to expect him. For everyone's safety it was best not to know. Many of the young men, Polish and Ukrainian, had taken to the "underground" quite literally, using tunnels and burrows in the dense and inaccessible geography of the forest, not only to hide and avoid being forced into the Soviet army or being deported to brutal work camps, but to organize and fight back in any way they could.

The Polish youths fought for Poland, of course. The Ukrainian youths dreamed of an independent Ukrainian state. Their common despise of all things Nazi or Soviet, bonded them in purpose and gave them cooperative efforts but still, their specific goals were distinct.

For the Ukrainian youths, the desire had been planted during the years before the war, when Polish control had repressed the Ukrainian peasantry and then it had grown steadily with the threat of German invasion and even greater repression. Ultimately, seeing their helpless people now under full Soviet scrutiny and harsh treatment, had made them steadfastly committed and loyal to their cause.

They were not yet known as the Ukrainian Insurgent or Liberation Army, but their acts of bravery and cunning were well known to the peasant population and recorded in secret underground newspapers and folk songs.

"Uncle Mykhailo!" Danyk rushed forward and flung his arms around his uncle's neck. Without a father's daily love, he relished the attention Uncle Mykhailo bestowed on him, though it was now only during infrequent visits.

Uncle Mykhailo had a very serious side to him as did most adults confronting these difficult times, but he always managed a short romp or ride for Danyk on his shoulders before he got down to more serious matters with his sister-in-law, Danyk's mother.

Danyk's respect bordered on worship, and he was always careful never to ask for more attention than was given him. Somehow, he instinctively knew it was all the time his uncle could spare, and that Uncle Mykhailo would have given much more if time and circumstances had allowed.

Uncle Mykhailo always brought a present, even if it was just a potato, which actually became more and more precious as the war went on. He always stayed only for a notably short time. But first, he would confer with Danyk's mother either in the house behind a closed door or preferably out of ear shot in the tall grasses of the fields, where if needed, he could slip quickly back into the forest.

Danyk was always given the important position of "look-out" and he took pride in doing the job well. He would scan the horizon and report even the slightest movement he saw in the distance, nervous that he might overlook any possible threat.

Never was he scolded for false alarms, which they always were. Rather he received a pat on the shoulder and a "job well done" wink from Uncle Mykhailo and his mother, who appreciated his caution and too, was painfully aware that it was a heavy chore for one so young to bear.

Then the visit was too briefly over, and Uncle Mykhailo took stride to leave heading back into the forest which seemed enchanted and mysterious to the young boy. Always, Danyk accompanied him to its edge and stayed with him until he could go no further for fear of being lost.

"Uncle Mkyhailo...?" Danyk inquired at the utmost final moment, a split second before Uncle Mykhailo would once again disappear into a world with which Danyk could not imagine or connect. He wanted desperately to share his secret for surely it was safe to discuss with Uncle Mykhailo, who risked his life to fight for all that was good.

Surely, too, Uncle Mykhailo already knew, Danyk reasoned to himself. After all, he was his father's brother.

Uncle Mykhailo knew Danyk's father was in America. Wouldn't he also know Danyk had been born there?

Danyk went to speak of it, using boyish reasoning; the need to share and delight in it was just about to control this impulse to tell, when he suddenly stopped. His mother had said that he dare not speak of it.

Suddenly the breeze that had pushed them to the forest entrance moments before stilled and he knew it was his warning. He dare not speak of it. He must trust his mother's caution.

And he must keep his mother's trust.

"Yes, Danyk. What is it?" Uncle Mykhailo questioned, unsuspectingly. Then he looked at the boy and knew. Danyk needed to say nothing else, because of course, Mariya had told Uncle Mykhailo privately of their conversation, and the boy's beseeching look spoke volumes.

Uncle Mykhailo kneeled down and looked at the boy at arm's length. Silently they conversed and Uncle Mykhailo ended it with a prideful wink.

Suddenly, Danyk had no need to share it aloud with Uncle Mykhailo. They had connected and it was enough.

Uncle Mykhailo stood and was off; seconds later so was Danyk. He returned home proudly knowing he had not shared the secret... even with one he trusted completely.

Mariya wondered if she were imagining it, or did there seem to be more Soviet soldiers passing? They were paired or in small groups and their murmuring and abrupt speech had woken her from her uneasy sleep. Growing increasingly louder were low-toned vibrations that seemed to make her feel as though she had a bee in her ear.

She peeked through the lines and crevices of her crude front door. She didn't want to be noticed, but she did want to detect signs of any danger as soon as possible. She wished she could shush them, so they wouldn't awaken her mother or Danyk, and felt pangs of frustration and anger, knowing that she could not. Soon, Soviet soldiers began to ride by on horses with rifles strapped to their shoulders and then on dilapidated, creaky tanks that looked older than she was.

Perhaps it was just her nerves that kept her looking through the crack. What did it matter what they were up to? It would probably be some new and terrible deed they had thought of to offend or terrify the people of her village. She would surely hear about it in the morning. She should only concern herself with the safety of her family. It was the most control she could hope for, if that much. It did not matter if it were ten Soviets or a hundred, as long as they did not stop at her farm this night.

It was early summer and if not for the possibility of a threat that might surround the four mud walls of her home, it would have been a beautiful hot summer night. She might have taken a stroll outside and enjoyed a gentle breeze, cooler in the darkness than in the heat of daylight to relax her until sleepiness took her again and... why was the buzzing louder? Her thoughts were interrupted. Was a bee in the house?

Mariya quickly circled the room and now felt fully awake, as well as alarmed. The once distant sound now roared and rumbled to an ear-piercing level, but she couldn't detect what it was or from where it came. It grew so loud that the dirt floor and walls began to shake from the vibration, causing dust and bits of hardened dirt to loosen and cloud the air.

She ran to the door and flung it open. Her eyes were drawn upward, and she caught the tail end of a low flying aircraft. Illuminated in the moonlight, she saw many more, all flying brazenly low in unison as though they were a flock of geese. Over the house they flew. The wind shifted and her nightgown bellowed out as they gushed by with hurried purpose.

Foolish Soviets, she thought. Weren't they afraid of crashing into the high trees of the nearby forest?

There were many such trees in the ancient forest that surrounded them. She was not at all surprised when her mother and Danyk joined her, mystified, curious and still half asleep, standing awkwardly outside in the dead of night just outside their home. No one spoke. No one knew quite what to make of it.

Danyk and his grandmother had never really seen a plane before and that alone would have been enough to take in. The metal birds overwhelmed the sky. Hundreds were overhead and they seemed on a steady determined course.

Danyk took in what a sleepy nine-year-old could. "Are more Soviets coming?" he questioned as he tried to rub sleepiness from his eyes.

It began to dawn on them from the reaction of the soldiers that they could still hear and dimly see in the distance that the Soviets were running... away? The soldiers readied their rifles and aimed their tanks as they continued to move down the dirt roads and across the fields away from their farmhouse.

Mariya was still confused. If it isn't the Soviets, who is it? Was this good? What should she think? She did not want to be overly hopeful and jump to the wrong conclusion. Especially, she did not want to say the wrong thing in front of Danyk or her mother.

Within the next half hour furious fighting could be heard as the Soviets tried to maintain their position.

The planes were now dropping bombs and the Soviets were trying to fight back. The shots could be heard echoing through the night. Where was it safe to go? Should they hide in the forest? Should they stay in the house?

The noise was too deafening to run out into the night so, they retreated to the back corner of the house and huddled together. Mariya drew Danyk as close to her as possible and covered his ears to shield him. It was all she could think of doing, though she knew it would do no good.

The three formed a warm ball close to the dirt floor, each with their arm around the shoulder of the other. At first, each explosion or shot made them grip and pull closer together, but then the noises joined by shouts of urgency or screams of pain, began to run into each other and became a single sound - the sound of war.

Their faces were barely a breath away from each other. "Maybe," Danyk whispered, "... the Poles come to rescue us! They will beat the Soviets and then..." Mariya ran her fingers through his hair, thinking she would allow him this brief hope. "...We'll go home to my father in America!"

Even his innocent enthusiasm did not hold her back from reacting.

"Danyk!" She was already kneeling in front of him with his face to hers. She grabbed both his upper arms in her strong hands. "You must not say such a thing! The Soviets will not be happy to know you have a father in America. They might do terrible things to you... to us... if they knew. I thought I had made you understand! You must never talk of it, even in this house, until I tell you it is alright. Do you understand? Never speak of it! Do you understand!"

He wanted to defend himself. He wanted to tell her he had not spoken of his American citizenship. He had not spoken of the secret. Not even to his Uncle Mykhailo, not even though he was desperate to do so!

Even his mother talked of his father in America. However, his mother rarely spoke to him in such an urgent tone, and he knew she would only do so to impress upon him the importance of holding his tongue. He needed to remember not only that he must not talk about the secret in front of the Soviets but that he must not talk about it in front of anyone or anywhere, including with his own mother and in their own home.

The secret was that important... and that dangerous!

"Yes, mother," was all he said but it reflected the tremendous respect he held for his mother.

For his mother, it was enough. She hugged him to her so very tightly, partly because there was a war going on at their doorsteps, partly because she was so sorry that his childhood was as it was and partly, mostly because she was so incredibly proud of him. She loved him so very much.

They listened to the fighting throughout the night. It remained the background of Danyk's private thoughts as his wheels turned. Danyk did not want to give the Soviets reason to seek him out.

When the Soviets came for you, they sent you to Siberia, they took you away from your family, or worse they took your entire family away, as well. Such were the sights he had seen every day with increasing frequency and increasing brutality. He must protect himself. He must protect his family.

He would never speak of the secret again, unless it was with his mother's blessing.

He would not make the same mistake twice.

By morning, they knew who the Soviet's enemy was... it was the Germans! But weren't they the Pole's enemy, as well?

The Soviet's response had at first been dazed disorganization. They shot at the low-lying aircraft with pistols and rifles pitifully unable to reach their targets. The weapons which had appeared so intimidating to the Polish peasants were embarrassingly inadequate to hold off the superiorly equipped Germans.

Hastily, able-bodied locals were recruited to portray Soviet soldiers and forced to choose between fighting against the Germans or instant death. Often, they served as body shields and were the first to die. So, it was to be for Sam's brother, Ivan, although they did not hear of it or what happened to him for weeks after.

Within a short two days, the shooting had stopped and an eerie quiet fell upon them. The people waited, not knowing what would happen next. It all seemed to be such an unexpected turn of events.

Ironically, Stalin had been well-warned of the Germans' betrayal and plan for attack.

However, he had refused to tighten security or even alert his troops for fear Hitler would interpret it as a sign of aggression.

Literally, at all cost, Stalin wanted to avoid Hitler's wrath. Although he was quite certain Hitler would eventually turn on him and attack the Soviet Union, as was the case now, he wanted to delay it as long as possible to continue building up his own forces.

For a day the people were left ungoverned as the transition of power occurred.

Displaced Soviet soldiers tried to regroup, tend the injured and leave for safety in all haste. Generally, they ignored the Polish peasants as they left hurriedly, but did take, or attempt to destroy, everything worth taking that fell within their path.

It was only their frantic need to depart that saved minimal resources for the Polish peasants. The Soviet soldiers didn't want to be spotted by a German airborne unit which had landed on the outskirts of the village the night before or be taken by the German foot soldiers that were soon to swarm the area.

The Polish peasants were not sad to see them go, only feared what was next to come.

It was a period of utter lack of control and helplessness. With little else to do, the Poles watched the Soviets flee.

Poor communication with higher officials made the Soviet soldiers' departure slow despite their urgency to exit. Each soldier gripped his rifle or pistol as though he might need to fire it at any given moment. They left, trudging down the road in much the same weary fashion as they had arrived, only now they jerked their heads quickly and nervously in every direction and at any sudden movement. Their eyes darted back and forth frantically in anticipation of the enemy's appearance.

Some disgruntled Soviet soldiers grumbled their private thoughts when they stopped to take three potatoes, all that they could find, from Mariya's food supply. The rest of her family's meager supply was safely hidden and stored in the hole they had dug and covered on the edge of the forest.

"Perhaps the Kremlin has forgotten about us." To the Poles who heard him, it was as though the Soviet foot soldier whined like a spoiled child.

This was, however, the general feeling of the average Soviet soldier, who indeed was Stalin's last consideration when he planned his strategies or considered the toll of his actions on human lives, even those of his own citizens.

The Soviet soldier's departing words, spoken in his limited Ukrainian, were, "My orders are to burn every house I see and leave nothing for the Germans!"

Mariya held her breath as she watched him walk away, knowing that it meant nothing would be left for the Ukrainians either. In the distance, black clouds formed from other homes that had met just that fate.

She watched him take a bite of the potato, still covered with the dirt from which it had been pulled. He turned back to look at her, and took a glimpse of the rest of the family whom he planned to spare from a great tragedy.

Potato spit from his mouth, as he informed them in weak Ukrainian, "Lucky for you, I am in too much of a hurry!" He turned back, somewhat satisfied by a temporary sense of control and perhaps because... he had denied the Kremlin!

The countryside continued to be painted with scattered activity as each man, woman, child and beast of burden played out their befuddled role. Families searched for loved ones who had either been taken by the Soviets to provide cover or were killed by the Germans. Those left homeless tried to resettle themselves with other family members.

Under Soviet authority, wealthy businessmen were in the most jeopardy of being deported to Siberia as the Soviet Union hoped to indoctrinate the area to the communist philosophy, and considered them, especially the more outspoken ones, a threat.

However, with Eastern Poland now under the jurisdiction of the Germans, it was the Jews, who had the most to fear. In Western Poland, hundreds of thousands of Jews had already been rounded-up in the streets and deported to Germany as slave laborers, executed or sent to concentration camps like Auschwitz, Majdanek or Treblinka. If the Jews of Eastern Poland had avoided the Germans once when the Soviets had taken over this section of Poland, they could not hope to be so lucky again.

They took to the roads and even less obvious paths, through the woods, hoping to make it to the border before the German authority was established and the borders were closed.

Of course, they could not be sure that neighboring countries would accept them, but there was hope. Whatever meager possessions they still had, they tried to carry with them in carts or on their backs.

Sometimes entire families could be seen leaving on foot, many barefoot. By this time in the war, shoes had become a precious luxury for many.

Fleeing Polish Jews, Soviet soldiers, arriving Germans and homeless Poles seemed to cross paths at random over and through the fertile fields, beautiful forests and meandering rivers. None were sure of the other's identity or knew who might have the upper hand at any given moment, so each avoided the other whenever possible. As the Germans secured each area, the visible evidence of their army's presence and their comfort level grew. They began to stop travelers and demand papers. Soon, word spread that it was safer to turn back, return to one's homes or go into hiding.

It was time to get to know a new enemy.

Slowly, news made its way to Mariya's farm. Another family casualty? Ivan, Sam's twenty-four-year old brother had not returned or sent word. A small hope was left that he had survived the invasion, but it was minute. Too many reports had indicated that the German attack had been very strong and forceful.

It was suspected that Ivan had been captured in Kiev by the Germans as the Soviets were running away. Those Poles serving in the Soviet army as forced recruits were used as little more than body shields for the Soviets fleeing back to the motherland.

The German takeover would continue to be swift, methodical and effective. Its execution would leave no strand of Polish life untouched. However, first they would make order. They would calm the residents to avoid hysterics and bedlam. They would proceed as planned, down to the last detail.

Many of the Jews, who weren't able to get out of the country, returned to their homes.

They found that not much had changed. It was reassuring and at the same time suspicious.

Ultimately, it created vast confusion as the Poles wondered... were the Germans friend or foe? For most, it was only a momentary consideration. For others, it was a time to appear loyal to the Nazis and gain their trust, in the hopes of gaining favor or position. In the end, the Germans would make them their greatest fools.

It had been about two years since Sam had last heard from Mariya and Danyk. He knew nothing of their whereabouts or well-being. He only knew that if they were alive, he had no way to go to them.

Each night he prayed for help and forgiveness from God. He had made a mess of his life! Perhaps this was God's way of punishing him. Perhaps he had asked for too much from life with his dreams and aspirations. Now, God had taken his wife and child from him. God had given him the cruelest of punishments and Sam was not sure he could bear it.

He still lived alone and filled his days with work to secure his family's future, should they have one.

Nightly, he followed the news of war in Europe obsessively, especially for any reports of eastern Poland and his village. There was of course very little.

His good friend, Mike Shegren, was a shoemaker on 6th Street and he shared with Sam an intense interest in news of the area. Much of his family remained in Wolodymra (might be Volodymyr), Galacia, a neighboring area to Sam's homeland. The two spent many quiet evenings together sharing silence, each pensively considering the fate of loved ones.

Within two years, the Germans had taken over Norway, Denmark, Holland, Belgium, France, Yugoslavia, Greece and his homeland, Poland.

Still the United States was not involved.

In New York it was a warm summer morning and Sam had oddly overslept and risen later than usual. He almost never did, but his stomach had bothered him long into the night and had kept him from falling asleep. Slowly, he lifted his head and then drew his legs over the side of the bed. As always, his first thought was of his family. Where were they arising to begin this new day? Were they alive to greet it?

His calloused hands scratched his outer eyelids as they rubbed, hoping to bring his half- asleep body to further consciousness. Absent-mindedly, he began his routine. He reached for the radio to turn it on and then brought his body to stand before a hanging mirror. He filled a stationed bowl with water and began to splash his face. He lifted his head, his eyes now meeting his own gaze in the reflecting mirror. He saw a stranger with bloodshot eyes and a pale, almost grayish complexion, staring back at him. It was numbing not to recognize oneself.

Then the radio announcer's words broke his daze. Was he surprised? No. Panic stricken? Yes.

More bombing, more fighting with his family right in the middle of it! Please God, let them live, let them survive this as well.

He had known that since the first German invasion of Poland, the Soviet Union controlled the area from which he had come. However, it had given him little comfort, or surprise. That Hitler and Stalin were two devils working together, was to be expected - at least it was by him.

Hearing that Germany had now attacked the Soviet Union's army occupying Poland was also to be expected. Neither could be trusted and he wondered why Stalin, a bully himself by nature, had not prepared and foreseen this inevitable event. Knowing this did not make accepting the event any easier. Now, not only did Hitler have another notch to add to his victories but his family's fate was now in his control.

There was no easy solution for which to hope.

What else was there to do but follow the news and the German's progress deep into the Soviet Union? Loss of control can be devastating to the human spirit. When a man is helpless, it is a brave task simply to go on.

That is what Sam did... until America offered him an opportunity to help.

Chapter 14

This Time... It's the Germans!

The Germans arrived in July 1941, and it appeared they planned to stay. They brought a well-equipped army. They had more machine guns than the Soviets had rifles. Their tanks looked new and invincible, not like the old-dilapidated ones that the Soviets had used.

Their approach was orderly and methodical, unlike the haphazard approach of the Soviets.

They expressed themselves in exaggerated enunciation and with obnoxious determination, but one thing did interfere with communication. No one understood German!

Ukrainian and Russian languages had certain similarities, but German was very foreign.

This made the people more afraid because they feared being misunderstood. A carelessness could mean the threat of death with no way to apologize, explain or offer a bribe.

The German soldier had a confident air. He stood more erect, held his posture profoundly straight. National pride radiated from his solid healthy body. His teeth gleamed white; his eyes were bright from good nutrition. What a stark contrast he was from the hunched-over townspeople or the haggard Soviet soldier who had been so easily conquered.

After an initial honeymoon which somewhat soothed the frightened Polish population, the Germans proceeded to establish structure and regimentation. Their first action was to search the area and take inventory. It was an orderly process as each villager and his resources, which at this point were minuscule, were tallied and recorded. Of course, the Soviets had left little behind them, even burning Polish homes and villages as they retreated so as not to leave anything of use for the Germans.

The work horses were long gone; the Soviets had confiscated them nearly two years back, almost immediately after their takeover. Some families still had one or two other farm animals left, a chicken, a cow or a pig, that allowed their food supply to be replenished.

The Germans were even less concerned than the Soviets about feeding the Polish population. At will, they took what they wanted, as they wanted. Usually, the peasants from whom they had taken the prized livestock were told to prepare and cook it. Then, they were ordered to serve it and watch it consumed under the very noses of their hungry family.

What was left to them would become part of the village's inventory. They were not to use it for themselves unless given direct permission. To be caught doing so commanded immediate execution, possibly for the whole family.

The searches by the Germans were more methodical and thorough than the Soviets whose primitive existence and ignorance had left them short-sighted. A detailed German inspector could easily find a family's hidden wheat supply which had gone unnoticed during Soviet searches.

The German's record-keeping was impeccable. At one point, the entire village was rounded up for a group photograph. No excuse was acceptable for not being present.

Every man, woman or child was expected to appear. Personal information was cataloged for identification purposes and aid in tracking each villager by first and last name with the precision of a rancher keeping track of his cattle. It was very quick, impersonal, formal and rigid. It exemplified how life was to be from now on under German authority.

The Germans had plans for Poland, and it was thought, "Why waste time waiting for the war to end? We shall be the victors in the end, best to get to work right away."

They quickly settled in for the long haul, establishing the way things would be now and post-war, once the superior Germans had finally won. German comfort was to be considered of paramount importance and it was expected that each Pole would recognize this as a natural phenomenon.

Many of the German soldiers stationed in Poland were those with a special disposition for cruelty and brutality. They had been handpicked by Hitler in anticipation of needing a special breed of men to carry out his orders of extermination without question. It was most unfortunate for the Poles that these would be the men to introduce them to the concept of Aryan Supremacy and the outline of a hierarchy not to be questioned.

The Germans were the superiors and to be served in all ways. The Poles would be the servants.

Disappearances did not stop when the Soviets left. Who was taken first and to where they were transported were the only differences. Consistently, Poles were deported to serve in slave labor camps in Germany. One might be taken while in the fields working, on a street corner or while praying in a church.

These occurrences were random and unpredictable. It did not matter if it was day or night, if one held a toddler in her arms or was attending to a sick parent. It mattered not and certainly no explanation needed to be given, nor was one expected. Usually, families were never informed or permitted communication. If a loved one did not return at the end of the day, it was assumed they were taken by the Germans.

Appreciating that one had not yet been taken away from their family to a work camp made the daily chores of cooking, cleaning, doing laundry and other responsibilities assigned by the Germans easier to accept, though not at all pleasant. Of course, there was no payment given for services rendered and one still had his own basic survival requirements and that of his remaining family to contend with at day's weary end.

Poles in the Ukraine had before led simple lives, but now during this time period, they found they had to be grateful for the simplest of simple things: a roof over their head, a crust of bread, a shoe, a piece of soap.

Families who had managed to keep their houses standing were now being evicted without notice. Where would they go, how might they stay warm, how might they carry their sleeping children was of no concern to the Germans. A care for them was wasted energy; it was not programmed within the plan. The mind of the German soldier at this time, in this place, reflected no conscience.

At the bottom of the German hierarchical structure, was the Jew. A hair above him was the Ukrainian. Commonly posted were the orders of the German Marshal, "Ukrainians and dogs, not permitted".

This ideology was uppermost in the minds of the people of Mariya's village, during any interaction with a German. It was best to be unnoticed. To be a target of a German was ultimately to be his victim.

Searches of Mariya's farm were a quivering, mind-numbing, frightful endurance test. Not only did she have to fear that the Germans would uncover some undeclared item, which would mean instant death in front of her family or perhaps along with them, she had to bear their untethered creativity for humiliation and cruelty. Worse... so did her son and mother.

Their arrival was unexpected... as expected. Their stay at

Mariya's small, once productive potato farm would be brief though catastrophic to her small family.

The Germans knew exactly what they had come for and seemed to go straight for it.

They did not ask for permission to enter the house nor did they offer any greeting or acknowledgement whatsoever. They simply commenced their business without explanation.

In commanded submission, Mariya, Danyk and her mother stood about fifteen feet from their front door. They did not attempt to move, speak or ask questions. Everyone's eyes were cast downward in a pose that had become familiar to them. Mariya studied her bare feet which were hard and calloused from going barefooted often. The family shared but one pair of mud-caked boots between them.

Danyk watched as a large spider made its way across the lumpy earthen floor. Wouldn't it be wonderful to be a spider? To be too small to be noticed, to freely explore as one liked? It was entertainment and an escape for a child caught in the chaos of war. It helped him to remain still.

Suddenly, a loud clanging metallic noise startled his thoughts. From an imagined world of freedom to a real life of restraint, he was now grounded in place by a perplexing racket that had struck his mother into a violent, impulsive reaction. He couldn't imagine what had caused her to mindlessly and boldly react so, but he knew her unpermitted protest would not be overlooked by the Germans.

He had been fearful. Now he was terrified. His mother had made it up to the door before she had been overpowered and dragged back and dropped to the dirt like a heavy laundry bundle.

There she sat in a puddle of despair, her protests now a loud distorted whimper. He didn't dare ask what had gone so wrong. In fact, he couldn't move. His grandmother began to cry and reach for his shoulders, drawing him into her skirts.

Then, a hurried German soldier carried out the hunk of twisted metal and gears that had once been the machine they used to turn grain into flour. Countless times the Russians had searched the house. Not once had they thought to touch it. The Germans had gone right to it, this ancient piece of farm equipment that so far had helped to keep her family alive.

Danyk forgot to breathe when it occurred to him what the twisted pieces had once been.

At the same moment, he understood his mother's immediate, desperate reaction and did not understand why the Germans had left the demolished metal scrap in a discarded lump in their front yard as they sped off. It was obvious they had no intention of using it, or they would have taken it with them. Nor did they intend to allow Danyk and his family to use it.

He did not understand their thinking, nor reasoning, nor words, nor especially their boisterous laughter as two of the soldiers had recreated a mock scene of Mariya's shock and protest. As an afterthought, they added to their performance a Pole holding his stomach in hunger and begging for food. This they thought was the most hilarious of all and they turned to Mariya as if to suggest that she should join them in their laughter. Impulsively, with no fore-thought, she could not help but to give them a guarded, though disgusted look.

Danyk's stomach was empty, so his nauseousness showed itself with the dry heaves. Before the truck had begun to make its way down the road, he had reached his mother still lumped on the dirt ground and put his hand on her shoulder. He did not know what more to do to comfort her.

Minutes passed, grimly they looked at each other. Each could hear the other huff and grab for air to fill their empty lungs. Their gasps were almost empty sobs that knew their own futility.

Finally, after several seconds of reckoning, Mariya decided it was time to go about their day. It was time to accept what had happened.

She lifted herself up, went to her mother and hugged her, then told Danyk to follow her to the fields. They had work to do.

"We will manage," she called out, turning in courageous afterthought. The will to survive was all that was left.

Propaganda against the Jews was a priority undertaking for the Germans which never ceased. It was no secret how Hitler felt about the Jews. Now, with absolute German authority over Poland, each Jew felt Hitler's hand sealing his fate. Most Jews had already done whatever they could to leave, but of course many had been trapped and now their only alternative was to hide. The Germans quickly used their methodically detailed resources to try and find them.

It became a common sight to peer out into the night and see the Germans marching Jews to the trains. No one knew for certain where they were being taken, just as they had never been sure where their own loved ones had been taken by the Soviets.

Some of the Jews who passed wore remnants of wealth as they trod under the watchful eye of roughly commanding German soldiers and dogs. Some were shoeless or ill-clothed when the weather was harsh. Children were among them. Women carried crying babies. It was a heartless scene that repeated itself with each passing night.

Mariya watched most often through tears, making sure she was not seen. To show them any sympathy or kindness whatsoever would mean immediate death.

It was a senseless world. How could one human treat another with such cruelty and hatred? Where had such brutes been before the war? Had they hidden behind the faces of loving fathers, did they buy flowers for their girlfriends back home, did they kiss their mothers and show respect toward their grandparents?

Where had Germany hidden so many monsters?

She only knew that God should never forgive them. Perhaps death would be the only place in which these monsters would get their just deserves. For it did not seem they would be served justice here on this earth, in this lifetime.

Mariya had not seen so many Jews at one time before. Although, perhaps now, she only knew they were Jews because they wore the required yellow star. Most of the Jews lived closer to the factories and their synagogue by Hanonicha or Chunishchee. Her own village had had only five Jewish families. The nearest synagogue was in Skalat, a district in eastern Galicia.

Approximately three-thousand of the six-thousand residents were Jews.

Archbishop Andrea Shiptikzsky from Lvov provided his following a heroic example. He took his cross and gallantly stood in front of a train transporting Jews to make it stop. The Jews were taken off the train and led to a monastery. He told his fellow Ukrainians, "Take them in, feed them and hide them."

Many Ukrainians did so, but they had to be quite cunning. It took a cooperative village effort to keep a Jewish family in hiding. They had to be kept moving from house to house. To remain in one house too long could mean detection and place the accommodating family in great danger. Some succumbed to the promise of power and gave away the Jews in hiding along with the Ukrainian families that hid them. Most, however, did not.

Some Jews were led to the underground fortresses of the Ukrainian Insurgent or Liberation Army (also known as the UPA or Ukrainian Peoples' Revolution Army) which had been formed to fight back in any way they could. It was a continually growing underground army of desperate young men and women willing to give anything for a free Ukraine.

After the overwhelming horror of the summer of 1942 people were reacting with anger and desperation. They formed an intricate network of communication and relied mostly on their own intuitive resources to make life as difficult for the Soviets and then Germans, as possible.

They tried and at times did make contact with the outside world and allies for support, but of all the underground networks forming throughout war-torn Europe, they were the most isolated and the most self-reliant.

By 1943, when the Germans were at the height of an intensified occupational regime, it is estimated that the Ukrainian Insurgent Army had nearly 20,000 members. Their performance and contribution under this strain would much later gain them world recognition and awe. To this day, the region remembers and commemorates them in songs, stories and legends.

> *"Three days fighting Three days not giving up*
> *Going to war and still smiling For Ukraine*
> *For our right We go and fight*
> *For our country Fight for freedom*
> *We fight together..."*

Many of the active participants and agents were Jews themselves making great contributions particularly in the areas of medical and strategical support. In addition to the predominately young local Ukrainians originally from Poland, there were Ukrainians from the Soviet, Polish and German armies and older men who had served in the Ukrainian army from 1917 to 1920. As well, there were Uzbeck, Tatar, Azerbaijan and other detachments composed of former German prisoners of war.

The Ukrainian Insurgent Army lived by a strict regiment and behavior code that could be traced to Kievan princes and their armies which encompassed a standard for bravery, dedication, self-sacrifice, endurance and "readiness to face hardships of military life."

They rejected a privileged class and imperialistic concepts and detailed their policies and philosophies in underground brochures and publications which they readily, though secretly, circulated.

Their fliers and brochures often provided the only updated news or information about the war that the peasant Ukrainian population could expect to get.

Considering their limited resources, similar organizations were later to marvel at their detailed planning and structure which they all hoped would lead them to an independent, thriving Ukrainian state once the Germans and Soviet Union wore themselves out.

Their weapons were often whatever the volunteers brought with them, could gather from the local population or could capture from the enemy. Generally, they were rifles, machine guns and grenade launchers.

The UIA used simple but well-thought-out strategies directed at keeping the enemy within their bases as much as possible and away from or leery of interacting with the local population; concealing harvest yields in well-camouflaged bunkers and a system of observation and signalization to warn the local population of approaching threats.

They would attack jails and release the prisoners, blow up supply depots or set up ambushes. When German units would come to retrieve their dead, they would catch them unaware and overtake and acquire their weapons.

It was a long laborious process, but the people understood the consequences of giving up.

They were not in any way ready to do so.

When news came to the village that entire Jewish towns were being rounded up and murdered it was practically unbelievable in its absurdity. Even the Germans could not be so mad, could they?

But the Germans' madness seemed to have no limit. Such was the part of history that Danyik was witnessing. What must be his view of the world? He was just ten years old.

Mariya had failed her son, because the world had failed her.

Eventually, they stopped marching the Jews to the trains as often. Barbed wire went up around Skalat which was a small town but well known as an old fortress built in the 16th century. Here, the Germans began to pack in the Jews.

In 1941, Skalat had 8,500 Jews. By 1942, it had been reduced to 4,600.

"Too many people, too many people." Danyk would murmur over and over again to his mother.

Bearing witness to the degree of inhumane treatment of the Jews created a sadness that was too overwhelming for anyone to understand if they had not themselves experienced it.

Children with forlorn faces, some Danyk's own age, were packed so tightly they literally made one sea of endless sadness. It was unspeakable! It was beyond human understanding and certainly well over the understanding of a young boy.

But then, the capacity of a child to compensate or cope should never be underestimated, even or perhaps especially, under the circumstances of war. It was often a mistake made by the Germans.

Children often made the best agents, for delivering messages, sneaking or hiding food, as they were the last to be suspected. Not only did the Germans believe the Poles and especially the Ukrainians to be mentally inferior and not as intelligent, they assumed the children were even more so.

Too, they did not believe a Ukrainian parent would be brave enough to permit his own child to perform such a courageous act. After all, anyone caught deceiving a Nazi would be shot without question. Children were no exception.

So, to feed a Jew one needed to be particularly cunning, fast and of course innocent looking. The church was urging action and circumstances were so dire that even fearful people dared to act.

Danyk's education living in war-torn Poland had included all these things. With his mother's blessing he would slip long narrow pieces of precious bread up his sleeve, then he would walk at a consistently even, fast pace parallel to the barbed wire fence. With his eyes straight ahead, he would near its edge as though he were briefly distracted, open his sleeve wide at the wrist and let the morsels slip out. He would maintain his steady pace, not go any slower nor faster to avoid attention.

Also, he would need to continue on his way, as the children who had spied the bread would come clamoring. The stirred activity could be enough to cause detection. Not having the children notice until he was out of sight was the most difficult, as well as, the most dangerous part. If he was caught, even just for depositing a morsel of bread, he would be shot on sight.

Each time, Danyk wished he was fearless like his Uncle Mykhailo, like the men of the forest who fought for all the people. But he was not. He was scared to death each time he gathered the courage to do it.

Maybe, someday he thought, when... if he became a man, he would be brave, too.

It felt good to deceive the Germans, though he felt far from celebrating as he knew his efforts were pitiful...far from adequate. These small personal victories were all one could do. But of course, these efforts would not be nearly enough.

By the war's end over six million Jews, including most of Poland's Jewish population, would be dead.

Chapter 15

Toll of War

On January 21, 1941, Immigration's extensions and patience ran out. Sam was ordered deported to Poland. He was not eligible at the time to file a petition for naturalization under the Nationality Act of 1940. However, there was also no place for him to go and no means for him to leave. A war was on, and the Polish Consul, represented by a staff of one, would not issue him a passport. As well, Gdynia American Line was still holding his ticket for transportation on the Batery but because of the war they were not yet offering passage.

His life seemed to be at a paralyzing standstill with no legitimate way to turn. He was between a rock and a hard place which seemed to raise havoc with his "nervous stomach".

Although the deportation order was a cloud that darkened his life, he was not otherwise directly affected. Life went on as it was because simply... there were no choices to make. His life was out of his hands.

Sam's friend, Mike, worried about him constantly. It was at his urging that Sam bought his own shoe repair business for $1,500 at

128 1st Avenue in New York City from a friend who was being inducted into the army.

Mike had wanted to celebrate and declare this development as a dream fulfilled, but Sam could not be swayed or distracted from the feeling that he was always trying to climb out of a sinking hole. Sometimes he wished he could crawl out of his skin until an idea grabbed hold of him and seemed not to let go.

Was it possible? Could he do it?

~

He was an illegal alien, but one with much love for the country he now resided in. Would a country that had ordered you to leave allow you to serve it instead? Could he be of any use?

Ironically, it seemed to be the one place that America would want him - the United States Army! Finally, he found a niche that felt right.

~

Everyone was watching what was happening in Europe. As the months followed, there would be daily reports, always in the Germans' favor. Sam, knowing the area well, surmised that Hitler was rushing, hoping to conquer all, before having to deal with Russia's harsh winter. Although it was not known at the time, Hitler had expected his superior army to overtake Russia in six weeks.

On Sunday, June 22, 1941, Hitler found an excuse to attack his ally, the Soviet Union, claiming it had reneged on an earlier agreement. This was not a surprise to Stalin, but his greatest fear was realized. He had wanted to avoid or at the least delay war with the Nazi's as long as possible, while he prepared for what he knew would be an inevitable betrayal. His advisors had warned him, including his number one spy, Richard Sorge, to expect the attack. Stalin had even been given the exact day, time and location of the invasion. However, he had so greatly feared antagonizing Hitler should he recognize a building resistance, that he left the area totally vulnerable. At the last possible moment, he changed his mind and frantically attempted to prepare his troops. But it was too late.

It would be the largest military operation in world history. Eight and a half million soldiers, 5,639 tanks, and assault guns, over 10,000 planes, 61,000 guns and mortar, 217 fighting ships and 161 submarines would be used to batter Russia.

Hitler's plan directed three army groups. The first heading for Moscow consisted of 50 divisions with 1,630 planes and 15 armored divisions. The second was headed for the Baltic republics aimed at Leningrad and the Soviet naval stronghold of Kronstadt. The third consisted of 57 divisions, 9 armored with 1,650 planes advancing toward Kiev and Odessa.

Ukraine, of course, would be easily overrun; it would be taken in a matter of hours.

Over the next six months the German soldiers would advance into the Soviet Union an average of ten miles per day. By July, Hitler's army would be dropping bombs on Moscow.

Within a fortnight of the invasion, half a million Soviets had been killed. Of the 170 Red Army divisions that had been stationed near the western frontier on June 22nd, twenty-eight had ceased to exist. Seventy had been halved in number and equipment. By September, Germany would take Lithuania, Latvia, Estonia, Bellorussia, Moldavia, Greater Russia, and the Ukraine.[1]

The United States was not yet in the war but seemed determined to

---

1. Karpov, V. (1987), *Russia at War 1941-45*, The Vendome Press, New York 1987 p.21

prepare for one, nonetheless. Aliens were not turned away from service, under the 1940 Selective Service and Training Act, even illegal ones such as Sam, as long as they were able-bodied. The Immigration Department, however, maintained authority and ordered that they were to be notified of Sam's address upon his discharge, so that proceedings could be resumed. If Sam had entered the country legally, his service would have qualified him for citizenship. As he had entered illegally, his service would not.

Still, at almost 39 years of age, Sam Szafranski left behind his bank account of $2,311.07 at Central Savings Bank on 4th Avenue and 14th Street and was officially inducted into the U.S. Army on September 17, 1942, at Fort Jay, New York. As a private he was stationed in Company F, 6th Quartermaster Training Regiment in Camp Lee, Virginia.

Half a world away, his wife and eleven-year-old son too, prepared for war.

~

Leningrad had been one of Hitler's original objectives and by September 8th he had isolated the city from communication with the rest of Russia. By October the citizens of Leningrad were starving to death.

Hitler then directed his attention to Moscow. The city had already been turned upside down by nightly air raids. All mass transit had been stopped. The platforms and passageway were used for shelters with families getting the highest priority. Single adults had to sleep right on top of the rails. All shop fronts had been boarded-up and sand-bagged to prevent danger from broken glass. It was a city prepared for attack but not really expecting it.

When the Germans rolled into Orel, 200 miles southwest of

Moscow the local citizens cheered them at first, too stunned to think they could be any other army other than Russian.[2]

Each day the headlines reported news of the Soviet front and easy German victories. For Sam, neither victory would delight him. His concern was only for his family and friends in the Ukraine who he knew were suffering much worse than the average citizen in Moscow.

In October, Hitler's army finally hit a glitch. Heavy rains had hit the area. Most roads were not paved. With heavy rains, the compressed dirt quickly became thickly mudded. German tanks sank into them as though they were quicksand. Unable to find traction, the glimmering new ready-to-attack German tanks stayed where they were. This would cause their army dangerous delays and cut their gains down to four miles a day.

Still, by mid-October they were attacking Moscow. The city was in a panic. Civilians were evacuated or organized to build anti-tank defenses around the city.

Another glitch in German planning occurred in November when the temperature dropped. At first the Germans rejoiced for the frozen ground was much more accommodating than the mudded road left by the rains.

But then the temperature dropped 20 degrees below zero. The vehicles and artillery were unable to function in such freezing temperatures. More urgently, however, was the lack of proper clothing for such treacherously low temperatures. German soldiers were literally freezing to death. Hitler, however, was not willing to allow a retreat. It was the first major defeat for the Germans who had grown over-confident with endless victories.

This presented a timely advantage for the Soviets who had taken

---

2.   Karpov, V. (1987),*Russia at War 1941-45*, The Vendome Press, New York, p. 22

every initiative to step up their readiness for a war they stood a chance of winning. They had already stopped the German advance. Luck had helped with that. They needed to swiftly mobilize their country for victory. The economy had to be geared for a country at war. Important resources needed to be relocated eastward away from western borders.

Mentally, the Soviet soldier prepared to fight to his death. Not necessarily due to a devotion to protect Stalin's Russia, but because of a full and complete recognition of his own vulnerability. He had long lived under the cruel hand of Stalin and knew that a defeated Soviet soldier was a dead soldier or at least better off that way. Stalin would not show any sympathy to him or his family. Earlier purges, ordered by Stalin of his own Soviet officers for inadequate performance or questionable loyalty, gave each soldier a crystal-clear vision of his fate, if they retreated in defeat.

Morale was at an all-time low for both German and Soviet soldiers when Stalin launched his first Soviet counterattack at 3 a.m. on Friday, December 5th. His spy, Richard Sorge, had assured him that Japan, an ever increasingly aggressive threat to the East, was busy attending to affairs elsewhere, which enabled Stalin to relocate his troops to the west and attack with a well- manned army.

The results were successful. For the first time, the Soviet army held the upper hand.

The Soviet army, feeling they had nothing left to lose, fought ferociously to save themselves and their countrymen, who sometimes joined them on the battlefield. They were withered, worn, tired and desperate but warmer and for once more prepared than the Germans who were literally freezing to death. By the end of November, the weather had killed more Germans than the Red army. By January 1942, Hitler relented and finally allowed his troops to retreat, with plans to try again in the early summer. Hitler's grasp on victory was no longer assured.[3]

---

3. Karpov, V. (1987), *Russia at War 1941-45*, the Vendome Press, New York, p.23

Although the German soldiers knew of the difficulties on the Russian front, they appeared stupefied when the Soviets returned to reclaim German-occupied Poland.

How could a dirty, ill-equipped, inferior army defeat them? No matter for now, they would retreat in a most obnoxious manner and of course return when the time was right. They would retreat as they had arrived, with total self-absorption and no care for the peasant population.

At this point the Ukrainian peasantry was worn thin. Hundreds of thousands of Poles had been deported in mass to labor camps in Germany. Over six million Poles, three million of them Jews, had died in death camps.

Factories, buildings, hospitals were shells, barely frames of structures which had once existed. The cellars, all that were left, were now used to house twenty-five million people.

The Ukrainian people felt stripped bare. Yet, still the Germans thought to take more.

They would slaughter or carry off twenty million pigs, seventeen million heads of cattle. They left no useful resource untouched. Crops were burned and water supplies contaminated, as they quickly and methodically made their way back toward Germany.

Many Ukrainian peasants were left only to scratch their heads when they realized the Germans were stealing, of all things... their dirt.

Nothing, it appeared was too sacred for the Germans to rape. Literally they scooped up the fertile red soil of the Ukraine for transport back to Germany.

Sam departed Fort Jay, New York and arrived at Camp Lee, Virginia's Quartermaster School. Camp Lee had re-opened in March of 1941, to provide an army installation equipped to meet the rapidly growing need for Quartermaster training. Here, there was adequate room to spread out for a growing population of enlisted men, staff, faculty numbering 362 officers, officers in training, officers visiting from foreign countries to attend courses, members of the Women's Army Corp. (WAC's) and civilians. A.P Hill Military Reservation was within sixty miles and provided the extensive terrain needed for training under actual field conditions.

Initial remarks were given and Sam listened intently. The overall function of the Quartermaster regiment was reviewed, though Sam expected to serve the regiment as its shoe repairman. Expectations of being personally responsible for issued items and a warning in terms of up-keeping appearance were barked-out by very crisply dressed officers and then, he was taken to a building to stand in a long line. There he was issued a barrack bag and told to fill the bag with all the essential items detailed on a list he had been given.

Before he was done, he had filled his barrack bag, as well as another of the two additional bags he had been issued. He had never had many material possessions in his life so, lugging the bulging bags with the brand-new issued items, at least for the moment, made him feel like a rich man, undeserving, but rich.

No sooner had he settled in his bunk than the rigors of army life began. His days were immediately filled with exhaustive physical maneuvers which were carried out over the beautiful landscape he had so admired when he had first arrived.

It was a busy time surrounded by focused people and high energy. For a time, it helped him forget but not for long. If he saw an officer's wife carrying a child, heard a war report over the radio, or listened to a Sergeant's forecast of what war could do to an ill-prepared soldier, he remembered what was going on in the world; that he was a man separated from family and not claimed by any country. Yet, he spent his days serving them both the best way he knew how.

For now, America needed his service, but they had not forgotten his status as an alien under deportation proceedings which were to continue after the war and his discharge. Sam was aware, as specified in Section 701 and 702 of the Nationality Act of 1940, that his service would not have any bearing on his eligibility for naturalization.

Sam was approaching forty but was physically training like someone in his early twenties. He tried never to complain, but he fell quickly and easily to sleep each night and struggled to rise every morning. At least there was no energy for nightmares; instead, the imagery he feared followed him through his days, increasing as time passed and he became accustomed to military life.

Often, Sam's hand could be found rubbing his stomach, trying to ease the tenseness that lodged there. Perhaps he had tried so hard to dispel his worries from his mind that they had found a new home in his mid-section. There, they managed to aggravate him just as effectively giving him frequent recurring stomach trouble. Ultimately, they would cost him a brief stay in the military hospital. Instead of being concerned about his medical problems, Sam in his typical appreciative immigrant-way, just felt relief and gratitude that he didn't have to pay the bill.

America had given him so much. That was the way he saw it. And he would continue to serve it, until it didn't want him anymore.

He prayed his future would also include a reunion with his family.

Live Mariya... live Danyk!

Let me live to see an end to this war... and our lives made right!

The first order of business for the Russians was to identify and round up anyone who had fraternized with the Germans. First, they would be publicly humiliated, then shipped to Siberia or assassinated.

Mere suspicion was enough to make one vulnerable. It became a fact of life that was to be endured for years to come in Stalin's Russia.

One day in March 1944, one hundred armed Bolsheviks arrived

in Mariya's and Danyk's village. They ordered all the men, sixteen years and older into two buildings.

Mariya, her mother and Danyk joined the others being escorted down the dirt road leading to the village. The rifles which slanted off the shoulders of the soldiers surrounding them, reminded Danyk of a lopsided picket fence that he dared not cross. Above him he noticed a flock of birds free to fly and go where they pleased. It would occupy his mind for a while to pretend he was one of them. Such imagined adventures were the only playgrounds for children of war.

Suddenly, the shots rang out and the people around him shuttered and then, oddly slumped in relief when they realized the shots had not been directed at them, but at the wild game which now fell from the sky and would be some fortunate soldier's dinner tonight. His mother's gentle hand reminded him to pay attention to what was ahead, and he was again in this time and place, marching on weary feet to the center square of his village.

Ahead he could see that the men and women were being separated. Instinctively Danyk reached for his mother. There was fear etched plainly on the faces of those who had arrived earlier and were now making room and surrounding those just arriving. The only other acknowledgement given were quick glances that danced, then skidded back to the ground where it was safest to be caught looking.

Soldiers were directing the slow, steady movement of tired bodies being pushed along by a tide. Men and older boys were being directed right into a building. Women and children were being directed left into another.

The soldier hesitated when he came to Mariya, who clutched Danyk by the collar as though she were disciplining a wayward child. But rather, it was the loving, desperate hold of an anxious mother and Mariya knew with all her being that if she let go, she would never see Danyk again. Relief swept through her when his bayonet directed them both left, following the path of the other women and children. Her mother was only a foot before them and as everyone regrouped the three made a closed circle.

187

When the screams began, their circle opened, and others took hold anchoring in. The crowd moved as a whole with a unified force that caused soldiers to stiffen and ready their rifles. Minds and hearts froze, overwhelmed with the gripping fear that they were all now in the last moments of their life. The circle waited for the soldiers to open fire. It is an odd sensation when one waits to die. The adrenaline runs furiously upward with no escape and the body stills with a helpless rush of acceptance. Then, time stands still.

More screams continued from inside the building and more time passed. Finally, the circle of women and children realized, as guards were being relieved with replacements, that they had been left to stand in their own bewilderment and fear for quite some time. The torture seemed endless and as the agonizing screams continued each was left to wonder if it was their own husband, father, brother, son that was the source.

One woman began to cry and wail openly, thinking that she had recognized her own husband's screams but was hushed and quieted quickly before she had time to be noticed. Such a display would have given a soldier an easy reason to shoot her.

It was difficult... more than difficult... it was unnatural to stand hour after hour listening to loved ones being tortured for... for nothing really, for being in this time and place... for being helpless against a giant foe. But everyone, even the children, even Danyk, stood silently as one scream after the other passed over them. Eventually, there was no reaction at all, at least not one that a soldier could see. When emotions are so overwhelming that they can not be contained but must be... one becomes blank... a sheet of nothingness. The eyes daze, and don't focus; the shoulders slump; the muscles of the face fall into a sagged droop and misery turns the complexions to a dirty white ash. Helplessness scars the heart and festers there as a recorded memento of war. It is never overlooked, not by the human soul, no matter how young or how old; it always hangs on. Those untouched by it cannot comprehend the depths of its full fury nor can its toll be escaped by those it has touched.

Long after night had arrived, the beaten and tortured men were released and their families permitted to take them home. Many could not walk, and the women had to help each other in any way they could to find ways to transport them.

Those of the village who had failed to show up as they had been told to do were the next to be rounded up.

Mariya did not know where Danyk was, and the shot had been so very loud.

Too loud, too close! Where was Danyk?

Mariya ran out the front door trying to focus on the direction of the shot. Her mother was quickly behind her, her arms raised pointing in the direction of where she had thought the shot had come. It was her confirmation, and she took off.

Moving quickly but wishing to be unseen she crept around the side of the house and then scurried through the open clearing until she reached a tangle of untamed young trees. She sensed the activity going on a hundred meters beyond and settled herself low. Softly, gently she moved the budding leaves aside for a sliver of view. She knew the two men being addressed by the Russian soldiers. One was Martin Lyholiz, a nearby neighbor and the other was Oleksky Tyholiz, his cousin.

Oleksky was panting heavily and holding his arm. Blood dripped at his sides. The Russians had only just begun. Before they were done, he had two broken arms.

They took Martin much more seriously, plowing him with bullets as though it were target practice or he was a terrible threat.

When they were done, Martin, riddled with holes, lay on the brown dirt. Blood flowed from head to toe and Mariya struggled not to heave.

Oleksky lay next to him moaning, which was a good sign. He was still alive.

189

As the soldier prepared to leave, one turned back and glared at the tangle of trees that had been Mariya's hiding spot. She recoiled quickly, realizing she had been discovered but still panic-stricken, she remained behind the trees. If she moved to the clearing there would be no mistaking her presence.

Then the soldiers loudly rang out a command, and she knew they spoke only to her. "Leave him here! You are forbidden to bury him. He will remind the villagers that they are to do exactly as they are told. You do not think for yourself. We will do your thinking for you"

He had known she was there the whole time. He turned and left. His men followed. Mariya was afraid to move, but Oleksky's moaning forced her to do so.

She let a moment more pass. She gathered her senses and began to creep forward. Oleksky's moaning grew louder, and an invisible force pulled her forward. She knelt down between the two men and reached for Oleksky.

"Why?" he whispered. "I have done nothing." His voice advanced and now shook with sobbing.

"You are a good man, Oleksky." Mariya's words were inadequate. "But that does not matter in this war, good men die... evil men..." She focused her thoughts. " Martin is dead; they've forbidden me to bury him"

"My cousin was a good man, too, he did not deserve this."

"I know." There was nothing else to say. So, they sobbed together for a while on the dirt floor with the dead man by their side.

Mariya jumped when she felt the hand on her shoulder. The movement made Oleksky gasp out in pain.

"Danyk! You startled me. Where were you?" She had forgotten him and was angry at herself for doing so.

He pointed to the branch where he had been hiding and she realized...painfully that, he had probably seen everything.

"The whole time?"

He nodded his head yes and waited to see if she was angry.

"Help me lift Oleksky. Slowly..."

190

Carefully they helped him up and began the slow journey back to his house. Each took a turn to look backward at Martin, the only one at peace among them.

~

The arrests and persecution continued. One day the Russians arrived with an unknown peasant. Neither Danyk nor Mariya had ever seen him before. They were forced to watch as the Russians made him dance to the firing of bullets at his feet. They did not kill him, which of course meant, they had never intended to. They had wanted to scare him, and break both of his arms.

Such scenes were commonplace; they were part of daily life.

Though the Soviets claimed they were targeting rebellious threats and dissidents; most victims knew no reason that they had been targeted. They were simple farmers doing their best to feed their families and stay alive.

Still, the arrests and persecutions grew worse and too numerous for the specifics of each to be recorded as memories of distinct separate events. They merged, intertwined and branded each broken heart a casualty of war.

The entire town was being rounded up again. It was always a chilling scene and by now the Soviets were perfecting their methods. One never grew accustomed to being brutalized and the people's fear was like an unleashed energy, static and vibrating through the air.

~

"Kupetzky, what is wrong?" Mariya whispered. At times he knew or had gotten word from the UPA or Ukrainian Revolution People's Army. This was an underground network that functioned independently of any foreign source. Sixty percent of their members were from the immediate Galicia area and most were simple peasants who armed themselves from stolen weapons or acquired from the enemy on the battlefield.

"Explosives were stolen; they are going to want a name." Kupetzky's voice was not encouraging. It was a desperate situation, and he felt a need to be truthful with her.

Armed Soviet soldiers circled the crowd. Growling dogs leaped in the air, seemingly eager to attack.

A stiff Soviet officer began to speak and immediately the crowd silenced. Often, they screamed orders at the Poles in Russian and without translation the Poles were expected to figure it out. But today, the officer wanted to be clearly understood and fully spoke his commands in Polish. Still, it was difficult to make out his words. They were thickly accented, and he spoke hurriedly.

"You are all aware that explosives were stolen last night. Don't deny it." He gave a long pause as if he were examining individuals in the crowd.

"You have five minutes to give us the name of the thieves. If you do not...," he hesitated again for calm effect... "every 10th person will be shot, until we find out who stole the explosives."

Almost collectively the crowd gasped.

Families clung together imagining that the end had finally come. It was such a helpless feeling.

One minute passed. Then, two. A woman wailed, a child cried out and panic began to descend.

Suddenly, the officer was distracted. His head jerked to and fro. The soldiers responded immediately and took random aim into the surrounding woods.

Something had been spotted, but it seemed to perplex the Soviet soldiers who had not been expecting a threat to surround them. Before the officer had time to command, and before the soldiers had time to find a target...a strong and clear voice came out of the forest.

Mariya, Kupetzky and Danyk eyed each other in shock. They recognized the voice; and they were certain many others had recognized the voice as well.

"Tell your men...", the words were directed at the officer, "... that they will not be shooting anyone today."

"How dare you interfere! Show yourself! Or everyone here dies!" Pompously, the officer continued to search the trees. "You dare to order me!"

"I'm not ordering you... no need to be offended," the voice threw back just as pompously, and the people could not believe their ears!

"... I'm just informing you."

Suddenly, further stunning everyone, the officer's hat was glazed by a bullet.

No one knew what to do for a fraction of a second and then an anxious soldier began to shoot aimlessly into the woods until his rifle was empty.

The other Soviet soldiers looked in vain for a target, a movement, a shadow. The officer had fallen back and was clutching his chest as if to pump air in and he gulped huskily as he tried to catch his breath. Embarrassed at his lack of composure, he quickly gained it back, simultaneously ducking backwards for cover.

But still the Soviet soldiers were at odds. Where had the voice come from?

All this occurred within seconds and then the brave voice spoke again from the shadows. "You don't need to hide!" The voice spoke with amusement and Danyk was at once soothed by the familiar tone. What a delicious scene, to see the officer so fearful!

"Those bullets weren't meant to harm you. If they were you would be dead. We just wanted to be sure you would believe us. We want to be certain we make ourselves clear."

"At least a dozen, perhaps more..." the voice teased, "Schmeisser's 9mm MP 38/39 sub machine guns are pointed right at your head, at this very moment.

The officer was visibly shaken. Again, he moved for cover, but a dance of bullets tapped at his feet, and he couldn't move. He began to look like a caged animal and his haunted eyes searched desperately for his insolent tormentor.

"Superior weapons!" the tormentor called out. "Did you get them from the allies? I know the Soviets don't usually have the luxury of such precise arms? Oh, but I forgot, you don't have them ... not any longer, do you? We have them." The tormentor exuded satisfaction.

Mykhailo knew his obnoxiousness could bite him back at any moment, but it felt too good not to play the game for a moment longer. He had worked long and hard to be in such a position and have the upper hand. Still his people were in a dangerous situation, and he needed to control himself and move this along, most especially because his sister-in-law and nephew were amongst the hostages.

The officer weighed his words before he spoke. He was in a precarious situation; he needed to maintain his dignity, yet he wanted to live to tell about it. Too quickly the invader issued his orders, and he lost his opportunity to respond.

"If even one villager is harmed... you die! Today, right here. Your men, as well, perhaps, but the first bullet will be yours. You die first!"

The voice waited for the officer to absorb his situation.

The officer was frightened but also outraged. "You insolent fool. Do you realize who you are threatening!" He spat out each word as though he were issuing a death sentence.

Everything grew very still. A minute went by, then two. The officer continued to search the surrounding area, as did the villagers and Soviet soldiers, who minute by minute were becoming more nervous realizing the insurgents were probably far more armed and equipped than they. The officer sensed this but as the minutes went by and nothing happened, he began to feel relieved as though he were back in control again. However, he remained on high alert.

Unconsciously, the officer took a step, but again a barrage of bullets bounced uncomfortably around his feet, and he began to dance reactively.

The firing stopped, then so did the officer. If a twig snapped the crowd would have heard it; it was that still and quiet while everyone waited.

"Release everyone, let them go back to their homes." The voice was loud but calm and determined. "There are still at least a dozen guns pointed straight at your head. What will it be?"

"Do you really think a dozen guns are going to deter the Soviet army?" The officer chuckled and then more incredulously... "or Stalin?"

"We seemed to be doing well against your heavily armed unit right now, no?" Again, his voice was making fun!

Silently, the officer who had lived now too long under Stalin's iron rule, envied the man who was brave enough to try and fight an unbeatable foe. He was naïve perhaps; he had not yet met the fire-breathing dragon that ruled his country. He would learn... but perhaps not today.

"It is not the entire Soviet army that I am assuring will be killed; just your death I will guarantee."

It was one thing to be arrogant and defiant with twenty soldiers surrounding you, ready to do your bidding, but it was another when someone held a gun to your own head and had you dancing to the tune of artillery, not once but twice.

The officer began to blink tensely, jut his jaw and to squeeze his lips into peculiar shapes.

The intruder's army was going to pay for this, he swore to himself. But not today. "I will release them..." and then he threw in absent-mindedly, "for now."

"Just remember Kapitan, my guarantee does not expire. If even one dies at your command ... so, do you. You will never see it coming."

At once, everyone sensed the voice had retreated. Yet, its presence was still oddly felt. The officer must have felt it too because the villagers were indeed released.

Tired and worn, the people began to disperse and rush for their homes. Everyone hurried, fearful that the soldiers would change their minds.

Mariya had recognized the voice immediately and she was sure Kupetzky and Danyk had too. Yet, no one spoke a word of it as they followed the dirt road and sloping pasture home. It was silently agreed that it was best not to.

They would live another day... at least for now.

~

It was now April 1943. Sam had been honorably discharged from the United States Army on March 26th. For a short time, he'd found a sense of peace in the total absorption of army life and service.

Thoughts of Mariya and Danyk were of course always with him. They were like a packed suitcase he didn't want to put down or lose, but the army allowed him to put his bundle down for a bit as he carried out orders and served America.

He'd reopened his shoe repair shop at 128 1st Ave. and would soon be making $100 a month.

Of course, he was not eligible to petition for citizenship. He had known this before entering the army, but it was now time to put his affairs in order. He would leave that to the authority of the U.S. Immigration Department.

Though he had served in the U.S. Army, he was a man without a country, without a family. At times he felt he did not care what they decided to do with him. As much as possible though, he kept these thoughts to himself. He was not one to bother others with his troubles.

Today, however, he was going to.

He was going to see Miss Larned at the International Migration Service.

Sam knocked softly, perhaps so softly she had not heard him, so he knocked again more forcefully. He cleared his throat, which felt dry from nervousness.

"Yes, come in."

Miss Larned was wearing glasses and reading something on her desk as he approached. They had not seen each other since he had enlisted in the army, and he wondered if she would remember him.

"Mr. Szafranski... how nice to see you again!"

"How are you, Miss Larned?" His English had much improved since she had last seen him.

"Fine, fine, please, have a seat."

She set aside the papers she'd been studying and eyed him with tremendous interest.

To Sam, she seemed like such an important woman. She was dressed so finely and had her own desk, and office, yet she always listened to him so intently. This was a fine, good woman, he thought as he gave her a respectful smile.

"I have come to finish being American citizen. If possible? Or I wish to know what America wants me to do. I do what they say." He spoke with a conviction she had not heard from him before.

Her heart melted at his resignation.

"Have you heard from your wife, Mr. Szafranski?" she asked as gently as she could. "No... no, nothing has changed. I go into the United States Army." He straightened momentarily with pride, "but in all that time, I hear nothing. I feel... " He looked her straight in the eye, while he searched for the right words.

LOST. ALONE? she wondered.

"Broken, empty... nothing there." He patted his chest as if to soothe the pain in his broken heart. "Nothing there... no more. You help me?"

He was so humble, so sincere and not the first immigrant to touch her heart.

Sam had pegged her well. Miss Larned was a good woman devoted to serving others.

"I will do my very best, Mr. Szafranski." She answered with the assuredness of a caring friend.

Motions. Correspondence, forms, crossed back and forth between Sam, Miss Larned and the International Immigration Services until every "i" was dotted and "t" crossed.

Each step of the way, Miss Larned assisted Sam in understanding the wheels of the Immigration Department process. She checked each application, made copies and kept him on schedule with reminders.

On August 10th they received notice that his case would be further considered. This was not a stamp of approval or an "O.K., you're in," but Sam was thrilled nevertheless. It was the spark of hope he needed to lighten his load. It was the first time in years that he felt a reason to get up each day.

There was quite a bit of "red tape" with which to deal with. Motions needed to be filed in triplicate, warrants needed to be withdrawn and the Department's orders amended. He needed to be given permission to apply for voluntary departure and reexamination before he could do so.

He also needed to apply for a Visa first by written request, then in person.

On November 5th, Sam's sworn statement was recorded at the N.Y. City Clerk's office.

He reviewed the events of his life since he left Poland in August, 1928.

It was a factual declaration but also a personal and emotional one.

In closing, Sam's eyes reddened and watered, his voice shook, yet marched on steadily... "THAT I have and my family have suffered much because of the wrong I did of entering the United States without inspection, and I earnestly petition that I be permitted now to take steps to regularize my status in order that I may eventually qualify for American citizenship."

The process continued on into 1944. By March, Sam had been fingerprinted and had proven that he had no criminal record.

On May 9th, he was given a Reopening Hearing. He now lived at 421 East 5th Street. He did not ask Miss Larned to come to avoid the cost, which she more than understood. She prepared him as best as she could, going over the questions he was sure to be asked. He had done well.

Both looked at each other and sighed at the same time, then giggled from nervousness at the coincidence.

"You are ready, Mr. Szafranski."

"Thank you, Miss Larned," he responded not as certainly, but determinedly. "You have all your papers?" It was a vague reminder; she was certain he would.

"Oh yes... I have everything!" In this he was certain that she did not have to worry. "Well then..." She sent him on his way.

Sam arrived the next day two hours before the appointment. Sitting stiffly outside the Hearing Room on a wooden chair, he alternated between holding his breath and taping his foot to the beat of a busy typewriter. He was oblivious to both, but those around him eyed him with annoyance and seemed as relieved as he when he was called in.

He suddenly realized as he took his stance that he was sweating profusely, but he didn't dare to adjust his tie or loosen his collar for momentary relief. Instead, Sam politely took out an ironed handkerchief and gave his brow a brief wipe.

The inspector waited patiently as Sam hurriedly stuffed what was now a rolled ball of stiff white cotton into his pants pocket and shakily arranged his important papers before him.

As if asking if he was now ready the Inspector's assistant began, "Mr. Szafranski?" Sam's shoulders jumped forward as he settled in, swallowed hard and took a huge breath.

He was as ready as he would ever be. Presiding Inspector Gustav Lazarus began.

Sept. 10, 1945, Sam was granted pre-examination at New York, New York and given a letter for the Inspector in charge at the Canadian Immigration Service, Lacolle P.Q. Canada. It stated that Sam was desirous of proceeding to Montreal, Canada for an immigration visa at the American Consulate.

On Sept. 12, 1945 Sam reentered the United States at Rouses Point, New York and was admitted for permanent residence.

Happily, Sam Szafranski was on the verge of citizenship. Ironically, so was Mariya.

Chapter 16

Uncle Mykhailo...To Trust or Not

Mykhailo's senses filled with the familiar sound of a spring shower ending.

Drip. Plop. Drip. Plop.

The last of the downpour was now making its way off the rooftops in droplets that loudly claimed the earth below as puddles. He couldn't see the day transforming outside the damp walls because of the scratchy blindfold, which covered the upper portion of his face.

He could, however, feel it, from a ray of stolen sunlight. It warmed the tip of his little-exposed nose, which had crusted with dried blood. Its warmth was nurturing yet irritating, as it left him with an urge to wipe away the scabs and stroke back the wayward strands of dirty hair, which poked annoyingly at his cheek. That of course was impossible, what with his hands tied behind his back.

He knew, after what must be days of interrogation, it was best not to think about it. It was best to, instead, distract himself, to think about what he could do... not what he could not do.

That left Mykhailo few choices. He could think about his family, but then he would also have to think about how worried they must be, if they had been told of his arrest. There was a possibility that they had not been told and for now, that would have to console and comfort him.

He could think about the cause... the fight for his people! It was, after all, what most drove him and indeed, fueled his strength.

His reserves were low. He was weary to the very core. For days now, he had been abused, tortured, humiliated and he knew there was even more to come.

He ignored the exhaustion and willed himself erect. His forehead beaded with sweat as intense pain radiated through his body with even the slightest movement. He knew that if he slouched, it would encourage his jailers to return and inflict more pain.

Mykhailo's ankles were bound to the chair which helped keep his lower half rigid, but his upper half was desperate for support. He spastically weaved back and forth, leaning to and fro. He felt like a buoy rocking submissively in an ocean storm, being tossed and submerged but ultimately bouncing back up right. He wanted more control and knew of only one way he might harness it. It had worked before. He began to concentrate on the very breath he drew to ease him. He'd used the strategy before, discovering it by accident.

It was, for now, his only sustenance and he had learned to use its life-giving power to focus his will. He had been denied food and water. But until they decide his time on this earth should end, they would not deny him the air he breathed.

Innnnnnn......,! He filled his lungs.

Outttttttt...! The air was released slowly with great control. It was about all that was left that he could control.

With each breath, he forced parts of his body to relax. Each muscle fought him, determined to remain tense and stressed. But he was equally determined to win.

It was a game he played, his mind over his body and at least to this point it had helped him from going totally senseless.

He wasn't sure how long he had been in the cell, how many times the interrogators had come or even if in the end, he would ultimately surrender in mindlessness and tell them what they wanted to know but, for this moment in time, he would be the master of his own mind... and his body would be willed to follow suit.

Each minute that passed, without his submission, was a victory. The secrets he held saved lives, as long as they remained or... died with him.

It was a frightening responsibility and his plan was to fulfill it, even to his death. If he didn't... the consequences would be devastating to the cause.

Step. Echo. Step. Echo

The taps of the footsteps were making their way to him.

More pain! More pain!!!

Mykhailo braced himself. It would start again. He tried to prepare... except that there was no real checklist to prepare for being tortured. His heart raced, his breathing quickened but these were not conscious responses.

The sweating accelerated and his clothes stuck to him like evidence markers of fear.

It was not his obvious fear that mattered most, he reminded himself. It was his courage! He had proven that he had a great deal of that, with every mission he had undertaken. He had hidden undetected in the surrounding forest for months, joining fellow patriots in the dead of night to perform a variety of activities, all with one goal: make life difficult for the Germans, or Soviets, whoever was the more immediate threat to his people. He had stolen artillery trucks, ambushed transports carrying medical supplies and explosives, and then he had joined parties of his comrades to use the weapons and explosives against the Germans and the Soviets.

Though he and other young people, both men and women, did everything in anonymity, their compatriots knew of their existence They quietly cheered them as heroes and honored them by writing songs about them. Their persistence and determined presence offered hope to a people battered by its enemies and even by their supposed allies.

"Courage." He whispered it aloud, unaware that company had already arrived.

The soft voice that responded back to him was more unnerving than any thunderous calamity could have been. This was not routine.

Interrogators did not usually begin so mildly.

"Indeed!" the Soviet officer spoke just above a whisper, but Mykhailo quickened to it and raised his level of alert. He could not see that the officer had waved away the guard and come to stand by him alone, unarmed.

There Mykhailo sat, arms bound behind him, ankles tethered to the chair legs, blindfolded, hurting, hungry, thirsty... miserably vulnerable.

"You've done well. You should be proud." Again, the voice was just a whisper.

Mykhailo was perplexed. What was going on here? What was this gentle approach? Who was this man who whispered? And why?

"Do you know how long you have been here?" the whispering voice inquired.

For a moment, Mykhailo hesitated, but when he was not slapped or kicked for taking too long to answer, he decided to respond.

"A number of days." He guessed.

"Over two weeks," the voice responded with a bit of respect. "And we've not gotten anything useful out of you. The voice spoke in perfect Polish with a thick Russian accent and a refined tone.

Mykhailo searched his memory to identify which interrogator this was, but he realized he was totally unfamiliar.

"The Allies need men like you." The voice waited for Mykhailo to digest what was a sincere compliment. He knew Mykhailo would be distrustful and disbelieving. If he wasn't, he would be a fool... and he would not be recruiting him.

"I want you to listen to me carefully because I won't be able to approach you again." The interrogator had Mykhailo's full attention as he wondered what new game was being played here. What was his purpose?

"You and your people have not been forgotten. The world is coming to your aid. There are people... good people... who have been as unwillingly drawn into this mess as you, your family and your people have been. For now, they must play their parts and at times ruthlessly disguise what is in their hearts." There was much regret and sorrow in the voice; there was almost anger.

"I am a part of an organization dedicated to finding these individuals and recruiting them for an underground network."

Mykhailo began to laugh, not for the humor of the man's words but for the fool this man must think him to be, to be so easily taken!

"Underground network? What does that mean?"

"It is no different than what you do now... only it will put you in contact with the Allies... give you and your friends the support you need to do your activities... more of your activities. Until now, we realize the Ukrainians have acted almost completely on their own. Communication has been difficult to establish, but you know this already... you know your organization has tried to make contact?"

Yes. Mykhailo was aware that they were trying to work with the Allies but throughout the war, contact had been near impossible. After all, the Soviet Union was now a supposed ally.

But they were the enemy, as far as the Ukrainians were concerned. The Poles, particularly the Ukrainian Poles had been forced to rely almost completely on their own ingenuity and determination, but they had been a force with which to be reckoned! They had been able to maintain a degree of control in the mountains, the forests and the rural villages during both German and Soviet occupation.

Still, Mykhailo was not going to be so easily won.

"And this... support... will come from who...you... a soldier... forgive me... an officer, at least I assume so...in the Soviet Army?"

"No, it will come from the Allies, via me... an officer in the Soviet Army."

"You are an officer? Show me, remove my blindfold."

"You are a strong young man. You have not given away names or information to save yourself now. Which is why I trust you. But I know you don't trust me yet. You would be a fool to, and *that* I know, you are not. Should you give me away either purposely or in a later interrogation, many lives would be affected. Sorry, you will have to respect that I can't unveil myself, not now, perhaps not ever. But, you and I are on the same side."

Mykhailo quietly absorbed what the officer had to say. What made him believe the man was an ally, he wasn't sure. But he decided to listen with an open yet guarded mind.

"Today, you will be released." The officer informed him.

"And you think I will lead you to my comrades. But I act alone."

"Of course," the voice assured him, and then continued as though Mykhailo had never spoken. "You will be given two weeks to recover from this interrogation. Sleep. Eat.

Gain back your strength." "And then..."

"I will arrange to deliver you a stockpile of German machine guns that I want you to hide in the bunkers of your forest. I would prefer you not use them on Soviet soldiers..."

"Oh, of course not..." Mykhailo agreed sarcastically.

"At least not yet, unless absolutely necessary," the officer seriously advised. He stunned Mykhailo.

"You mean you want me to shoot Soviet soldiers. But you are a Soviet. Are you an enemy of your own people?" Mykhailo did not understand this lack of loyalty, even if, he did hate the Soviets, for the treatment of his people.

"No, I'm not the enemy of my own people. Hitler is their enemy. Stalin is their enemy." He spoke Stalin's name as though he would spit it on the ground if he could.

"I am like you. I was born into and live in circumstances I did not create. But if we are patient, if we work with those of similar intentions, join together; these circumstances will not necessarily control us all. We can rationalize the world once again. It is my goal. It is what I live for. And I have many friends, in many places, who believe as well. We, who believe in human dignity and the sanctity of human life, must find each other... and work together... or God help us all."

"No! Poland asked the world for help. They refused. When the Soviets arrived, we were hopeful, but they are no better than the Nazis. They want to steal our land, our food, our dignity. They leave us nothing. Our children are starving, and still, they take!"

"I can't deny the truth. But there are many men who fight in Stalin's army who would give their life to see him dead. I could be shot for saying that. However, it is not so easy to take arms against him. You and your people have only seen a small fraction of the misery Stalin is capable of causing. You and your people may think it can be no worse but just wait. If Stalin does indeed acquire Poland or the Ukraine, he destroys families, villages on a whim! His own officers live in fear of him. Your people have only known this misery for a few years. We have endured it for decades. It is difficult to be brave in the Soviet Union right now, but some of us are trying. I fear the hell on earth that he has created will go on for generations, unless carefully, thoughtfully and above all else, patiently, he is opposed." The Russian voice strained to make his point.

"And my people and I are part of your plan..."

"You do not understand! Yes, we must triumph over Hitler, but we must also lay the groundwork now, to defeat Stalin, or it all means nothing."

"I work for a free Ukraine!"

"Then, I would see you have it. Help us and we will help you."
"How do I know you will not arrest me again if I pick up your guns?"

"You are under arrest now, why should I let you go at all? Only to re-arrest you?" He wanted to make Mykhailo think he was being senseless, but the reality was that he was thinking clearly.

"Because you think I will lead you to others and a secret location," Mykhailo accused.

"Possibly, but you and your men are smart enough to outmaneuver us, don't you think?" He challenged Mykhailo.

"I told you I work alone."

For the moment, the interrogator decided to assume Mykhailo had agreed. After all, there was no real way to prove himself except perhaps to let Mykhailo know he was aware of his organization's attempts to contact the Allies. But then again, that could be knowledge the Allies had volunteered to share with the Soviets, or information received by Soviet informers. Mykhailo would only trust him after he had taken a chance and had promises delivered. He would need to leave it to Mykhailo to test him with a plan, which, of course, would not put Mykhailo or his friends in jeopardy in case he proved to be a false friend.

Perhaps Mykhailo did not trust him, but he trusted Mykhailo enough to believe that he was capable of developing such a plan.

"In two weeks, you will be given two dozen MG 34 machine guns and fifty round saddle belts - the ammunition I mentioned. They are German, far superior to anything the Soviets have. They can deliver 820 rounds per minute and have an effective range of 2,000 meters. You will hide them and use them if necessary. I only ask that you make them available to my organization when the time is right."

"Where? How?"

"Two kilometers due north of your friend Kupetsky's farm."

He knows of Kupetsky, Mykhailo thought cautiously. He must be careful not to draw any further attention to his friend.

"That location will be one kilometer into the surrounding woods, offering you protection from discovery. There is one small clearing, you know it?"

Mykhailo nodded.

"They will be buried in the ground and covered by a huge fallen log."

"I see. And how many men will I need to move the log?" Mykhailo did not try to hide his suspicion.

"It will be huge, but hollow. When you are fit again, you will be able to do it yourself with a bit of strain. I do understand ...I need to build your trust. I'm hoping the guns will establish the start of a long-term relationship between our organizations."

"I told you I work alone!" Mykhailo was determined not to be tricked!

"Of course... come alone. You will need to make many trips; the guns will be too heavy to carry all at once. You'll need to remove and recover the log over the hole, as well as, sweep the area clean each time, but I'm sure there is no need to tell you how to do your job. I say it only because we will use the location many times, as need be, and I want to keep it as secure as possible."

"Of course." But Mykhailo was not yet convinced by the man's words. His actions... they would be the convincing factors.

"If all goes well, there will be another drop off soon after. You will be given instructions and taught how to use an explosive compound that can be molded and disguised as everyday items. No one will suspect."

"I have never heard of such an explosive." Mykhailo's distrust was presented as amusement. "And what other support... help do you intend to give me for my purposes?

"Machine guns and explosives are not help?" The interrogator sounded almost insulted.

Then he relaxed his tone. "All in good time."

"So would the contact be through you?" What the hell was he getting himself into? Later when his head was clearer, he would need to rethink all of this and decide if he was going to go along with this. For now, he would play along.

"Not necessarily." "Which means...?"

"You shall see... we are a very secretive lot... again... for everyone's protection ...you will see. First, let's see if you show up for the guns? Ummm?"

"Are you saying you don't trust me?"

"I trust your integrity, but you did get caught. You aren't infallible."

Bull's-eye.

Mykhailo couldn't argue the point. "We can teach you a great deal. You have great potential, or we wouldn't be bothered with you. I think this is going to be a mutually satisfying relationship. Now if we can just live through all this business."

Mykhailo had much to think about as he felt a metal cup reach his lips and was offered a most satisfying peace offering - cool water.

Chapter 17

Thank you, Satner

Marion opened his eyes to the pitch-black night and was suddenly blinded by the rotation of the camp's searchlight. He held up his arms to block it as he again heard distant artillery, which over the last week seemed to be getting closer and closer each night.

The camp had been given evacuation orders the evening before, confirming the POW's suspicions and hopes that the Allies were near, and the Germans feared their prisoners' ultimate liberation... and of course, their own defeat.

Some of the POWs were talking of using this time of turmoil and confusion to escape, but Marion wasn't sure. Perhaps the war was near its end, and it wouldn't be necessary... and he remembered the fifty Americans who were shot under the direct orders of Hitler to pay for the attempted escapes of others.

He was also so very weak, a mere stick of the man he had been before captivity. He wasn't sure how long he could last without at least the limited rations he received as a POW.

Satner crouched near to whisper, which perhaps was unnecessary with the backdrop of combat noises, but it was a habit from years of caution that he followed automatically. Besides, some of the prisoners who had awakened previously had already turned over for whatever shuteye was still left to them, deliberately ignoring the war which had gone on without them for the past five years.

"Did you think about it?"

"I'm not sure, Satner. I'm not saying no, but I'm not ready to say yes either. We've survived five years of the war in this place. Perhaps it is best to finish it here, as well?"

Satner looked disappointed.

Marion didn't wish to let his friend down, for indeed they were true friends, more like brothers, in fact. They had guarded, protected, nursed and comforted each other as though they were family throughout life in Stalag IIB.

"I'm not a coward," he said flatly, "but I don't want to be a fool either. If the moment is right, we'll know it." He hesitated as a thought occurred to him.

"If you need to ... if the moment presents itself, go without me. I'll watch your back as much as I'm able."

Satner's nod was a "thank you."

The compromise did not minimize their partnership; it solidified it. Marion knew his friend was eager, whereas he was not. But that did not mean he would not support his friend's decision in any way he could.

Satner held up his hand and Marion grasped it between both of his hands as though they were about to arm-wrestle.

"After the war my friend." Their hands shook solidly.

"After the war, my friend." They had used the gesture and phrase often to remind each other to keep hope alive, to dream of the future when they could return to their farms and families, and visit as friends should in celebration and good times.

Satner crept back to his bunk and Marion rolled over on his. He sighed and felt the cloud of his breath thicken in the air. Perhaps he should enjoy tonight's paltry comforts. Who knew what tomorrow might bring.

It would be one of the coldest winters Germany had ever seen. At first light, they were ordered out for roll call. They had few possessions to pack for what they feared would be a journey similar to the transport that had brought them to Germany five years earlier. They knew it would be a march under strained conditions. They just didn't realize how strained the conditions would get or how endlessly long the transport would be.

They were used to minimal rations, cold water, little heat, few blankets, lice ridden overcoats, inadequate medical care, typhus, pneumonia, diphtheria, pellagra and a multitude of other illnesses born from malnourishment, overcrowding and filthy living conditions. But this would be worse.

First, they were marched one way only to be marched back over the same path the following week. The POWs marched as few as five kilometers on a good day and as many as 30 kilometers on a horrendous one. Marion's feet blistered quickly in the wooden shoes issued to him, a month before by the Germans.

At night, they slept out in the open, on frozen ground covered by one blanket shared with another prisoner. For Marion, it was always Satner with whom he paired off. At times, they and the other POWs all slept in huddled bunches on purpose to share body warmth. Fingers and toes began to feel the full effects of frostbite, and infections set in, making some too weak to continue moving on. For a time, the Germans permitted the weak to be transported in wagons pulled by other POWs, but as time went on, they became impatient and the weakest were shot and left unburied on the side of the road.

For once, the Germans seemed frazzled and undirected, second-guessing decisions.

Some guards were especially cranky and easily angered; those that suspected their defeat was on the horizon were uncharacteristically friendly and accommodating.

As they crisscrossed Germany, they encountered other subdivisions of prisoners on similar marches looking just as weak, ill, tired and malnourished as they were.

Eventually, it was beyond the German's ability or caring to meet even their most basic needs. They drank from contaminated rivers and still ponds. They foraged for wild plants to eat and hoped they weren't poisonous.

At times, they took shelter from air raids to avoid bombs dropped by the Allies. Attacks, which killed livestock or animals, provided that night's dinner. German soldiers were so perplexed they didn't even try to stop the prisoners; their last measure of control served only to prevent escape.

They began to walk through towns and villages that had been completely leveled by Allied air attacks. The depression, which had long been part of their world, now began to show on the faces of the German soldiers who had once thought Germany invincible.

German families took to the roads, fearing the arrival of the Soviets. Their deserted farmhouses and barns became their shelter for the night. Silently, the POWs rejoiced knowing the growing evidence indicated German defeat was near. Dare they think it!

Hope grew with each German civilian wheeling all of their belongings in tow. Women, children and old men were fleeing, walking, pulling carts, riding in wagons, and desperately trying to stay ahead of the advancing Soviets.

Marion had a severe foot wound that was developing an infection. His once sturdy frame had dwindled down to skeletal proportions, and his immunity along with it was now almost non- existent.

Would he perish just as victory knocked? Amazing, the turns in life that he should now die at the war's end, not because of some heroic act but from a foot infection!

He wanted to lie down on the side of the road and refuse to go on as many others had already done, but Satner insisted that he go on, knowing he risked being shot.

"I can't go on..."

"Yes, you can!" Satner insisted, but Marion's body was quickly becoming dead weight.

What to do? Satner thought quickly.

The march had come to an abrupt halt and the POWs were trying to take shelter from the wind in any way they could. The Germans were concerned about the cold themselves and were distracted by their own discomfort.

Satner spotted a trench to the side of the road and instead of stopping at its side, he continued into it, almost dragging Marion's body.

"Help me, help me get you down here," Satner begged Marion to do what he could.

Marion heard his pleading through fogged consciousness and tried to help his friend as best he could. He didn't realize it was for himself that his friend begged.

Satner laid him down, none too gently behind an evergreen bush and quickly covered Marion with their one blanket, followed by nearby rocks and branches. It would have to do, there was no more time.

Marion had a strange sensation of being buried, but he was too weak to care.

"Stay here, don't call attention to yourself, and please God... Marion stay alive. I will be back."

Then, Satner was gone, back up to the curve of the road, ready to march again when orders were given.

When others started to ask for Marion, Satner shushed them with a look, a signal they had used over and over again during their years of captivity to maintain a brotherhood of secrecy.

They immediately understood and fell into the usual drill. They trusted Satner and knew he would be doing what was best for Marion.

Suddenly there was a turn of events. It would work well for his plans, even better than what he had schemed.

The Allies were attacking from the air, purposely missing the POWs. They were intent on annihilating the German unit, which had passed them, heading east.

The POWs were not their target, but they were close enough to force the prisoners to run for cover off the road. The scattered commotion was just what Satner had hoped for... a distraction.

Satner scurried into the woods, but once there, he changed direction ninety degrees and headed westward, to the dip off the side of the road where he had left Marion. He ran like a rabbit, ducking, crouching, swerving, and hoping to go unnoticed amongst so much disorder. He stopped cold when he realized he might have passed the spot. He looked right. He looked left, then doubled back processing quickly, thinking... What is the same? What is different?

"Marion?" he chanced. If the wrong person heard him, he could be shot on sight. "Here." A miracle! Marion. Sweet Marion had heard him. He hadn't even been sure if Marion would be conscious. Like a bird swooping down, he landed by Marion's side.

"You didn't leave me?" Marion asked innocently as though his answer didn't matter. "No, you ass," and Satner looked at him, saw how very sick he was, and decided not to be insulted.

"I needed to hide you for a while, that's all."

Satner waited for the artillery to die down and prayed that the POW March had continued forward, not doubled back, possibly looking for him or Marion.

When the opportunity seemed best, he lifted Marion up over his shoulder and began his search for the nearest farmhouse. His frequent work detachments had made him familiar with the general area they were now in, particularly the farms and barns. For all their marching, they had been led in circles and they were probably still within five kilometers of Stalag IIB, where their march had begun.

His exertion made him warm with sweat, which he knew was not good in the frigid weather. He needed to find shelter quickly. Marion's foot was desperate for attention.

Then he saw it!

The familiar farmhouse. It was like a mirage on the desert and he hesitated for a moment, not sure of what to make of it. He and Marion had returned to it more than once, season after season, to plow and reap as prison laborers.

The barn had a loft, perfect for a hiding place. How would he get Marion up the ladder? He didn't know yet. How would he get Marion food and medical supplies? He didn't know that either.

One thing at a time.

He was ready to rush through the clearing. It seemed quiet and he hoped the family either had deserted the farm or was keeping warm in the house, unaware of his approach.

One, two, three. Goooooo!

With strength that seemed miraculously bestowed upon him, he scurried across an open field which was as hard as stone from the cold, carrying Marion. His overcoat flung open from the wind but he resisted falling backwards.

When he reached the barn door, he flung it open wildly, aching to be inside. If the farmer was there, if he was caught, he would simply fight to the death.

Nothing else to do. No alternative.

Safely inside, he quickly circled in all directions, taking in his surroundings. He stiffened as he made ready to dump Marion on a clump of hay.

"Uhhh." Marion grunted.

"I'm sorry my friend," Satner apologized between the intakes of air. Then for a full minute, maybe two, he rested.

Marion didn't stir. Satner checked. At least he wasn't dead.

Yet.

Just like his friend to sleep while he was being a hero, Satner thought. When Marion woke, he would need to fill him in on every detail.

Well, maybe not, he reconsidered.

He realized he loved Marion, his one true friend through this whole ordeal. He didn't want to make it through the war without Marion. He wanted their children to grow up together, to share holidays with him and his wife, to grow old and share war stories once they became old, far-off memories.

Suddenly, Satner was startled. The barn door creaked and before either had time to prepare, Satner was face to face with the farmer. He had no gun or weapon of any kind, so he used what was left of the farmer's surprise to jump him.

In the air he flew, knocking the farmer off his feet. They recognized each other. They had never spoken, not a single word, separated by privilege, class and order, as well as a language barrier.

Satner had him in a chokehold and was squeezing his neck as hard as he could. "Surrender," the farmer groaned out in Polish.

How could that be, but Satner quickly realized the farmer, though much older, was twice the size of him, well fed, healthy and not going to die because of his chokehold. Suffer maybe, but not die. Then what? Without realizing what he was doing, his hold lessened enough for the farmer to gasp air and dart away.

They circled and eyeballed each other. Satner used every muscle in his face to look terrifying and felt somewhat satisfied that the farmer did indeed look terrified right back at him.

Problem with that was so was he!

The farmer breathed in, bending at the waist, pounding his knee as though it would help the air fill his lungs more quickly. Finally, he seemed to recover.

The farmer raised his hands as if to explain something.

"Surrender," he said again and pointed to his own chest. "Me."

Could it possibly be? Could the Allies be that close that the farmer was actually surrendering to him?

The farmer pointed to Marion passed out on the hay, and gingerly made his way to him. Satner leaped protectively, unsure, not knowing what to believe.

Again, the farmer's hands went out as though to explain, as though to reassure him.

Cautiously, the farmer walked toward Marion. Once there, he quickly dropped to his knees and felt for a pulse. Then, he surveyed the emaciated form and saw a bandaged foot. He was prepared for what he might see as the smell of the festering flesh permeated the air.

The farmer grimaced with concern, which Satner didn't trust, and pointed to the house. "Let's go," Satner commanded. "Nazi... don't set me up. You try and trick me and I'll kill you if it is the last thing I do." Satner was trying to act tough, but tears came to his eyes.

Could there be a flicker of understanding in the man's eyes? It couldn't be. Satner thought that perhaps his mind was playing tricks on him. Whatever, he let the man pick up Marion.

He followed as the farmer led. First, slowly, then as the farmer gained confidence, they both picked up speed.

He wanted to tell the farmer to slow down, he needed a minute to think, to plan his next move should there be company in the house, but he couldn't think or express himself fast enough with the language barrier. Instead, he hurried and overtook the farmer, beating him to the door.

The farmer looked sincerely burdened and Satner worried that he might drop Marion.

He motioned for the farmer to go in ahead of him. Children's things were scattered on the floor, a woman's apron rested on the back of a chair. Where was the farmer's family?

They were gone. It was not surprising. Half of Germany had vacated, heading west to avoid the approaching Soviets. Year after year, the Germans had treated the Soviet POWs pitifully. He didn't have to wonder much why the Germans feared them so greatly and preferred to surrender to the British or Americans.

With Marion placed on a couch, Satner made his way through each room, checking closets and looking under beds, then quickly returned to Marion's side.

The farmer seemed headed for the kitchen. Satner didn't want to leave Marion again, but he didn't trust the farmer, so he followed him.

When he took out a large knife from a drawer, Satner shouted at the farmer who immediately backed away, dropping the knife then raised his hands to emphasize his harmlessness.

Somehow, a little Polish here, a little German there, a hand gesture just so; they communicated just as thousands of prisoners of war from varied nationalities had in the POW camp over the last five years. When the farmer felt it was reasonable for Satner to no longer feel threatened, he slowly, carefully, purposefully moved to reclaim the knife. Again, not wanting to startle Satner, he moved slowly and pointed to the stove. He lit the first burner and a flame appeared.

Satner realized the farmer was going to heat the knife. It made sense. There was no medication of any kind available and something was needed to kill Marion's infection.

Marion seemed oblivious. Perhaps it was the right time to get the job done. Lord, help him, if Marion woke.

Maybe it would be a good time to remind him of his heroic deed!

He couldn't bring himself to do it. Nervously, he let the farmer approach Marion to perform the chore.

Marion's scream needed to be stifled by three kitchen napkins stuffed on top of his tongue and then a pillow from the next room. It had been loud enough to wake the dead, but as long as it didn't awaken any passing German soldier's curiosity, it was tolerable.

Hours passed and it seemed that all had gone unnoticed. Germans were known to patrol on motorcycle or even bicycle, since they were much quieter but no patrol had taken notice. All of Germany seemed intent on their own survival.

Satner didn't feel secure yet. He still didn't trust the farmer, but he knew he couldn't remain awake indefinitely. He fought it as long as he could, but finally he drifted blissfully off to sleep, warmed by the farmer's fire and a feather quilt.

He woke to crackling bacon and the smell of sweet pork. He hadn't had the pleasure of either aroma in many, many years. Have I died? Have I gone to heaven?

He jumped to attention when he realized where he was and that he'd spent the night totally vulnerable to the whims of the German farmer. He was still alive, however. So was Marion, who was already awake, sipping broth. When he faced him, he received an amused look charging him with neglect.

"So, you leave me in a ditch to fend for myself, hum?" His voice and chuckle were weak, but his spunk was glorious to Satner's ears.

"Then, you bring me to a German farmhouse to have half the flesh burned from my body and the first thing you do is fall fast asleep. Remind me never to count on you... unless of course, I need someone to save my life."

"I think I'm waiting for a simple... thank you!"

"Then... you shall have one." His voice grew serious, sincere. "Thank you."

"Perhaps we are safe. The German didn't turn on us in the middle of the night."

"It appears not." Marion was back to his mild manner.

"How do you feel?"

"Don't bother me with questions that you know the answer to."

"Cranky, are we?"

"I do think the infection is a bit better. That torturous act may have done the trick... but it hurts like hell. Sorry, you don't deserve to hear me complain."

Satner eyed Marion suspiciously, then got up and took a whiff of his breath. "Are you...?" He came in closer to examine him further. "Are you... drunk!"

"Quite! Our farmer dressed the wound with alcohol and to keep me being a good boy... he gave me a swig... or two."

Satner tsked. "I can't leave you alone for a second, can I?"

"Remember... the hellish pain! No, I suppose you should not."

Then, the two looked deeply at each other, long and hard. Simultaneously, they bellowed out in laughter like schoolchildren who had successfully carried out a prank.

Today was going to be a good day. The first one since the start of this damn war.

Tomorrow would be another day.

Chapter 18

War Ends, Chaos Follows

The German farmer was now known to them as Otto Lang. For the moment, he was out tending to his few remaining livestock while Satner and Marion were relaxing and enjoying their noon meal around a wooden table that wobbled. It was the only imperfect thing that they had found on this farm. Otherwise, it was immaculate and well-tended. Greased and polished.

Orderly. Everything was tidily in its place as though the war had never happened. Just like the farmer himself.

They expected Otto to join them at any moment, as he had for every meal since they arrived well over a month ago. At first, he had made every meal and tended to Marion around the clock when he lay ill and helpless. However, Satner had also kept a protective eye on him and observed how Otto tended to him. That had seemed quite unnecessary even early on, as the farmer had tried to do everything possible to accommodate them. He had graciously offered them the beds of his children, extra pillows and evening tea. Their lazy days were helping to restore their health and vigor and they had begun to help with meal preparation.

They still enjoyed and savored every bite of nutritious food but their eyes, especially at first, had been bigger than their stomachs. Quickly, they realized that the smaller portions which they had been accustomed to and known pre-war could easily satisfy them. As their appetites grew, so did their strength and their appreciation for the luxury surrounding them.

"Do you ever feel... guilty?"

"For what?" Satner questioned as he slurped a messy spoon of noodles and chicken soup. "That we are here... warm and gaining back our health, day by day, while the others may still be marching around Germany?"

"No." Satner gave a quick reply. Then, he thought again and put down his spoon."

"I try not to think about it. There is nothing I can do about it. I pray for them though." Marion eyed him with surprise.

"I did not know you were a religious man."

"I didn't know myself. Then the war happened."

A low rumble seemed to be approaching the house and it occurred to Satner that Otto had not yet joined them for the noon meal.

"Speaking of war... what is that? And where is Otto?"

"He'll hear it and be back soon, don't worry."

"Don't worry? How often has my worrying kept us both alive, my friend? I need to worry and every time I do, I need to do it for two!" Satner tsked as though he was reminding a mischievous boy to behave. "What do you think he is doing?" Satner's tone suggested suspicion. They had developed a sense of comfort with the farmer... but not trust. That was how war worked.

"Don't worry!" Marion began and then caught himself. Satner was quick to give him an annoyed eyeball for so absent-mindedly repeating something so dumb, so soon.

The rumbling noise grew louder.

"What? Do you think he's betraying us?" Marion asked incredulously.

"Marion, don't be so naïve. That's exactly what I'm worried about."

Once again, he would need to protect Marion from himself and needed to take a hard direct stance. "Do you think the farmer cares about us? That he has taken us in out of the goodness of his heart. He knows the war is nearly over." Satner shook his head, hoping it would put sense into his friend. "When it is, he thinks we will be his bodyguards."

"Then..." Marion began, not totally catching on, "why would he betray us now?" By mid-sentence, they had both turned to the window, compelled by the sound now vibrating the house and making Otto's fine china rattle.

They gripped the sill and tried to make out the approaching army.

"My god! Oh my god, my god, my god! He's done it, he's turned us in...runnnnnnn!!!!"

One turned right, one turned left. Both ran... right into the other. Unscrambling themselves quickly, they ran for the back kitchen door. They had no plan, no forethought. They only knew a large army was parking on Otto's front lawn.

They could hear the hum of the tanks and the metal of a creaky truck door slamming.

The whole German army? Were they so notorious that a whole regiment had come to recapture them?

Marion, who had been barefoot, had been sharp enough to grab a pair of shoes before heading out the door. He didn't dare stop to check that they were his. Satner grabbed an overcoat.

The door flung open and out they dashed, overcoat and shoes waving in the air behind them as they headed for cover in the nearby forest.

However, they did not get far.

First, they had to round the back of the barn, and that's when the encounter occurred.

Crack.

Groan.

Crash.

Splatter.

Drip!

Milk was everywhere. Otto was soaking.

Milk dripped from Marion's eyebrows and down Satner's front making him look like he had soiled himself.

Satner tried to punch Otto, but Otto was quick and on his feet ducking, which made Satner begin to lose his footing. Marion grabbed Satner's arm first steadying him, then pulling and almost dragging him into the forest.

Otto was running after them, yelling and screaming in German, which made them run faster.

By the time they reached the first tree, they were panting wildly, almost sucking in air. Marion grabbed a tree trunk to the right. Satner grabbed the trunk to the left. Both hunched over.

Suck in air! Breath, suck in air!

Listen. Think. Translate. Comprehend.

Eureka!

Otto's words were sinking in. Though far in the distance, he could still be heard.

"Americans! Americans! Americans!"

At least for Satner and Marion... the war was over!

How fortunate were Marion and Satner to have been picked up by an American combat unit! All along the way to Paris, they witnessed Germany's consequences for having caused havoc and harm throughout Europe.

The German people were desperate to run from the Soviets who were fast approaching. At first, military vehicles had been rushing past shouting warnings through loudspeakers, "The Soviet tanks are approaching; expect them in half an hour."

Thousands had begun walking, raggedly carrying or pushing their few belongings.

Babies were being born on straw in the back of moving wagons, which passed people on the side of the road who had died of exhaustion or exposure. Some merely rested for a moment and then rose to be on their way again. Some had been on the road for weeks; others had recently responded to orders of evacuation. All were terrified, homeless and mystified as to what the future held for them now that their once invincible Germany had fallen.

When possible, the parade of refugees followed the American units, comforted by their presence. It was not so odd and unreasonable as it might have seemed.

The Americans, of course, were Allies and had been the Germans' enemy. However, with the war so close to its end, the average German saw the Americans as the closest thing they had to a protector from the Soviets, who were sure to seek revenge for Germany's betrayal. The Germans had treated Soviet POWs brutally throughout the war, countering Stalin's inhumane treatment of German POWs.

As well, the Germans had annihilated much of the western portion of the Soviet Union. There was hardly a Soviet citizen who had not been touched by great personal loss and sacrifice, including loss of home or family members.

At all cost, the Germans wanted to stay out of the Soviets' way. German soldiers were surrendering in droves but only to the Americans. It was considered a death sentence to surrender to the Soviets and, as history indicates, that was for the most part correct.

There was a massive exit and everyone was heading west. Onward they trudged, meeting and overcoming obstacles as they went... fallen cables, toppled trees, roads sunken by bomb craters and dead bodies.

It was beginning to look like Poland all over again, except the cries heard this time were in German.

Some had lived through WWI but none had lived through a World War with such far- reaching and devastating impact.

POWs were being liberated, but they ambled forward with great caution, hesitancy and physical depletion. They were perplexed by their new freedom, and most chose to listen to the Americans who were telling them to head towards Paris for mass repatriation. However, everyone had more immediate needs. They needed water. They needed food. Many were sick from ill-treatment or mentally drained and fatigued to the point of not functioning.

The Red Cross and YMCA, which had helped to sustain them during their years of imprisonment, were not to be found as they were evacuating and avoiding the final blows of war themselves. It was bedlam of the highest magnitude.

Marion and Satner were lucky to have had a head start. For them, leaving Germany was a much easier journey than the one, which had brought them to it. They had joined the American unit early on before the other POWs had been released and had had the luxury of being transported along with the Americans. While their physical frames still displayed years of malnourishment, they had been well-fed and nurtured under Otto's care during the last month.

Many POWs had been forced to march senselessly back and forth across Germany, as it panicked in its nearing defeat.

It was difficult not to enjoy it a bit, seeing the Germans put upon, as they passed towing their families and life's possessions to ... nowhere. Perhaps some were headed back to their homes now that the fighting and artillery had ended but only if it was westward... away from the Soviets.

Perhaps Otto's family was reuniting, and Marion felt a momentary mix of emotions. After the Americans had offered to let Marion and Satner join them en route to Paris, they had said good-bye to Otto with a firm handshake.

Marion was relieved to be leaving Germany, this he could do without one look back, but he was also grateful to Otto for helping to save his life.

He was sensitive enough too, to sense the farmer's fear and vulnerability at now being defeated and surrounded by his enemy. Indeed, the tables had turned.

Perhaps the farmer had only used Satner, himself, realizing the end was near, and it would be good to have a friend amongst the Allies. However, Marion chose not to believe that. So, he strongly gripped Otto's hand in his own, holding tightly rather than shaking it and patted his back with his free hand. He wished him good luck and stopped short of calling him friend. Then he turned and got into the jeep in which Satner already sat.

From the back of the jeep, Satner merely gave a slight wave which he felt was more than adequate; after all, he was saying good-bye to an enemy. And then they were on their way.

Conditions would still be primitive, but to those who had suffered so severely for so long, it felt like they had just begun a holiday.

Along the way, they encountered white flags hanging from almost every window, as well as stragglers, beggars and orphaned children. Certain streets, except for what remained of painted swastikas, reminded them of the Poland they had left behind five years earlier, with crumpled, dusty, messes at the foot of arched doorways, which had survived the bombings. The American bombing at the war's end had been very effective at shattering the German country and its materials, and it had demoralized the people, once so assured and empowered. They were humbled, but embittered and their sentiments were difficult to disguise.

Germany was becoming saturated with Soviet infantry accompanied by tanks. In the aftermath of war, their fury was being taken out on the civilians. Reports of looting, rape or even execution of civilians were common.

Allied armies were also uncovering death camps and conditions so cruel and inhumane; they were unfathomable even to POW camp survivors, even to most of the German people.

Marion counted his blessings with so much fear, terror and decay around him. They were relatively safe surrounded by the American GI's who to a certain extent had befriended them.

They were routinely included when C and K rations were handed out and had gotten quite used to canned pork loaf, candy nuts, chewing gum and chocolate bars. They were also offered cigarettes and though neither of them smoked, they took and hid whatever they were offered in the hopes of using them to barter with the general population.

Fresh produce became available, though not plentiful as they neared France. One could find fresh pears or grapes in one village, fresh apples and potatoes in the next.

French farmhouses were often built of stone and into the slope of a hill. Livestock lived in the cellars while kitchens and living rooms extended out above them. Each house generally had its own water pump out in front and rarely did anyone object to sharing, especially because they were in the company of the United States Army, their liberators.

Some of the Americans would complain about the smell of manure, which the French farmers kept piled high in front of their homes and considered a sign of status. To Marion it was like the sweet smell of home, and he longed to be there with his family.

The French civilians often requested medical aid from the unit, so brief stops were made with long lines forming to see the American doctor. The French loved white bread and often offered it as barter or gifts of gratitude. They also had black or pumpernickel bread but white was their traditional preference. They thought of it to be like a cake.

On they went towards Paris, and little by little, they saw less manure-filled lawns and more cobbled streets and attached homes.

Finally, in Paris, they received soap, hot showers, and delousing. American and British radios with contact to the BBC had provided them with updates of the war during their years as POWs, but they had missed much of the day-to-day events of the war. Now they received regular reports of what was happening worldwide.

They continued to be well fed. The food was not as good as Otto's home cooking but compared to prison camp food, it was gourmet. They had no complaints.

The mood was festive,but interrupted with tidbits of real life ... a missing limb, a weeping widow, the uncovering of a concentration camp.

It was organized disorganization as the world tried to remember what it was like not to be at war.

Satner was walking in leaps toward Marion. His strides resembled a German march and then he fell into Marion's arms. His hands clenched a paper in his fist, a letter... his first piece of mail or word from home in five years.

"They are alive, my friend, my wife... my son!"

The two began to dance wildly around, still holding and clasping the other's elbow.

Satner's eyes were wet with relief and Marion's were gleeful in joy for his friend.

"You got mail!" Marion exclaimed hoping that soon he too would learn the fate of his family.

"I'm happy for you, my friend!" And he was deliriously happy! He was happy just to have a reason to be happy.

Then, ever so subtly, his concerns for his own family returned. His face betrayed his thoughts and Satner, who had come to know him so well, read his thoughts.

"Tomorrow will be your turn, my friend!"

Satner wanted his friend to remain hopeful especially because he was feeling so fortunate now.

"Yes, tomorrow." Marion agreed but he was not convincing.

"We'll go look for your brother, Paulo." Satner suggested. He had had his own joyful moment, and now he was determined that his friend should have one as well.

"I don't know Satner, we've looked and looked. Perhaps he left Paris long ago. I have asked and asked but no one knows him."

"This is not Horonitza. This is Paris, a large city! You can't expect to find him so quickly especially with so many displaced people. But I have a feeling. Tomorrow, we find him!"

Marion's brother Paul had gone to live in Paris in the 1920's. For years, they'd written and communicated. However, he could not remember his brother's address. In fact, after five years as a POW, laboring for Germany and fighting to survive, he had difficulty conjuring up his image. They had not seen each other in twenty years, and so much had happened during those years.

Suddenly, Satner did not feel like waiting until tomorrow.

"Please, don't give up. Come, I'll go with you now. We can at least do a few more city streets, today." Satner was eager to get started and use his exuberance and energy for something productive. He had already taken a few steps expecting Marion to follow.

"Fine, I'll go... but not you. I want you to enjoy your letter ... over and over again. I'll go alone."

"Are you sure, Marion? You know I don't mind."

"I know, my friend." Marion headed away from his friend. Oddly, he wanted to be alone. He was happy for his friend but could not help but experience a little self-pity. He would wander the streets of Paris by himself. In fact, the solitude was strangely comforting and now that the war was finally over, he found it exciting and peaceful to walk about feeling safe and adventurous.

His search had picked up momentum and before he knew it, he was on the outskirts of the city, knocking on the door of a French farmhouse.

"Mademoiselle," he began and continued in guttural French, "Do you know my brother...?" Marion was about to continue to give his name and to describe him when the French woman interrupted him.

"Pardon, you have an accent? Like my husband's. Are you from Ukraine?" The woman spoke quickly, expecting Marion to understand, but his French was limited and unable to comprehend everything she said.

All that he really commanded of the language was what a French POW had taught him in 1939 before being returned to France. He had seemed to know enough for other Parisians to understand him and for him to understand them when they told him they had no idea who his brother was or where he might possibly find him. However, this French woman seemed particularly confused by his request. She kept speaking French quickly and appearing to come to some baffling conclusion before she scurried off to the back of the farmhouse seemingly searching for something or someone, leaving him to stand awkwardly alone at her front door.

Marion had caught her reference to Ukraine and did hope she would return quickly to clarify or tell him that she knew nothing, so that he could again be on his way.

Had she been able to detect his nationality so quickly from his French? Why should he be surprised? He was certain his accent must be very thick.

It began to feel that she was gone so long that perhaps she expected him to leave. Had he frightened her? No, certainly she meant to return, she had left the door wide open. He had been very polite, and he was no longer the intimidating figure he had once been.

Then he heard her voice once again and that of another growing more and more excited, as they approached the front door. It was now obvious that the woman had gone to get her husband. He stopped for a moment at the end of a long hallway, which extended from the front door entrance. His wife stood behind him; both were somewhat hidden by the shadow of light. Then, the wife stepped forward wearing a wide, satisfied grin, dragging her startled husband behind her.

Even with the wife's dragging, the husband froze and looked at Marion as though he were the devil himself.

Somehow, unknowingly, I have offended her, Marion thought. For a split second, he prepared to turn and run. However, something caught his attention... something familiar.

Again, long seconds went by healing and soothing Marion, and he wished to enjoy every inch of the sight before him.

The French woman looked first at the man she had summoned, then at Marion, and it was obvious that she wondered why the two did not greet or acknowledge each other.

In French, the wife questioned the man as though he were a silly child. Marion recognized the tone. It was how Satner spoke to him on occasion. Then she pushed her husband forward.

Step by step, she watched one man approach the other, and finally when they were but inches apart, still staring at each other, though through tears, she watched as they stretched out their arms for the other to fall into.

Silently they cried, ignoring the French woman for a long time. She did not seem to mind at all. In fact, though she had made no physical contact whatsoever, Marion felt fully embraced by her, as well.

Disbelieving they pulled away, to look and study the other, only to draw in again for another brotherly union. One arm patted the back of the other, and they repeated their physical display until the French woman grew tired and pulled them to sit down.

"I've missed... you... my brother!" Paul spoke first. The two were still breathless, almost speechless. The woman offered them both wine, which when available, the French drank like water.

It was heavy but made Marion feel light and gay. Relaxed.

He was amongst family for the first time in many years. He felt at peace.

Satner had been correct. He too, would have his turn.

And now to be reunited with his wife, Anna? His daughter, Asana?

And the rest of his family, hopefully still alive in Poland.

He would not have complete peace until this had come to pass, as well.

Chapter 19

Mykhailo's Warning

It was early spring. Mariya had been the first to notice a figure ruffling the tall grass in the clearing, and when she recognized the outline of the form, she could not help but to rush forward to greet it.

Danyk, attentive by his mother's side, immediately noticed her take-off to the clearing and quickly jerked towards the direction she'd taken. Hurriedly, he was evaluating what had suddenly provoked her. Danger? Friend? It was always a first reaction whenever something unknown approached.

He used his hands to block the sun, then he too suddenly rushed off not far behind her.

The three met in a wheel of excitement, jumping up and down, joined by interlocking arms that seemed determined to swoop the other in... for comfort, for joy, for relief. It had been almost a year since they had last seen Mykhailo.

The adrenaline rush was exhausting and left them reduced to tears. "God bless...you are all well? Your mother?"

"Mykhailo..." Mariya reached up to soothe his stubbled face, so he would not assume the worst. "She is resting. She is well."

With that Mariya's mother appeared at the door to their mud home and when it registered who it was that Mariya was embracing, she smiled broadly and gave a frail wave.

It was joyous...it was exciting... it was an event to break the boredom of another predictable day. Mariya had not seen much of Sam's family during the war. At the beginning, it had been Mykhailo who had provided the brief and secretive but regular contact.

But then ... there had been that awful day when the villagers had been rounded up. The voice from the woods had protected them... then disappeared.

So had Mykhailo! She knew it had to have been a cautionary measure in case anyone from the village had revealed the source of the voice to the authorities.

It seemed, at least by evidence of his visit, no one had revealed his secret. Still, unable to help herself, she looked around to make sure no one other than the three of them had noticed his arrival.

It would have been surprising if someone had. Rarely did villagers stroll by without a practical or necessary reason. Contact had grown increasingly difficult, and the people avoided being out on the open road which would increase the chances of being noticed by the wrong person at the wrong moment. It was best not to be obvious and not call attention to oneself. This meant relying on the ancient forest paths when absolutely necessary, following the curfew, remaining close to home and relying on word spread neighbor to neighbor for news of relatives and friends. For too long there had been no word.

Miraculously, Sam's brother, Mykhailo, had managed to survive the war so far. Most males his age had not... or had long ago disappeared. In fact, except for Soviet soldiers it was odd to see any males of Mykhailo's age at all. This alone would make him suspect, if authorities were not already suspicious.

But he had not survived untouched. He seemed mature beyond his years and life for him was an unrelenting effort that had etched crow's feet around his eyes. She knew he held many secrets from her, but they had long maintained the understanding that he would only tell her what she needed to know. All else was better left unsaid.

Mykhailo's eyes betrayed his strength, determination and a keen intelligence. For the moment, his mere presence gave her great ease and she relaxed against him as they, arm in arm, made their way to the door of Mariya's small home.

From the door's shadow, came Mariya's mother who reached above her head to hug the neck of the tall Ukrainian who bent to meet her halfway and then rocked her back and forth like a rag doll.

Danyk eyed his strength and took in his gentleness. To say the least, he was proud that his uncle was a good man and duly noted that it was possible for a man to show both natures at once.

"I have news..." Mykhailo hesitated thoughtfully, and then announced, "There is good reason to believe that the war is near its end!"

Mariya dared not to ask how he knew this.

"Hitler has been pushed back steadily and the Allies have gained confidence." She merely nodded, accepting his news with reserve.

Mykhailo had expected more of a reaction, but he understood her caution. She had not followed the day-to-day events of the war as he had, and since he could not explain himself further, he left the news hanging in the air.

Mariya's trust in Mykhailo was absolute, but still...she could not believe it was true. And if it were, did that mean the Soviets would simply leave? She was no fool and knew there would be no easy conclusion to this war.

The last few years had been an endurance test, and should she interrupt her focus with hope... only to have it lost... she might not be able to go on again. Too much had been endured and become a way of life to hope for such a turn of events. She too, allowed the silence to say much between them.

"And I have more..." Mykhailo countered the mood that had just been set. "Yes?" Mariya prepared to be disbelieving again.

Mykhailo simply withdrew three large potatoes and two small

cucumbers from his pockets and held them up before her like trophies.

"Dinner!!!" Mariya declared and snatched them from his hands. "Where did you get them?"

"You know I do not give away my secrets." Mykhailo turned smugly and winked at Danyk. The simple interchange made Danyk feel a connection... a closeness to his Uncle Mykhailo.

Perhaps his mother had good reason to doubt Uncle Mykhailo's prediction of the war's end, but he in childhood adoration of his uncle, could not.

Danyk was not surprised, when soon after Uncle Mykhailo's visit, the war did end.

However, as is characteristic of all endings, it merely marked the beginning of what was to come next.

~

Roosevelt, Churchill and Stalin also foresaw that the war's end was near. In February 1945 at the Yalta Conference, these world leaders began to divide jurisdiction. It was decided the Soviet Union would annex some 180,000 kilometers of pre-war Polish territory.

In May of 1945 Germany surrendered and World War II in Europe was over. The Soviet Union, occupying all of Europe east of River Elbe, controlled Poland, Czechoslovakia, Hungary, Romania, Bulgaria, eastern Germany and Austria.

At Potsdam, Allied leaders established Poland's new western boundaries along the Odra (Oder) and Nysa (Neisse) Rivers.

Now, Mariya's and Danyk's village of Gorodnitsa, in the Province of Galicia, outside the provincial center of Ternopol, was no longer a part of Poland and neither were they.

Mariya and her mother were to be among 10 million other people who were to transfer their citizenship from Poland to the Soviet Union.

It took time and probing by Miss Larned to receive notification of the Board of Reviews decision concerning Sam's petition for naturalization under Provision 701 of the Nationality Act of 1940 as amended.

By March 4, 1946 Sam had received his Certificate of Naturalization. He had done as he had promised Mariya.

Only she was not to be with him to share in the joy of his fulfilled promise.

Would his life always be a mesh of gears turning with missing parts?

While the world rejoiced and anxiously awaited recovery, the people of Mariya's village knew only despair.

How naïve they had been to hope that once the war was over, life would return to their simple peasant existence and their occupiers would go home. If her acceptance of this would take time, her indoctrination as a Soviet citizen would not.

Stalin was feeling victorious. However, by nature he was also somewhat paranoid. He was particularly distrustful of the west and this view had been somewhat adopted by the average Soviet citizen, who had suffered the ravages of war with little or no help from the United States or at least so their government led them to believe.

Just before the war, all shortwave radios and private cars had been confiscated. News was received via loudspeaker only, under strict Stalin control of what was told and of what was left untold.

An entire nation had been drafted to serve as soldiers under the harshest of military officers or as civilian laborers, issued shovels and told to dig anti-tank trenches until their hands were meat-raw from the cold, blistered from overwork and sticky from blood.

A decade before, they had been lucky to have survived the

purges. During the war the slightest infraction such as being late for work could earn them imprisonment.

It was their children who had gone hungry, near starvation and lived through one of the coldest winters in Soviet history with little fuel or relief.

It was their sons and daughters who had taken to their city streets and been slaughtered.

There was not a family who had not in some way felt the hard realities of war and loss directly. Each counted its own casualties.

Hundreds of thousands of Soviet Union's soldiers had been POWs in Germany's prisoner of war camps and had been the most ill-treated prisoner of war ever known.

Stalin had not agreed to provide a fair standard of treatment for any captured soldiers.

In turn, this denied his own soldiers humane treatment by the Germans.

While the Germans allowed the Red Cross to assist, aid and provide for almost all nationalities in German POW camps, never were they given access to the Soviet POWs who were left to fend for themselves in almost all aspects of survival: food, shelter clothing and water.

At the conclusion of World War II, twenty to twenty-five million Soviets were dead and a disproportionate amount had been young males.

Justly or not, the United States was held accountable, by the people of the Soviet Union, and blamed for waiting too long to join the war effort.

This was the sentiment to be held for decades to come and encouraged through relentless propaganda by Stalin himself, who felt western influence constricted his own and interfered with his own total control.

His people were tired and bitter from years of Stalinism, repression and war. Anger needed to be directed somewhere, and to direct it westward was safest and enthusiastically condoned.

Outside, particularly western influence was not to be tolerated! Exposure was to be resisted even if it meant re-writing history books and regressing technologically. Even if it meant imprisonment or the execution of their own returning POWs, who having experienced outside exposure were considered disloyal, for having allowed themselves to be tainted.

Better they should have died for the motherland and for... Stalin.

What would become a particular focus for Stalin were the areas newly acquired from Poland after World War II where a strong underground network of resistors had developed during the war. Stalin, influenced by reality or psychotic paranoia, was convinced the CIA had infiltrated the area.

Soon to return, in a desperate strategy to reclaim the area, were the unrestrained purges of the 1930's. No one would be safe and those not yet in total and absolute mental and physical submission to Stalin would know no mercy. Those who had surrendered their own will, also, had much to fear for Stalin's unrelenting brutality did not cease just because their will had been broken. He believed in convincing reminders, so great was his paranoia.

One day, quite unexpectedly, Mariya and Danyk received a letter from Sam who had hoped with the war's end that he could reconnect with his family.

Mariya's first impulse was to hide it, which was somewhat silly as word had probably spread quickly through the village by now of the letter's delivery. She prayed her neighbors would use discretion. She was not yet sure of how her western ties would be handled by Soviet authority.

She was now an acquired citizen of the Soviet Union, but that meant little in terms of rights or protection even for a natural born citizen. Ukrainians, as during the war, were the least privileged.

Mariya chose to keep the letter pressed to her chest for most of the day, mostly because she feared that if she put the letter down it would disappear. It was not to be believed! She had heard from her Sam. He had not given up on them.

Although she wished she could, she was unable to withhold the fact of the letter's arrival or its contents from her mother and Danyk. Over and over again, she read Szymon's words to them. Each time she scolded herself for doing so. For the next few days, a blanket of serenity fell over the house.

Sam had promised to send papers to bring them to America!

He worried how they and the rest of his family had made out during the war and prayed for their safety.

He had made good his promise. He had made things right in America.

But who now knew about their contact? The war had made neighbors suspicious of each other. Now, even with the war over, information was often twisted, used as a weapon for desperate people to protect their families.

Everyone living in the Soviet Union occupied territories was now a Soviet citizen regardless of western ties or other citizenships held. Under Stalin, Soviet citizenship was more like a prison sentence, and it left the population scrambling to climb a ladder with a safety net. Everyone wanted to be just a bit higher up, just a bit more secure.

Ifs! There were a lot of them. If...Sam sent papers...if they were able to reach her hands...if she tried to use them... would it be safe? Would it be seen as treason, just to try? Would the authorities single her out? What consequences would there be, not just for her but for her mother and Danyk? How was she to respond to Sam? Did he realize that anyone could read their mail? Or that their correspondence was not for their eyes alone. There was much about her world that she did not believe he would understand. There would be much thinking to do before acting.

It was not until Mykhailo's next visit that she dared to talk to anyone about Sam's letter outside of her mother and Danyk.

"When did it arrive?" Mykhailo asked, referring to the letter he held in his hand. "Three days ago."

"Has anyone else seen it?"

"No." Then Mariya cleared her throat guiltily. "Except Danyk and my mother, of course."

Mykhailo did not look pleased. She tried to explain herself.

"They knew about it already; it made no sense to hide it from them."

"I'm surprised you felt that way." He was very disappointed in her. His voice was low and heavy as though she had suddenly placed a huge burden on him.

"Mykhailo, I know I shouldn't have. But I was so happy... not to share it with anyone..."

Mariya's eyes watered as she tried to explain.

"Do you understand how dangerous this is?" Of course, he knew she did. Mariya was not a stupid woman. He didn't mean to sound so angry, but he couldn't help himself.

"Hopefully, the authorities missed it. I can't believe they would have allowed it through, if they did. Unless, it is a test." He stared off pensively.

"You mean they will be watching me?"

"Perhaps."

"But, if he sends papers, official documents... wouldn't they have to uphold them, recognize my right to leave?" Her voice was unusually hopeful as though she was begging him to validate that the possibility existed.

"If I could give you hope, any hope...I would. But for right now, there is none." He took no joy in telling her this. It was just one more job to be done in this business of day-to-day survival.

"You are right. What was I thinking?" Reality hit her like a slap in the face. It would not be wise to chance putting her family in danger. They had been through too much.

In her next letter she would tell Sam that she did not want him to send papers.

He would send them anyway.

Chapter 20

Reality and Consequences

It was again a tense time for Mariya and her family. Many people were disappearing, including her own family members.

In order to survive and triumph, the Allies had to be cunningly clever, and one-step ahead of the Nazis throughout WWII. For a number of reasons, they were able to do just that.

Early in WWII and even just before, the Allies had carefully monitored possible Nazi informants. The Germans, in turn, followed the movements of Allied informants, and when the war started both sides rounded up any and all possible enemy agents. Many suspected spies on both sides were judged guilty and executed.

Losing valued spies was, of course, a detriment to Allied forces; however, they were also able to gain a tremendous advantage during this time.

In order to please Hitler and his high command's impossible deadlines, German spies had to be trained very quickly. They weren't given much, if any training, in how to withstand interrogation. Being inadequately prepared, many "cracked" and gave away many of

Germany's most guarded secrets including the names of additional German spies and informants.

Those who the Allies considered "harmless" were given a special proposition. They were invited to be double agents.

A crafty system was set up which eventually allowed the Allies to take over the German spy system. In fact, it was so good that the Allies had to carefully weigh what information was to be used and what needed to be ignored. Events, information, casualties had to be carefully considered so that the allies could be as victorious as possible without letting Hitler know his top secrets were being leaked to the Allies on a regular basis.

If the Allies were always successful or prepared, then Hitler would become suspicious of his own spies. At times, the Allies knowingly sent their own soldiers to be ambushed because they had to pretend, they didn't know it was about to happen.

The Allies had also acquired the Nazis secret deciphering machine used to code and decode top-secret information. The original machine was called Enigma. The later model was nicknamed the Bronze Goddess. It helped the Allies access almost all top-secret German correspondence. This advantage was deemed so vital to the Allies that it was the most closely guarded secret of WWII, even more so than the plans for the atomic bomb.

All this was kept from Stalin, a man whole-heartedly distrusted by Churchill and not particularly liked by Roosevelt, either.

Stalin was not one to easily accept being fooled or disobeyed. He liked to give orders and have total control. The complex world of double-espionage and his own increasing paranoia left Stalin suspicious of everyone, particularly of anyone with western ties. Mariya's village and the surrounding area had until recently been part of Poland and open to outside influence. Thus, Stalin felt it best to use a strong hand, and squelch any notion of disloyalty, even if it did not yet exist.

His people would suffer greatly for his bizarre mentality and purges would become an everyday event. No one would be safe, not Stalin's highest-ranking officers, nor his most trusted confidants.

Anyone at any time could become the next casualty. And they all knew it.

~

Mariya's family was counting their own casualties. Szymon's youngest brother, Vasil, had been taken in early 1939 and forced to be a Soviet soldier when the Russians invaded Poland. Soldiers forced into service were generally used as bait or cover and rarely lived long. Such was the fate of Vasil who had been killed within the first few days of war. A friend who had been told about his death notified his family, retelling Vasil's final moments as they had been told to him. Vasil had just turned nineteen years old.

Szymon's other brother, Evon, was forced into the Soviet army in 1941 to fight the Germans. He was captured at Kiev but believed to be dead, as the conditions for Soviet soldiers in a German prisoner of war camp were well known to be unbearable. Had he been a Polish soldier, he might have fared better. He'd been twenty-four years old when taken.

Marion was still a question mark. Their hope for him was that as days went by, he might return as a released prisoner of war. But days went by, and then weeks, and still they heard nothing. Not many families were hearing from relatives who had been taken to Germany as POWs, servants or laborers. There was a good reason why, but they were not to learn of it yet.

Mariya poured her heart out in letters first to Szymon and then to Paulo, her brother in France.

Her first drafts were ones of anger, bitterness and hatred. Then, of course, she destroyed those versions and rewrote the letters to avoid censorship. It was tiring to communicate using carefully chosen words, but it was the only way. Then, one had to hope it didn't get lost in the mail or disappear altogether. It was quite miraculous that she had reestablished contact with Szymon in America and Paulo in

France. Paulo had not yet mentioned reuniting with Marion. There was a reasonable, yet... also, ridiculous reason for this.

Mariya worried that the authorities had too easily allowed her this contact and feared it actually meant she was being watched. She was a new Soviet citizen, but she had quickly learned to understand much that would never be explained to her.

Satner had joined Marion at Paulo's farmhouse just outside Paris. There the two continued to regain their physical strength, as well as their mental stamina.

The area swarmed with soldiers being repatriated. Satner was anxious to return to his family, and his departure was an emotional one.

Paulo, who had been told the story of how Satner had saved Marion's life, hugged him good-bye as if they too, were brothers. Satner expressed his gratitude to his gracious host and then went on his way to what he believed would be a joyous reunion with his family and friends. He expected Poland to be different, for sure. It had suffered through many years of war, and it was now part of the Soviet Union. But he expected, as many Soviets of the time did, that life would go on much better than it had pre-war. The Soviet borders had been opened and its citizens were anxious to begin life anew.

Paulo had wanted him to stay, to wait and see how the world settled first. He and many others did not trust Stalin and he was concerned about what awaited him at home. But Satner was too eager to see his wife and son.

Both Satner and Marion were sure that they would see each other again in their homeland and soon be introducing each other to their families.

Marion chose to continue his visit with his brother knowing once he left, he might never see him again. He also missed his wife and family but as he had waited many years a few more days would not make a tremendous difference.

As well Paulo had been in contact with Mariya, and Marion was sure his family now knew he was well and would be returning soon. He had also been given a blessing. He had received word of how his family had fared. There were many friends, and family members lost and much to mourn... but he could begin to do so here in the comfort of his brother's home.

There was also much to consider. He had a brother in France and one in America. When he had left Poland, it was a mound of rubble. Perhaps it would be wise to consider relocating with his family elsewhere.

Marion spent his days conversing with his French sister-in-law, Maria, using a mixture of gestures, smiles, French and Ukrainian. They were patient with each other and ultimately communicated quite well.

Maria was grateful to Marion for giving her husband tremendous happiness and relief to be reunited with a family member. Paulo had spent years agonizing over what might be the fate of his family. Finally, at the war's end he had received word making him both relieved and saddened by the news he had been given.

Paulo had remained particularly attentive to Allied redistribution of power and control, especially as it would have a great impact on his family. He had waited until, he was sure. The language barrier had allowed Paulo to protect his brother from what had recently become stunning and incredulous news. However, now, it was time to share with his brother what he had feared all along.

Paulo approached the subject gently, realizing that Marion had been away from home for a very long time, and as a POW he had been isolated and uninformed.

"There is talk of what is going on in Poland." Paulo spoke more sternly than he might ordinarily have, for though he wanted to protect his brother, he also wanted to make his point clearly. Marion needed to fully understand before he made the difficult decisions that lay before him. "The Soviet Union has taken control of our village."

"Well, they are our ally, no? I had my doubts about those Soviets... but as long as in the end, they took our side!"

Marion was not as worldly as Paulo. Before the war, he had rarely gone more than five kilometers from his village and because he had been captured so quickly as a Polish soldier, he had not lived there during Soviet occupation. The only Soviets he knew were the weak and vulnerable POWs he had met as a prisoner of war himself.

"No, I mean they are in control. A section of Poland, unfortunately the section where our family is from, has been given to the Soviet Union."

"Who gave it to them? Poland belongs to the Poles." This was odd talk coming from Marion, who had never felt national pride before the war. His pride was in his Ukrainian heritage, which mainstream Poland had always done its best to deny.

"Stalin and Hitler had divided up Poland, even before the war. That is why our village was controlled by the Soviets after you were captured, until Hitler betrayed Stalin, and then it was controlled by the Germans. With the German's defeat, it is once again under Soviet jurisdiction." Marion looked confused as to why his brother was telling him this. "Stalin is no different than before the war. He is as much a mad man as Hitler was, perhaps worse... and he is still the political power ruling our homeland."

"But he did switch sides. As an ally, won't he allow the world to return to its pre-war boundaries?"

"No. I wish I could say it was otherwise, but simply... no." Paulo allowed it to sink in a bit because it was not the worst he had to tell him.

"The Soviet Union will remain in power. But now... you must listen carefully! Marion... the Soviet Union... Stalin... in his paranoia is targeting returning POWs."

"I don't understand." And he did not, nor would he for several more minutes as Paulo tried to make sense out of something that even to himself, he found totally senseless.

"Anyone, who has crossed over the Soviet border... even captured Soviet soldiers, who have been outside the Soviet boundaries are being considered unpatriotic and enemies of the Soviet state."

"That is ridiculous!" Marion looked away almost amused. "You mean, if they were captured, rather than killed, they are regarded as enemies of the state."

"Yes."

"So......... Soviet POWs must not return?" Marion looked like a man who had just learned that two plus two actually equals five.

"Yes."

Marion shook his head at the downright indecency of it. "Have they not suffered enough already?" Images of the POW camp and the Soviet prisoners came to mind. They were, by far, the most inhumanely treated. No food, no water... sometimes not even a shelter over their heads. What is wrong with that Stalin? If these men had somehow managed to stay alive, they deserved their country's highest medal, not their hatred.

"But...," Marion began playing with a hodgepodge of ideas in his mind. "I'm not a Soviet soldier; I was a Polish soldier..."

"It makes no difference. I said, anyone, any Soviet citizen will be considered an enemy of the state. If they served in the Soviet army, the Polish army... if they have had western contact, they are considered to have been influenced... and are an enemy of the state."

"You mean..." Marion could not make any sense of this. He must be misunderstanding.

"Marion... you must not go back to our village in Poland, it is in the Soviet Union, and you are considered by Stalin to be a Soviet citizen now. If you return you will be arrested for treason!"

Marion felt as though he had stepped into a pit and was spiraling downward. There was nothing left to hang on to.

Not to see his wife... his family! Never to see his village again! A short moment ago, he was considering leaving his village forever to bring his family to France or America and now he only longed to live his days out there.

"Impossible! My wife is waiting for me!"

Sadly, Paulo needed to be truthful with him. "What good will a dead husband be?"

Marion could only stare back. He needed to digest all he had been told. He knew the Poland he had left would be different from the one to which he expected to return. But never to return?

Now a part of the Soviet Union?

"We will need to bring my wife and daughter here then...," Marion spoke to himself in a confused fog trying to sort it all out.

"Marion...," Paulo approached carefully, "that will be difficult. Remember... Stalin does not allow his citizens to leave."

"But we are not *his* citizens, we are Polish citizens... we are Ukrainian!" Could Stalin just demand citizenship? He stood up with his voice rising, wanting to fight, wanting to argue this point, but ultimately, there was no one there that disagreed with him. So, he took his seat, quietly defeated by having no opponent to fight.

Marion leaned forward with his elbows on his knees and held his hands in a single fist. They shook in anger at Stalin's audacity while the rest of him went numb. It was too much to absorb, simply too much!

And suddenly, another disturbing thought...

What of Satner! He had returned a few weeks ago.

Marion called out his name realizing his friend may have made a terrible mistake returning to their homeland so quickly. He had been so anxious to return to his family, and he had had no reason to stay as Marion did.

"I would have told him had I known! I knew about Soviet jurisdiction, but I did not know about how Stalin would treat returning POWs. I was only informed of that recently from British soldiers. I would have stopped him had I known." Paulo's voice begged for forgiveness.

The relief, which had lifted Marion's shoulders at the war's end, was now replaced by a shroud of darkness cast heavily over him. Paulo saw that Marion finally understood the gravity of all he had been told.

"I understand none of it," Marion contradicted, "not any part of the last five years. We live in a mad world!"

All Paulo could think to do was throw his arms around Marion.

Although they looked very much like brothers, Marion was a whole foot taller. Still, Paulo felt like the big brother needing to comfort and protect. Silently, Marion withdrew and his brother knew that if the war had not been enough to change his brother forever, this had done it. The toll was clear on his ashen face. Time and love seemed the only remedies to offer, though neither might change a thing.

Unfortunately, time was not theirs to determine, and after a short time, Paulo and Marion were to receive another blow.

Mail arrived from Kupetsky. Odd... Paulo remembered the neighbor well but did not expect direct communication from him. He opened the envelope hurriedly as unexpected news was often very good... or very bad.

This bit of news would be no different.

Chapter 21

Word from Sam... What to do?

All day his mother had been quiet and preoccupied. Danyk and his grandmother were careful not to distract her with trivial things as they might on other days.

This evening, a serious and secret meeting of grave importance would take place. A teacher from the neighboring village was expected and it was requiring all of his mother's energies to maintain her leap of faith.

It was not a time to trust an unfamiliar neighbor, but that was exactly what she was about to do.

Szymon had somehow sent official-looking documents. Earlier letters had instructed her that they were soon to come, and that when they arrived, she was to take the documents to the American Embassy in Moscow. But how was she to do that? There was much that her Szymon did not understand about their circumstances or the reign of terror that Stalin projected over their lives.

Could he understand that one feared even to leave his own farm to visit a neighbor or gather necessities? Mariya had barely gone beyond her own village, except to Skalat, since before the war had begun, and now Szymon wanted her to board a train bound for

Moscow, deep in the Soviet Union, a territory once forbidden to her and other Polish citizens before the war? Did he understand the bravery and courage it would take to accomplish this task, discreetly, secretly and alone.

And what was she bringing? She had been unable to make the documents out as they were all in English. It had been many years since she had entertained herself with her employer's used magazines back in New York, and while she recognized the print as English, she did not know where to begin to understand what it said.

Inquiring about and then inviting the schoolteacher who would be able to translate the document had caused a nervous frenzy in her chest that fluttered furiously, much to her exasperation. It caused her to doubt her resolve to follow Szymon's instructions. But she did so much want to be back with her Szymon in the protected world that she once enjoyed, however briefly. To do so, did she first have to lose all common sense and endanger her mother and Danyk?

What had she done? How selfish could she be? What had she done?

What-had-she-done!

Dusk had arrived and without soldiers to carry her off, to murder her family for doing the unforgivable... for inquiring about the impossible possibility, the glimmer, the speck, the minute dust particle of hope for freedom and return to America!

When the teacher, a sister of a friend of a friend, arrived everyone jumped at the first sight of her form striding off the dirt road toward their cottage.

She was quickly ushered in as Mariya, Danyk and her mother glanced outward, scanning the countryside, looking for anyone who might be watching, spying, witnessing the act of treason they were about to commit.

The woman understood the urgency and wondered to herself, if perhaps she should not have come.

The Szafranski's were neighbors of her friends and though Stalin had implemented a way of life that left neighbor unable to trust neighbor, the Ukrainians still felt an impulse to follow tradition and care for one another. Indeed, this particular woman had, time and time again, courageously done whatever she could for her people throughout the war. Now, she was demonstrating her courage once again, but she hoped it was only that and not her impulsive foolishness as well.

She was aware that Mariya was a close relative of a man she admired who worked for the Ukrainian Insurgency Army, also known as the Ukrainian Liberation Army. Had she allowed that loyalty to sway her? Should the fact have been a good reason to turn the woman down? Was the woman being watched? Might she now also be under suspicion... after all the years of escaping detection?

The low, hushed whispers and closed shutters drenched the cottage in a solemn tent of darkness that befitted the seriousness of their encounter.

Suddenly she wanted to see the papers, be done with her business here and be gone. It was best for all concerned.

Mariya was also growing more nervous and anxious, yet she graciously offered the young, attractive teacher one of the two chairs that furnished their home.

Mariya thought for a moment of Mykhailo and knew he would disapprove. Had she been unwise not to let him know and guide her as to how this should have been done?

Either way, it was too late now. She couldn't derail; she could not hit reverse.

It was all too important. She took a moment before she joined the woman to take a nourishing breath and used the time it took to exhale for evaluation.

War had sharpened her skill at making quick judgments, at least she hoped so, and right or wrong, she was about to rely on it.

Mariya searched the teacher's face, studied her eyes, watched her every movement for clues. Was she friend or foe? Would she help decipher the documents that Szymon had sent, or would she report them to the authorities?

The woman's eyes narrowed, not with opposition but clarity, recognizing leeriness and caution.

"I have papers, important papers that I need translated. Can you help?" Mariya felt slightly awkward and silly. Why else would the woman have come?

"Yes." The woman's eyes intuitively searched for the papers mentioned, but Mariya had not yet moved to present them.

"From English to Ukrainian? Are you comfortable translating them?" Mariya was trying to evaluate, confirm one last time that the woman could be trusted.

"Your brother-in-law, my friend, Mykhailo? Does he know you do this?"

Mariya realized instantly that the woman would not betray her to the authorities as she had feared, but perhaps she would betray her to Mykhailo.

Of course, that would not be as great an offense but one that could still have dire consequences. She did not want to lose Mykhailo's trust, but with great shame, she realized it was what she deserved.

This woman could have as easily been an agent for the authorities as she was a friend of Mykhailo's. Fortunately, she seemed to be the latter... but if Mariya's instincts were proven wrong, it was best that she made sure that Mykhailo was in no way connected to her act of treason.

"No, he doesn't know." Mariya's eyes pleaded for this to be a transaction between them only, but the woman's eyes did not answer or give away her thoughts. Perhaps, she had not yet made up her mind.

Was she also a member of the Ukrainian Insurgent Army? Mariya wondered, but of course would not ask.

"May I see the papers?" The woman knew she had given Mariya reason to think, to second-guess her decision and wisdom. For now, that would satisfy her. She had taught the woman to use greater caution and had done her friend, Mykhailo, a great favor. Too bad her honor would have to stop her from telling him about it.

"This is a copy of your husband's naturalization papers." The woman continued to review the papers as she spoke. "He is now a citizen of the United States of America." She looked to Mariya for her understanding.

"Yes!" Mariya beamed, though she didn't mean to. Before this moment, she had not been certain. He had sent a letter saying that he had 'made things right', which was an implication. Now, she knew most certainly. With that, Danyk stepped forward, drawn by the silent happiness he knew his mother was feeling. His mother glanced his way to share in their own private celebration.

"And this is Danyk's birth certificate. He was born in Man-hat-tan?" The woman realized she was sharing incredible and dangerous news.

"May I ask, what is it you plan to do with these papers?" Then the woman seemed to have second thoughts.

"No! Don't answer me." The young lady stood, anxious now to leave.

Mariya realized instantly that it was not the woman's fear for herself that made her quickly rise to leave but concern for learning what she need not know that prompted her hurried exit.

It was only for an instant that the woman's eyes met Mariya's before going. Much was said in their brief silent conversation.

You will be careful? This is dangerous information. Do you understand? Really understand?

Yes, I do understand.

Mariya felt relieved. She now knew the woman could be trusted. She would not go to the authorities.

But... would she go to Mykhailo?

Chapter 22

Soviet Paranoia

Mariya could not take the situation any further. She hoped Szymon could read between the lines of the letters she sent him, if indeed they were ever sent to him.

No, she would not be going to Moscow, 600 kilometers away, with the papers he had sent; the time was not right. There could be much to fear if she went.

No one could be trusted!

She couldn't even bring herself to imagine what could have happened to her, her mother or Danyk if the teacher had betrayed them and gone to the authorities.

What had she been thinking! She had trusted her family's lives to a complete stranger.

Fortunately, the stranger was a friend of Mykhailo's, possibly a fellow member of the underground. She had dared not ask the teacher for a confirmation of her suspicions. She did not need or want to know. The less one knew, the less likely he could betray a neighbor accidentally. But the fact that Mariya had been willing to confide in a person of whom she didn't even know the identity with absolute certainty, that the person could have easily been the authorities, was at once a slap in the face and a blessing all at once.

It was a warning sign that she dare not proceed. Too much was at stake. She would do as Mykhailo bid her and forget about the documents, forget about Moscow, forget... at least for now.

Would Szymon understand? How could she explain? For six long years, they had not been able to communicate with each other. When Mariya had received the first letter, her heart wanted to burst with joy and relief. But so much could not be expressed in the letters that she sent back to him, and it was a tremendous frustration. Not only could she not express herself as she would have liked, but she also didn't know if Szymon was aware that all mail was censored as another control that Stalin mandated over his people.

His people.

Were she, Danyk, and her mother truly Stalin's now? Would there ever be a way out?

Time perhaps would change things.

It had been the theme of her life, with its events veering her personal course this way and that, transfiguring her from a trusting peasant girl to this mutated self... distrustful, watchful, and calculating.

Time could change people and alter circumstances. Perhaps it was the only answer to her predicament.

When time is your only hope, you learn endurance.

The Austria-Hungary Empire, then Poland, then the Soviet Union, then Germany and again the Soviet Union had all controlled her small village at varying times, all during her lifetime.

Time changes things. There was always reason to hope.

For now, as the turmoil that surrounded their lives played out, she would wait. Once again, she was waiting for things to be made right. Her Szymon had done his part. He was now an American citizen.

Now, she must do her part, but she hadn't a clue as to what that was or how she might accomplish it.

She only knew what she most assuredly must not do.

She must not go to Moscow. She must not let the authorities know of her family's western ties. To do so would make her a traitor to the Soviet Union, which now claimed her as a citizen... and could have devastating consequences for her family. The risks were simply too great to contemplate.

"Danyk... where is your mother?" Kupetsky approached solemnly.

Danyk pointed and as Kupetsky turned, he realized she was not far away, working her fields.

Danyk did not have to be told that he brought bad news. Kupetsky had not given him his usual greeting and his tone was all business-like and serious.

Putting down his rake, Danyk followed his neighbor. They so rarely had company that he didn't want to miss this opportunity to visit ... or to hear whatever it was that Kupetsky seemed so intent on telling his mother.

"Stay here, Danyk... I need to talk to your mother privately...you understand?"

Of course, Danyk was respectful of Kupetsky's request and showed not even a morsel of disappointment. Instead, he nodded compliantly and picked up his rake to continue with his work. But his ears were perked to attention, and he could not help but stare at the two, a short distance away, as they spoke back and forth.

His grandmother too, knew something was amiss. She came behind him and placed her hand on his shoulder. For a moment, the two stood frozen trying to overhear what was being said.

He knew it was about Uncle Mykhailo and his grandmother, his father's mother, but he could catch little else. Nor could his maternal grandmother, who tapped his shoulder, hoping he could interpret for her what she could not make out. But he had nothing to offer, so he put up his hand gesturing that she should be patient and commenced to listen even more intently.

His mother's collapse onto a crude overturned bucket signaled the disaster Kupetsky's mood had led him to expect.

The intruding pair could hold back no longer. Danyk took off in a near run with his grandmother waddling hurriedly just behind him, panting to keep up, until they reached Mariya's side.

At first, she could not turn to them, fully realizing that the even greater agony was that she must now share the news with them, as well.

"Mariya... what has happened?" Danyk's grandmother begged with grim, panicked concern. She was weeping and reaching for Mariya simultaneously, preparing for the worst. How much more must they bear? Mariya wondered to herself. A long, pensive,

indulgent moment passed and then selflessly... even perhaps heroically, she began to straighten and wipe away her tears.

Her family needed her strength, not her weakness. Fulfilling a promise she had made to herself long ago, she stood and made ready to catch them as they too succumbed to the devastating news.

Kupetsky, the true friend that he was, spared her from making the miserable broadcast by repeating the news before she could speak.

Unfortunately, it distracted her from the strength she was determined to show, and she helplessly felt tears stream again.

"The Soviet police have taken your Uncle Mykhailo. They say he failed to report for military duty."

Again, knowing she must be the rock of her family, she wiped away her tears, took a deep breath and offered what was left of her strength. The three huddled together, offering support as they had so often throughout the war, bearing bad news once again, together.

Kupetsky waited, first letting them absorb this terrible tragedy. Only Mariya knew that more was to follow.

It was already a familiar situation to many Ukrainian families. Unfortunately, when the Soviet police arrested you, it often meant deportation to Siberia. It didn't matter how you were charged or the reason for the arrest. Most often, you simply disappeared... possibly never heard from again.

Then, Kupetsky winced. He knew he must wound again, stab this family in the heart once more.

"They also took Paranka."

"My grandmother?" Danyk whispered his shock. His paternal grandmother was nearly seventy years old. What possible offense could she have committed? His heart stopped and his blood rushed to his feet. He felt light-headed and looked it, as well.

His mother's arms reached out for him and though they shook, they were mighty enough to hold him up as they shared their sorrow.

"Paraskenia?" Suddenly, Mariya had realized that Paraskenia, Szymon's twelve-year old sister was alone... or had they taken her too?

"No, no!" Mariya fell back as though she were going to faint. She is just a child! But that never stopped the Soviet police before.

If this too had happened, would it be her undoing?

Kupetsky reassured her quickly, "No, Mariya, no, no, no. She is safe!"

That was good news, enough to let her remain sane, but... not enough to put the pieces of her heart back together again.

For years now, Mykhailo had been so careful and had never been detected by the Germans or the Soviets.

His home had been the ancient forest that he and the other young Ukrainian men and women like him knew so well. They had gotten limited outside help and training from undergrounds up north in France, Belgium and Holland whose connections could be traced to the CIA. The agency was more than anxious to teach them how to steal explosives from the enemy or blow-up bridges needed to transport the enemy's supplies.

They were equipped with rifles, grenades and even machine guns. Clever and fast, they moved mostly at night through man-made tunnels and dense forest... and always maintaining an element of surprise.

Ukrainian children were told legends about them and secretly sang songs about their bravery and victories. Stalin knew they existed, although the Allies denied knowledge of them. Although paranoid beyond reason, Stalin's fears were realistically founded concerning these patriots who had helped win WWII. He just wasn't sure what to do about them; they were that difficult to search out.

They added to Stalin's suspicions of the West trying to infiltrate and seize the Soviet Union. Above all else, these patriots were highly motivated, as opposed to his own army, which was apathetic and worn thin. His soldiers had not just endured the war but the demands of Stalin's harsh dictatorship and crushing, dehumanizing controls.

Mykhailo had only stepped out of the forest on missions, and on rare occasions, to check on family members. He had recently thought it safe to check on his mother, but much to his regret he had been wrong.

They must have been watching her house, as he hadn't been there more than five minutes when the house was surrounded.

He should have known better. For a long while he could, in part, count on the confusion of war to hide his identity. Obviously, the Soviets were taking root and were more methodically investigating who the troublemakers might be. He of course, if they had any knowledge whatsoever of his counteractivities, would be high on their list.

His biggest regret was that they had also taken his mother. She knew nothing, and he knew they would eventually find that out. But his heart sank for what they would do to her to discover that.

For himself, it was part of the bargain. He had given himself to the Ukrainian Insurgent Army, whole-heartedly and fully realizing and willing to bear responsibility for his dedication and actions. But could he bear his mother suffering the burden and consequences of a choice never given to or made by her?

He was fast learning that it was often the way the Soviets conducted interrogations. They involved a web of family members, so one would try to protect the other.

Mykhailo tried to think quickly. Was there something to do? Was there a way out?

Could he help his mother escape? Even if there was a way, where would she go?

There was nothing he could do. It was this exact feeling, a sense of swelling ineptitude, which had gotten him involved in the Ukrainian Insurgent Army to begin with. Never wanting the feeling to overtake him again was what drove him and his comrades as well.

Both had been blindfolded and were being driven for quite some time. Mykhailo tried to note the turns and twists, but the powers that be were determined to make it impossible to detect their route or direction.

He would do only what was left to do.

"Mother," he whispered, "I am sorry!" Mykhailo was much sorrier than he could ever have said, but it was expressed in the delivery of his heart-felt words and well received by his loving mother.

Hidden in the hem of his trousers was an "L pill", wrapped in a waterproof shell; it could cause instant death if crushed by the teeth. It was the only evidence of his identity as a resistor that he carried when he visited his family.

He fought the instinct to pass it to his mother. It was unbearable to think of her being tortured. As a good soldier of the insurgency, he knew at all cost... he must not. He had to save it for himself.

He had seen too much to act impulsively. God forgive him, but too many lives depended on him keeping valuable secrets. He and his mother were dispensable. The greater cause had to triumph.

At this moment, he felt as if the burden of the world rested on his shoulders. In the end, his early maturity and wisdom prevailed. He would keep the pill and if need be, take it himself. He also held a son's hope that somehow his mother could survive, and at some point, be returned to his family.

"Mykhailo... don't be sorry." Amazingly, even in such a situation, the small woman's soft voice soothed him as it had so many times throughout his life. "You are a brave man who has only tried to help our people. With all my heart, I know that."

Mykhailo squeezed tight his blindfolded-eyes and steadied his clenched jaw. "I am so proud of you, my son. I give you a parent's blessing." He accepted the blessing with a bowed head that his mother could not see, for she was blindfolded as well, and he felt very unworthy but totally forgiven.

The world was not so bad a place if a mother's love could be so unshakable.

It would be the last time they would speak.

When the vehicle doors opened, they were pulled in opposite directions, each to meet their own fate.

It began for Mykhailo with a walk down a long straight corridor. He was still blindfolded and handcuffed. The guard's ring of keys jangled the whole way, echoing and giving him his first impression of his prison. They uncuffed him, and he was allowed to take his blindfold off. He was checked for a belt, shoelaces or anything else that he could have used to commit suicide.

The cell was five feet by five feet and empty except for one dimly lit light bulb that hung from the ceiling. The door had an observation hole high above eye level that allowed guards to look in but didn't allow the prisoner to look out.

There he sat... then stood. Sat, then stood. There wasn't enough room for his near six- foot frame to lie down, not that he would have been able to rest if he had been permitted to.

Hours came and went; he knew because he grew hungry. Nothing was offered to him.

The concrete walls, which at first had been cool, now seemed cold. A frigid chill began to creep into his joints and bones making him involuntarily begin to shiver. He tried to imagine a warm blanket around his shoulders and the heat from the sun in the fields on a summer day, but his mind could not win over his body and still, the cold gripped him. He started to rub his feet hoping the friction would warm them at least slightly, but in the end, it did little good.

Finally, two guards came to the door. They placed the cuffs on his hands behind his back, and then pulled him out of the cell. While the cell was locked from the outside, he was forced face-up against the wall. This was how he was to stand when guards stopped, or another prisoner was being led across his path.

He quickly learned that prisoners walked with their faces forward, not turning or looking up or down. One guard walked in front and led the way. The other walked behind him. Back down the long corridor they went, until they reached an iron staircase and proceeded up its shallow steps.

They finally reached a large metal door with a small glass window. It was reinforced with thin crisscross wire that seemed to run through it. In the room were two chairs separated by a black metal table. He was thrust into one of the chairs. The back support offered by the chair gave him a moment of relief.

Then the interrogation began.

Hours later, he was taken and escorted to a cell on the second floor. They stopped at a metal door, unlocked it and shoved him in. This room was larger but just as blank as his first cell with the exception of green tiles running around the perimeter, a soiled tub with two handles that sat to the right of the door and … the forty pairs of eyeballs that all looked his way.

Compared to the other prisoners of various sizes and frames filling the room, he appeared to be in the best condition and health; although he might have felt differently if he'd had a mirror.

He wiped his chin to catch some blood oozing from his broken tooth, and a man next to him rolled away when some of the blood dripped on the floor. Other than that brief introduction, he wasn't given any notice at all.

His blood mingled with other stains of spit, urine and extinguished bugs that seemed to carpet the floor and permeate the room with the most-foul smell... or was it from the soiled tub, which seemed to have been recently used.

Mykhailo deduced quickly that the concrete floor was his bed and that the only open space not covered by a body, the one by the soiled tub, was reserved for him. It was the honor always reserved for the latest newcomer.

There was little one could do to get comfortable, no blanket was provided, and to have any possibility at all of finding warmth one had to close in on the prisoner lying next to him. No one seemed offended as it was a shared comfort and a code of survival passed down from one generation of prisoners to the next.

Finally, Mykhailo's weariness caught up with him. As a result of the stress of his arrest, concern for his mother, the interrogation, lack of food and warmth, he found himself drifting off in spite of the incredible pain in his jaw from his broken tooth. Perhaps he slept for hours, perhaps for only minutes. With a sudden swing, the metal door opened and two Soviet guards marched in.

"Dawai, bistre!" "Now get up on the double!"

Mykhailo was speedily roused with barely enough time to get his footing. He was then taken down the hall for more "questioning."

This would happen each day that followed, at 11 PM and 3 AM, although he had no way to know what the time was.

Sustaining him was one thick slice of dark bread, given to him each morning and three bowls of cabbage soup, one served at each meal.

Each time, the interrogations grew worse, physically and mentally. The worst by far was when he could hear the cries of his own mother pleading for mercy. It was standard procedure, a common element of torture. Eventually, her cries ceased, and he knew she had either been released, moved to another prison or simply was no more.

When what he believed to be his final hours arrived, he knew he could bear no more. Using his own ragged teeth, he broke the hem of the trousers he had worn since his arrest and quickly swallowed the pill dry without being noticed.

Oddly, he felt his mother's hands upon him, blessing him and calling him to her. In the end, after all he had endured, he felt a momentary hero's peace. For he knew he had done all he could to protect the weak and try to right a world gone mad.

For some men, this would have been enough. For others, the pill and the final rest it offered would have been a mark of failure and haunt them for eternity.

Such men don't die easily.

Danyk had walked down this dirt path a hundred... a thousand times over his short almost fourteen-year life span. It was quiet, rural, a mixture of open fields and the forest's edge. Villagers used it to go from farm to farm especially after the war began, and the open roads were to be avoided.

The smack of branches and twigs giving way meshed with the crunch of pebbles and dirt echoing his footsteps. The mesmerizing sounds made the soothing stroll his favorite activity of the day.

He was alone with his thoughts after a day of hard work at a neighboring farm. It had been a good day by all accounts. He had begun early as usual to milk and feed his neighbor's cow, followed by other routine farm chores. He'd been paid with a scant bit of wheat, which he'd managed to sell for a few kopeks and a bag of potatoes, which he was now carrying home, by its burlap handle.

He should have been distracted by the lull of a beautiful day, the rays of sunlight filtered by the tree branches that shadowed the forest's floor and the feeling of passing through a tunnel of nature's bounty.

But he wasn't.

Alert and ready as always, he caught the vague murmur of unfamiliar male voices coming from his home. It was still away in the distance, but it was enough to slow his steps and make his approach a cautious one.

Danyk stepped off the beaten path, so the trees could hide his approach. Slowly he continued to advance, being careful to lay his steps on the forest's bouncy humus floor rather than on the dried leaves or twigs which might crackle and give him away.

Then the clearing came into view, and he could see his farm and the mud-bricked house, which he shared with his mother and grand-mother. It looked quiet except for the two Soviet Army vehicles parked in front. Within minutes, one truck drove away in the oppo-site direction from where he stood. One jeep remained.

He couldn't detect anything of his mother's or grandmother's whereabouts; however, he could hear two soldiers talking in Russian. They spoke quickly and he couldn't understand what they were saying.

It was best that he waited for them to leave, he thought. He was certain his mother would not want him to approach with the soldiers there. So, though he was filled with worry and fear for his mother and grandmother, he took a seat on a nearby fallen tree and began what would become a very, very, long wait.

First one hour went by, then another. Still, he could not hear or see his mother or grandmother. "What could they be doing?" he wondered.

The soldiers seemed at ease. They were not yelling or shouting orders or tossing this and that as they did during searches.

The third hour came and went. Still no sign of his mother or grandmother. His seat was beginning to hurt and his legs needed to stretch. Soon, it would be dark.

When the sun began to fall, he felt like he couldn't resist any longer. He stood to relieve himself and shake his numbing torso.

What if his mother and grandmother needed help? He had sat doing nothing, not even getting help. But who could help? There was no one to stand up to the soldiers except... Uncle Mykhailo... and the other resistors. But Uncle Mykhailo and his grandmother had recently been arrested. No one had yet gotten word of what had happened to them.

Too often word never came. But that was not what he needed to deal with now.

Now, he needed to decide what to do. He fought with himself back and forth.

What would my mother tell me to do? Stay away, of course.

Perhaps the soldiers needed food and they knew her son would be coming home with potatoes earned from his day's work. Could that be all they wanted? Could that be what they seemed to be waiting for?

Ah! He remembered suddenly that he had planned to find wood after his chores. Would they be angry that his household had no food to offer...no fuel...and that he was so late? His mother had expected him hours ago. Was she frantic inside waiting and hoping for his return, so that she could feed the soldiers and send them on their way?

He was hungry, thirsty... and needed to know his mother and grandmother were alright.

His decision was made. He backtracked to the path, not wanting the soldiers to know that he had been hiding and watching them all day long. He pretended to be surprised when he came upon them. As respectfully as he was able, he asked if his mother and grandmother were in the house and if he might go in.

"No." the soldier replied. How quickly his manner had changed.

For the last number of hours, Danyk had watched the soldier relax in his front yard.

Now, suddenly, he was tense and his tone authoritative.

He grabbed the bag of potatoes from Danyk's arm and using a mix of Russian and Ukrainian threw it back at him with orders. "Go to the nearest house to boil these. Hurry! We are hungry."

The soldiers had obviously searched the house and knew that there was no supply of firewood. Perhaps, as he had suspected earlier, they had been waiting for him all along.

The two soldiers motioned him to lead the way and began to follow with pointed guns.

Danyk had been scared, now he was terrified.

Where were his mother and grandmother? What had the soldiers done with them?

He was hungry, thirsty and tired. He felt lightheaded with fear and his hands that carried the bag of potatoes shook visibly.

The three began the journey to the nearest farmhouse until there was a slight distraction. Overhead a flock of geese began to take flight, and the soldiers quickly lifted their rifles skyward and aimed at the squawking birds.

When they were finished, it took them a minute to realize...the boy was gone!

They would have gone after him if either had the slightest idea of the direction the boy had taken. Carelessly, they fired their rifles in various haphazard directions before realizing they were clueless and much more interested in tonight's goose dinner. Besides, the boy had considerately dropped the bag of potatoes behind him.

Had they known how closely the bullets had danced under Danyk's feet, they would have had their recaptured prisoner for their feast, as well!

Danyk wished he had managed to save even one potato from his bag for his supper, but he had acted too quickly and had begun his dash into the forest a split second after turning and seeing the ends of the soldier's rifles aimed upward.

He had been thirsty even before the dash and now he was sorely parched. He had gone, run as far away as he could and now needed to check his bearings. It was difficult to see in the darkness, which now engulfed him, but he thought he must be near his neighbors, the Shetnuks. He needed to rest, and he needed more light to make his way, so he found himself a bouncy seat on the forest floor, covered himself with thickly leaved branches and hid.

He waited for the first light of morning for a dozen reasons. He couldn't navigate safely enough in the dark, and he was afraid the soldiers were searching for him. He was also, for all he had lived through, still quite young and thoroughly terrified. Although tired and confused, he was a thoughtful boy, and he respected his neighbor's privacy and sleep.

With tremendous courage, he finally made his way out into the clearing of his neighbor's yard and lightly tapped on his door with his last bit of decency and reserve. Completely spent, he fell into the arms of Shetnuk's elderly wife as she opened the door.

She quickly seated him and gave him as much water as he wanted and a cup of cabbage soup. Between gulps, he told of the soldiers at his house, how he had waited and then decided to approach the house. His voice broke when he recalled his escape and fears for what might have happened to his mother and grandmother.

As soon as the farmer realized the authorities might be looking for Danyk, he somberly told the boy all that he could do for him.

"Danyk, hide in the forest behind our house. I will try to bring you food and water... whatever I am able to spare." The neighbor's face was weathered with age, but his eyes were kind and direct.

There was so much that did not need to be declared between them, including Shetnuk's concern for his own family or the risk he faced in helping him.

Danyk's downward gaze and then quick upward glance spoke both his appreciation and regret.

Already, the farmer was pushing him from the house, but he offered no apology. Danyk understood full well that the farmer was thinking sensibly and that he must not subject or endanger his family any more than necessary. It was enough that the neighbor would do all he could for him. It was an inadequate, though sincere, and loving offer.

There was a small group of neighbors that would be told and trusted to help over the next couple of weeks. It was not that others could not be trusted, but as war had taught them, it was best to tell only those that needed to know. Indoctrination into Stalinism had only emphasized and reinforced the wisdom of this communal policy.

Danyk survived the next few weeks on any food scraps he was offered; he knew full well that whatever he took meant his friends would do with less or even without.

Still, he accepted because he had no other choice. They gave because they too had no choice. A repressive Polish government and the occupation by foreign armies had not been able to break Ukrainian kinship and bonds. Perhaps they had even strengthened it.

It was a heavy guilt to carry knowing that he may have put his neighbors in such jeopardy. Even with the community's generous support, he had never felt as alone in all his life.

No one had heard anything about his mother or grandmother. Nor had there been any word about his Uncle Mykhailo or his paternal grandmother. Were they to be like thousands of others who simply disappeared, never to be seen or heard from again?

It was such a familiar tragedy throughout his youth, yet no one had found an easy way to accept it. Like so many others in this time and place, he'd lost many family members. They had died or perhaps even worse been forced to serve in the Soviet army, as German laborers or sent to Siberia for unfounded charges... without word to their families for closure, so they would know how to mourn or put their sadness into context.

It was Danyk's constant fear- not just to eventually know, but to never know what had become of them.

The weeks passed, and it seemed no one questioned his whereabouts. Had they forgotten about him?

Might it be safe to return home? Home? What did it hold for him now? At least, it would offer shelter to sleep in, a fire to keep him warm and a pot to boil a potato in. Otherwise, it would be empty.

He had lived a brutal existence inside its mud-brick walls, and yet it had been the only life he had known. His mother and grandmother were his world, and suddenly his world had evaporated.

It felt like an out-of-body experience, and he believed, wrongly so, that life could not plunge any lower.

It took another week to assure him that the authorities weren't looking for him, before he made the ultimate decision to return home. It was a shattering experience for him once he did.

He had waited until after dark, and then crept up on the cottage expecting...expecting... what, he wasn't sure. A regiment of Soviet police to burst out with guns drawn? A ghost? His mother and grandmother to be peacefully asleep in the beds? He just had no idea.

Or perhaps he did. Ultimately, he had expected an old sense of comfort and familiarity to return. Neither, however, any longer existed. They had flown away with the geese... with innocence and with his boyhood.

That evening the snap and crackle of the fire was his only company. Never before, not even for one evening, could he remember ever spending it in front of this fire, in this house, without his mother and grandmother by his side. Their voices lulled him to sleep at night and woke him to rise each morning. Now, those voices were silent and gone too was any sense of security or peace.

Those blessed enough never to experience this total abandonment and loss could never understand its depths of despair. Sympathize perhaps, but never understand.

He mourned intensely, and it was exhaustion that released him into a sleep so deep he would find it oddly refreshing when he woke at morning's first light.

First, he needed to dream of the fantasies and realities his mother had given him.

They all existed in a place called America, a land where his father lived, the land where he had been born.

It was a magical place, so powerful that he must guard it the way a magician would guard his trickery. Exposed, it would lose all its power and the strength he drew from it. He must protect it the way a mother guards her child; he must love it the way his mother loved him.

America was the land of freedom where people slept safely in their beds at night... lulled to sleep by their full stomachs and warm feet.

America was heaven on earth... and the best part was... it really did exist! His mother had told him so.

During these hours of deep sleep, he found peace.

Then, the soldiers returned.

Chapter 23

I'll Go to Moscow

D anyk was blindfolded and hurried into the back of the vehicle. It rode over rough terrain, bumping and swaying to turns and ruts in the road. He smelled gasoline fumes and struggled not to cough and aggravate his already dry throat or call any attention to himself.

The soldiers made small talk in Russian, not particularly concerned with their prisoner or affected by his terror. In fact, they had made this kind of arrest so often it was now routine and mundane.

At times, the vehicle slowed, and he could hear typical sounds like wood being chopped or a cart's wheels rounding over hard dirt. He could hear and even feel sudden changes in the wind's direction and the slight shift of the vehicle as it fought against the gusts, exerting force to continue on its way.

There was an abrupt screech. A stop. Then, Danyk was pulled from the vehicle. He gave a frustrated sigh and he hurried to in-take a lungful of fresh air. The sun stroked his forehead and he focused for a split second on its delightful warmth. Perhaps it was the last time that he would ever feel the sun.

Are they going to shoot me? He was right to wonder. The blindfold added to his fear. After each step he hesitated, not sure what lay inches in front of him. His hands were cuffed behind him and couldn't be used for balance or protection.

The soldiers weren't patient when he stumbled on a rock, and it was understood they expected him to recover quickly. He felt the jabs of the rifles' barrels in his lower back and did his best to keep up. They seemed to be taking a straight path, which gave his steps a bit more predictability.

He heard a door being opened and sensed it was large and metallic. Once they stepped in and the door slammed shut, he entered an echo-y world of clinging and clanging, soft moans and frightened whispers.

The warmth of a moment's sun was replaced by a mix of humid, muggy heat and the smell of human sweat.

His blindfold was whipped off, and he was instructed in Russian to step into the cell. Unblinded, stunned yet curious, his wide eyes darted around the twelve-foot square cell.

His first intent was to catch a glimpse of his mother or grandmother amongst the sea of sixty or so, dirty, bloodied, lice-infected men and women. His second was to obey the guards command and make his way into the cell to join the others, but there was little space left to do so.

The bodies all sat clustered in rows, knees drawn up and bent outward, to accommodate another human being between them. This allowed for too many people to be packed into too small a space. In fact, it was so inadequate noses pointed upward gasping for air and limbs extended out of the cell between the metal bars.

On the lap of one miserable prisoner sat the communal toilet, used and dirty. Its smell and stench reached every corner of the cell, but the pot itself was apparently unattainable to most of the prisoners, as they could not stand or roll, even to get into a more comfortable position. It was a barbaric scene, one difficult to adequately describe and even more so to comprehend.

Not even an animal would be expected to endure such pitiful circumstances, but it was the lot of thousands of Soviet prisoners, imprisoned sometimes for no more of an offense than existing.

Somehow, Danyk managed to squeeze in, accompanied by the unappreciative moans of those already imprisoned within. Numbly, he took his place behind the last prisoner. There he sat for hours, then days, sore and bruised from confinement and lack of circulation.

Some faces were familiar while others were those of strangers. Their cries, screams, and moans never stopped.

In the background, the sounds of those being interrogated could be heard. They denied, they begged, they pleaded, they screamed their agonies, but still the torture never seemed to end.

Each prisoner was taken in turn and then delivered back bloodied and broken. Their souls matched their physical states.

The only water or food they received was from the townspeople who were commanded or permitted - no one seemed to know - to share what they had.

It was almost a relief to Danyk when, finally the cell door opened, and the prisoner they wanted to interrogate ... was him.

He was already very weak and could barely stand when the guards told him to do so.

Though they hurried him, it did little to make him move faster. Like a newborn fawn, he struggled to find his footing and felt a surge of stinging yet desired circulation.

They brought him to a room and despite his ragged condition, he was told to stand. They would not accept any relaxed stance; he was to face forward with his arms at his side.

The interrogation began striking at the heart of his greatest vulnerability. "So... your father is an American?"

They eventually asked about every member of his family. Their main purpose, Danyk knew, was for him to betray someone... anyone. They wanted a name of an anti-communist.

They would continue to ask until they got one, killed him or believed he didn't know any.

Unfortunately, they would not think the latter until many interrogations had failed to yield a name.

One day between interrogations, Danyk was sitting in his cell. He heard a vague voice, an utterance really, but Danyk knew it was his mother.

~

She was nearby! His heart soared.

"Momma," he called, once, twice then waited.

"Danyk!" He heard her call back. But that was it.

At least he knew she was alive. For the next two days, it was all he could think about.

Then a miracle happened! He was roused awake and taken to another holding cell. It was very like his own cell, filled with frightened, battered people but with a bit more space and in the corner *sat his mother!*

She was thinner and had large-pronounced bruises against her pale, sickly skin. Black circles surrounded her sunken-sad eyes, which were cast out looking aimlessly.

He didn't run to her immediately as he was weak and stunned, unsure if he should trust what he was seeing. Was she a spiritual vision?

Then, the eyes that had been empty met his, and after a brief moment of astonishment Mariya's eyes reflected back great relief and joy.

Mariya's open arms called to him and then locked around Danyk with ferocity once he was in them. Only a mother's love could explain the strength her battered body found to enfold him so snugly against her. Danyk relished the security of her familiar embrace and sunk into its comfort.

"Danyk, my Danyk!" she cried over and over again.

For the remainder of their time together they held each other and cried. The other prisoners seemed just as frantic, crying and screaming. Not much else was left to be said. Tears communicated what words were too inadequate to say.

Too soon, a guard came for Mariya. But she refused to go, a most bold and audacious defiance. A guard had to pull her from her son.

Desperate to hold on to the moment longer, Danyk committed to memory her outstretched arms. They both bitterly knew they might never see each other again.

Then, they took her to a nearby room... and beat her!

The plan, of course, had been for Danyk to be the audience of his mother's torture. In some things, the Soviets could be very efficient.

The next morning...

A cherished crack of daylight rested on his nose and shadowed his eyelashes as he woke.

He strained to raise his body in the small bit of spare space allowed him, and with a limp wrist tried to wipe the strain and tension from his body to no avail.

He was surrounded by hopelessness and the smell of urine. The blank faces of the prisoners surrounding him spoke of their own misery. They cared little about the thirteen-year-old boy traumatized by the witness of his own mother's torture.

For the moment, it was quiet. No one moaned or begged for mercy. He didn't hear the thud of a bone cracking or the slapping of flesh. For one moment, there was complete silence.

This then amplified the interrupting, creaking sound of the cell door opening, followed by the soldiers' footsteps.

They motioned and he obeyed. He stood and walked out of the cell. If there had been anything in his stomach he would have vomited, but there was nothing.

One swallow, two and then he entered a small room. By now his shaking was ferocious... his knees wobbled, his teeth chattered, and he began to gag, all in anticipation of what was next planned for him.

Before him sat a vision so beautiful, so unexpected that his mind fought against recognizing it. His mind fooled him, he thought surely. He blinked but it didn't disappear, instead it reached for him. The old peasant figure, weak and weary, worn and limp began to cry and call his name.

He could not move; he could not answer her. Then, she cried again, this time with strength and she commanded him to her with both pleading and demand.

"Come, Danyk!"

Finally, off he went, to seek comfort, to give it, to feel love surrounding him ... in his grandmother's arms.

They were both released that day almost as abruptly as they had been arrested.

Unfortunately, Mariya was not.

It was a lonely walk home. Danyk's grandmother had aged ten years. So had he. He was a man now.

Arm in arm they made their way home. Neighbors waved but were afraid to speak to them, openly at least.

He checked their provisions, but of course, there was nothing. Not a single potato.

Whichever of their possessions had been left, had been strewn about in disarray, scattered as though the soldiers had been searching for something.

He knew he must make his grandmother as comfortable as possible and then go out to beg help from his neighbors, but a thought occurred to him. Did they now know he was an American? Would they be too afraid to assist him?

And the documents? Had the soldiers taken them? He held his breath as he checked their hiding place.

Gone!

All of them! Danyk remained still for a moment, not as surprised as he was panicked.

He would have shared the news with his grandmother, but for two reasons he did not.

It was a death to him ... and he needed to mourn alone. His grandmother also did not need another tragedy to dwell on. He alone would bear the knowledge, for now at least.

He left the house hunched over and clutching his stomach as though in pain to gather fresh hay. It was comforting to do a mundane chore; one he had done many times before. But it didn't distract him from his agony, and before he returned to his grandmother and placed the hay in the corner of their home for her to rest upon, his grief and misery were released in ragged sobs. He didn't stop or slow but continued with his errand, all the while wailing relentlessly. He quieted to sniffling by the time he returned, and he suspected his grandmother had released her own distress and sadness similarly while he had been out.

Both were weak, tired and hungry but he knew their needs would not be satisfied until he visited the neighbors and begged for whatever they could spare. Even before he had completely gotten his sniffling under control, he prepared his grandmother for his departure. She blankly nodded with a soft expression, which told him she greatly appreciated his care... and took great pride in him.

Danyk had walked only a few steps out the door when he saw a familiar and welcomed figure approaching in the distance. He recognized Kupetsky immediately, but Kupetsky was caught off guard. He had not yet learned of Danyk or his grandmother's release and had expected the cottage to still be empty. Kupetsky froze, accessing if he was approaching friend or foe.

Recovering quickly, Kupetsky took off, racing up the slight slope of the hill that led to Danyk's front door. Danyk wanted to rush into Kupetsky's arms, but his advance was staggered and reflected all he had recently endured. Kupetsky's momentum made up for what Danyk's lacked, and ultimately, they collided into a crushing embrace.

Kupetsky held Danyk as a father would and the endearing gesture gave Danyk permission to sink into the depth of his despair. He sobbed and sobbed while Kupetsky rocked him back and forth. Intermittently, Kutpetsky patted his back with a tenderness and sincerity that fed the boy's hunger and need like a plate of food never could have.

There would be no one else to show his tears to... not his grandmother...not his mother should she be released... for they would not need any further burden placed on them. Nor his other neighbors... for to them any weakness on his part would only make them more vulnerable.

In Stalin's Russia, weak people were intimidated into betraying others.

Only Kupetsky could see his weakness, not even Kupetsky's wife could know.

Danyk sniffled, signaling the end of his unraveling. He did not tell Kupetsky what he'd seen or been forced to endure. During this barbarous time, it would not even have been news. It was a way of life rather expected, unfortunately. However, he did tell Kupetsky that only he and his grandmother had been released.

"I'm sorry Danyk, but maybe..." and then Kupetsky's voice trailed off.

So many were taken prisoner and interrogated, never to be seen or heard from again. He hesitated, wondering if he should give Danyk false hope.

Danyk caught his hesitation and now, being wise beyond his years, fully understood.

"Did you look for your documents?" Kupetsky asked seriously. "Yes, but..."

"No, no, don't worry. I have them. When the soldiers left, I took and hid them for safe keeping."

Danyk collapsed again into Kupetsky's arms. Kupetsky explained further, "They were scattered about, I hope I got everything."

"Why? Why didn't they take them?"

"I think, Danyk, they were illiterate and didn't realize what they had found."

Finally, something had gone right. He still had the documents, and he felt a small, satisfied relief wash through him. Then, Kupetsky confronted him and once again, he felt on edge.

"Danyk, do you trust me?"

"Yes, of course!" You are all I have left to trust in the world. Where would I be this moment without you?"

"Then, you must let me oversee the care of your grandmother and you...you must make your way to the American Embassy in Moscow!"

Danyk stared at Kupetsky as though he had two heads while he desperately tried to make sense of Kupetsky's request. Demand?

"Go to Moscow? Alone? Without my grandmother? How can I do that? I have no money... my village is the only thing familiar to me. Which way would I go? What would my mother think? I leave without her? And my grandmother? Who will care for her? She needs me." He could have rattled on in panic, but Kupetsky interrupted him.

"I will care for her." He countered like a slap. "Listen to me. How long do you think you will be able to keep those documents? There will be more searches. It is better to burn them now if you don't plan to do anything with them."

"I do want to do something with them! I want them to help me get to America! I want to see my father! But... I want my mother to go with me; she will go too. How can I go without her?" Danyk had never really spoken these words out loud before and it startled him to have them announced so, on an impulse.

"It may just be... the only way you will ever get to go." These were such disturbing facts for one so young to grasp. Kupetsky did not like himself very much at the moment for being the one who had to say them. But the reality was that the boy needed to hear them. So much was at stake. "Think Danyk. What would your mother want?"

Danyk shook his head violently in confusion. Moments before he had thought the documents were lost to him forever. Was this another chance?

But without his mother?

"Danyk... perhaps you are your mother's hope?" Danyk's eyes locked with Kupetsky's and he searched for clearer understanding.

He knew then, at that moment, that Kupetsky did not believe his mother would ever be released.

Kupetsky continued on, but it was as though a biting wind was reeling, blurring his words.

Danyk struggled, forcing himself to focus intently and listen.

"Doskoczynski's sister-in-law, a teacher from Moscow, is visiting. Within the week, she plans to return by train. I will ask her if she will show you how to get there. You can travel separately... for her protection... but she can guide you. We can trust her, but... once she leaves, the opportunity may be lost forever."

Finally, he had given Danyk a stern ultimatum, fully regretting that it was necessary to ask a boy to make a man's decision.

All the while, they had been no more than arm's length away from each other. Suddenly, Danyk thrust himself away from Kupetsky. He looked off into the forest for a long time, searching as though the trees would have the answer he needed. But they were silent. He alone needed to answer.

It was a long time, but Kupetsky simply waited.

Eventually, Danyk turned back and Kupetsky knew he had decided upon his destiny.

"I'll go." The whispered words stung both, and again they embraced to comfort each other.

Paulo read the letter three times before gleaning that Mariya and her mother had now been taken by the authorities and soon after, Danyk, too.

It was a bad dream, a nightmare! The letter could not give details.

It had been difficult enough for Kupetsky to relay the information in a way that the censors would not touch his written word. He had underlined letters, which at first glance appeared to blend with his handwriting. The message itself made no sense, so Paulo knew to examine it more carefully, almost immediately. The decoded message was deciphered. It said:

MARIYA, MOTHER ARRESTED. THEN DANYK. UNSAFE. STALIN CRAZY. SORRY.

The one positive note of the letter was it would convince Marion it was unsafe to return to Poland... or what would now be considered part of the Soviet Union. Paulo knew Marion had still been playing with the possibility... the hope of returning and being reunited with his family.

That hope would now be shattered. It pained Paulo greatly to share this news with his brother and even more so, to realize his sister-in-law, mother, nephew and other family members were still in terrible danger.

Paulo would do only what he knew to do. Go on... just like the rest of Europe was attempting to do.

Would his dear sister-in-law, mother and Danyk be able to do so as well?

Chapter 24

Meeting on First Avenue

S am and Joe were so involved in their exchange, they missed the stares of waitresses and the annoyed lunch crowd.

In front of them sat empty coffee cups that had remained there since early morning when they'd first been served. However, they had been so interested in what the other had to say that they had completely turned away from the outside world. Other than to politely accept coffee refills when they were offered and one or two unavoidable pardons for a bathroom visit, they hadn't allowed anything else to distract them.

Sam had filled Joe in, as much as he could, not just to satisfy Joe's curiosity, but so that the updated information could be given to Danyk and hopefully, eventually be shared with Mariya when she returned.

Joe was able to give Sam a personal account of Danyk. Was he a quiet boy? Or was he talkative? How tall was he now? Was he strong? Not just physically but would he survive emotionally the loss of his mother if that was to be?

Sam was not expecting to hear from Joe that his son smiled and laughed easily, loved to thumb through American car magazines and could listen endlessly to stories of America. He had expected to hear about a timid child, saddened and worn, lost.

At various times, Danyk appeared to be all those things, but they did not define him. He had depth and character, conviction and loyalty, humility and courage, things unveiled early in his life because of his circumstances. Intertwined with all these virtues, he had a typical boy's heart, a desire for adventure tempered by a longing for home and his mother's safe arms.

They both sat quietly, pensively contemplating the likelihood of the boy's desires being fulfilled.

Neither, with all their dedication, had been able to move Danyk's cause forward and sadly, they both realized... the odds were against them.

They both knew it.

And both knew the other knew it.

Joe had made a few stops during his journey before meeting Sam at the diner. Each had been on Danyk's behalf, and it appeared that the results were going to be fruitless. It had seemed the proper thing to do considering Danyk's dire circumstances. He was a natural born American, he was a minor living in the American Embassy in Moscow, his mother was either in Siberia or dead and his father here in America was doing everything right. But nothing had worked!

The United States was admittedly powerless to do anything about it, as Stalin had remained totally unmoved. He was iron-willed and he wasn't changing his policy for anyone... even children fending for themselves.

It had also become a known fact (within the Soviet Union, at least) that he wasn't above torturing children if they or their family members had western ties. That... Joe didn't have the heart to share with Sam.

In fact, it had been difficult to say the words aloud when he had approached influential and powerful people in the hopes of gaining their interest and support. Indeed, he had gained both, but their influence just didn't cut it when it came to Danyk's situation. Joe began to realize that even President Harry S. Truman couldn't or wouldn't productively intervene.

It didn't make a lot of sense to Joe. Stalin and the Soviet Union were so damaged and weakened by World War II, Stalin could have been easily intimidated, but those who had seen him triumph over the Germans and help win the war were not so easily convinced.

Suddenly, Sam and Joe each seemed fascinated by the tabletop as they stared at it intently.

"How about a hamburger?" Joe asked, partly because he was hungry, partly because he thought they both finally needed a change of subject.

"No, no." Sam waved the invitation away.

"Come on, it's on me? I'm starved and I'm not eating alone."

Sam hesitated a moment longer thinking how he could respectfully decline. "Waitress?" Joe called one over.

"More coffee?" she asked with a hint of sarcasm.

Joe was quick to notice it and reciprocated with a double take.

"Yes." Joe confirmed a little more forcefully than he had intended, which made the waitress slouch in disappointment.

"And two hamburgers with lots of fries, Add two salads to that, too.

'Iced tea, Sam?" Joe glanced Sam's way, but really wasn't expecting an answer. Sam felt compelled to nod appreciatively.

The waitress finished writing up the order on her pad. Then, she used a pointed finger to lower her eyeglasses down an inch to look over them. She glanced pointedly at Joe. "No offense mister, but I thought you'd never get around to ordering."

"No offense taken," and he meant it. He had things more important on his mind, "just make it quick, we've developed quite an appetite!" Joe winked at Sam and rubbed his stomach.

"Yeah, right. Sitting in the same booth for hours will do that to you."

This time Joe didn't appreciate the sarcasm or her tone, and a quick sharp glance told her so.

"It will be right up." The waitress perked up realizing she had probably just lost her tip.

~

Before Sam was contacted by Joe, he had simply been going through the motions of life. After his honorable discharge from the United States Army on March 26, 1943, he had reopened his shoe repair shop at 128 First Avenue. Frugally spending his average monthly income of $100, he kept his life simple and focused on "making things right" for his family. He had hoped by mid 1945, with the war's end, that he'd be able to make contact with his family. It had been so long without direct word, and he knew that facing the bitter reality of the war's culminating devastation might also mean facing the fact that his family had not gone unscathed. Who lived? Who had died? Who at this moment still suffered?

Almost never did these thoughts leave his mind. Only good friends, at times, gave him distraction, but they too had family back in the mother country and on occasion spoke aloud or shared their own fears.

A letter, a telegram making its way through, news of the health of a loved one or a desperate plea for help from a distant cousin always loomed in the background of a friendly checker game or round of cards.

By the spring of 1945, Sam had received a letter from Mariya's brother in France. It had lifted his heart because it had been the first bit of wonderful news he had heard in a very long time. Marion, Mariya's brother had had a terrible time of it... but had lived. He had survived being in a German P.O.W. camp and was now safely under Paulo's care just outside Paris. It was blessed news. Nevertheless, it was to be carefully shared. Paulo had given a brief explanation of Stalin's Repatriation Program.

Sam didn't want to doubt Paulo's words but could such a reckless regard for the human life of one's own citizens exist? Unfortunately, indeed it could, and as word spread, it was greatly discussed by the immigrant population with families affected by its lunacy and absurdity.

~

Paulo's letter read:

"This dictator, Stalin, is recalling all his displaced soldiers - those who have somehow miraculously survived German P.O.W camps in which they were the most mistreated of all because of their country's refusal to sign the Geneva Convention's guidelines for the treatment of Prisoners of War. He demands their return. There is no option or choice. Should they not return of their own accord, he has ordered them searched out and forcibly returned. Most outrageous is his reason for their return... so that they can be imprisoned! Their crime... "their displacement"... and exposure to the outside world... their sin for not having died for the motherland!

Marion had very much wanted to return to his family, but I delayed him...thank God! He still talks of it, but I am determined to persuade him otherwise. It is much too dangerous... he must not be found. He must not take any chances, after all he has been through."

Then he warned, "Mariya must not be told! The Soviets might read her mail or use their methods to trick it from her. I can not stress this enough. She must not know. Do not share it with your neighbors yet, not until we are sure Marion is no longer in danger. Eventually, Stalin will forget about him."

His final words, at least, were hopeful.

Sam knew that for the moment, Paulo had no need to worry. He had no contact with Mariya, at least not yet, though he tried weekly. But he knew her brother was optimistic, as a brother should be.

If a blessing should happen, should he finally make contact, then there would be reason to worry. For how could he deny letting his beloved Mariya know that her brother lived. What of Marion's wife and daughter? This meant that they too, could not know. The burdens of their lives were heavy, and God forgive him, at times seemed too much to bear.

～

A few months and many days later, Sam indeed heard from Mariya.

She lived! Danyk lived!

It was a moment of unparalleled rapture... the greatest joy he had ever experienced in his lifetime.

Further, she cataloged the circumstances of each family member and friend, though she was brief and did not give many details. He supposed that would come later when she was sure her letter had reached him. He hurt when she spoke of Marion and her uncertainty of his condition or whereabouts, and he longed to reach across the world and soothe her, tell her he was not only fine, he was safe with Paulo in Paris.

He had heard from his Mariya and there was hope for life to be good again, if he was patient. He knew his real Mariya was somewhere behind the direct words... hurting...and longing for his comfort...as he longed for hers. Wasn't she?

Considering several years had passed since their last communication, she had been brief.

But as he had considered, perhaps she was not sure he would receive her letter. Or was she cautious with him because she felt he had abandoned her? He could not help his guilt. Or was it the censoring of the letters that he'd heard so much about, but was thought by Stalin to be a national secret?

He had sensed her nervousness and considered her fear before hurrying off his first letter to her. He had hesitated before enclosing the important papers she would need to pursue bringing herself and Danyk back to him in America.

What was she trying to tell him...not to send her the papers? Could she be rejecting him?

No.

Even if she was rejecting him, she would not reject bringing her son to safety in America.

It was their only opportunity.

"Take these to the American Embassy in Moscow," he added to the letter's last page.

"Then..."

Into the envelope, he stuffed the papers, licked and pressed closed the flap.

He addressed the envelope and added a stamp. Before he could change his mind, he was headed to the United States Post Office to check his postage and hurry off the letter.

Years later he would realize it was one of the most selfish things he had ever done!

Again, there would be long stretches of thin communication, until one day, Sam was contacted by the United States Embassy in Moscow.

Sam's son had arrived alone, with valid papers indicating United States citizenship. The boy, Danyk, was requesting that he be joined with his father in America, as his mother's whereabouts were not known.

"Why was Mariya not with him!!!???" Sam wondered but only in the back of his mind where his secrets are hidden even from himself.

Sam continued to read what it said further, all the while pulling his jacket and hat on. That done, he headed out the door to find Miss Larned at the International Migration Services.

It was not a light tap on her door. When she opened it and

found Mr. Szfranski with a letter in his hand and jabbering incoherently, she knew he needed her immediate attention. In the first place, even under the most stressful circumstances, he always presented himself as a mild, polite unobtrusive man, and his behavior was so contradictory to that image that she was enormously curious as to what brought him here without a scheduled appointment.

Breathlessly, he handed her the document that he had been waving and she instinctively began to review it, steadying his hand that still partially held it ... and shook, making the reading difficult.

"Well, it seems your son, Danyk, is at the American Embassy in Moscow and they are asking you if you are willing to support him while he is there!" Miss Larned was jubilantly elated for Mr. Szafranski and near jumping up and down with him in excitement and victory!

Sam, of course, had already gotten that from the letter, but it had not seemed truly real until Miss Larned had confirmed it. Now it was real.

What to feel first?

Gratitude... that his son was safe and perhaps on his way to him?

"But?" Now, Miss Larned had begun to get down to business. He could tell that she was hesitating with more to say. Whatever it would be, it wasn't going to be good. The crunch of her eyebrows told him so.

"Yes, something?" Sam knew it. It was too good to be true.

"I don't understand why they don't mention your wife."

It echoed through Sam like thunder. He had held his joy in check until he saw Miss Larned, and she confirmed his hopes. Could it be? He had dared not believe it could be so!!!

Now he understood why. He had known it, just not been able to deal with it. In his subconscious, the unanswered question had loomed. He had felt it with every bone in his body but, he had hoped it was simple disbelief that such a wonderful thing could have finally happened to him, that had kept him holding back.

Miss Larned was calling his attention to the very thing he did not want to acknowledge.

Despair returned. Mariya was not there with Danyk! Why wasn't she? What had happened to her?

Again, he was back to a life of unanswered questions.

When Joe Malaznik had contacted Sam, he thought it was the answer to his prayers. He knew that Mr. Malaznik was an official United States something, obviously a very important man to be an American stationed in Moscow.

Mr. Malaznick not only knew and understood his family's situation; he was eager to help and most importantly... had been with his son, under the same roof with him and seen his living quarters. Maybe the gentleman had influence and could hurry things along. For he, a simple immigrant, even with the kind support of Miss Larned had not been able to accomplish much.

He was paying the American Embassy for Danyk's financial support; at least he could take pride in that, but it could not go on indefinitely. He was depleting his savings, and if Danyk was not released soon, he might not have enough left to see to his transport to America. Excuses for delaying Danyk's departure for the United States were not really offered. No reasons. Just that he couldn't come... yet.

He comforted himself thinking friends would help, but still it added to an anxiety that was already consuming him.

The night before he was to meet Joe, he had laid out his Sunday best and ironed his white shirt. He wanted to make a nice impression for the man who was coming so far to help him and his family, especially his son. There was a bit of fantasy to it all. It didn't seem real to finally be meeting someone who had had contact with his son and might have an understanding of where his wife was and what had happened to her.

So many years had gone by. There were so many unfulfilled dreams and unanswered questions playing havoc with his psyche.

Would Joe be able to answer them?

Many, he could. Patiently, Joe had reviewed Danyk's existence surviving, filling in many of the details he'd longed to know. Communication was never an issue as Joe also spoke Russian and Polish. Even so, there was still so much that only Mariya could have answered, and she was not to be found.

Even Danyk was not certain what had happened to her, which in itself was another pain for Sam to bear. That his son should not only be alone but left fearing for his mother's life was simply unbearable and exceeded any father's worst nightmare. Sam, of course, faced this torment daily.

Was he stronger or weaker for it? Well, he'd continued on, he'd not ceased to exist.

That alone showed great strength of character. However, he appeared to be growing old before his time. The show of gray. The circles beneath his eyes. All the things noted by Joe when he was trying to identify Danyk's father from the crowd. Yes, there! That would be Sam. A man who had suffered greatly.

Joe reviewed Soviet history for Sam with a mixture of eloquent textbook accuracy, some of which Sam knew already from the local Polish and Ukrainian newspapers he read daily and personal familiarity.

Perhaps, he should not have been surprised at all that Joe knew; after all, he worked for the American government in the Soviet Union. But Joe had an understanding of local customs and traditions that most immigrants had come to not expect from natural-born Americans. His knowledge base and ability to help Sam grasp the total picture of his family's circumstances within the present-day Soviet Union was somewhat startling.

Joe had an amazing ability to communicate, to explain, to clarify, to elaborate and to understand what was not understood by others, so he could explain further; that simply put him in a class by himself.

It was not beyond Sam's comprehension or intelligence to realize that the man sitting across from him was not simply kind or compassionate, not just extraordinarily intelligent or honorable but perhaps a great man. Something radiated from the man who had traveled so far to see him, and it couldn't be missed. It was a comfort to know that such men in the world existed.

Miss Larned had explained it all before, and Sam had read about the Soviet Union bit by bit in the information gathered about Stalin as the war had proceeded. Still, Stalin's Russia had seemed so senseless to him, and he had been sure he had not understood, or it had been exaggerated.

He was not unlike most other Americans at the time who didn't want to believe such horrible acts against mankind were occurring. They had gotten through World War II and it was time to dwell on happier times ahead.

Joe had left nothing to doubt, however, and Sam now understood the world in which his family had to endure. The only thing Joe had not extensively shared with Sam was that the KGB had taken Danyk out of the American Embassy and into their custody for interrogation and the conditions Danyk had endured when he was first arrested.

Soviet law dictated that Danyk be held and not released to America, due to his newly acquired Soviet citizenship obtained through his mother. His mother, a former Polish citizen, was now a Soviet citizen due to the expansion of Soviet jurisdiction and boundaries into what had been Poland before the end of World War II.

A second citizenship, such as Danyk's American citizenship as a natural born American, was not recognized by the Soviet Union.

Though Joe didn't know where Mariya was, he did suspect that her western ties were what had gotten her into trouble, although it could have also been a thousand other senseless infractions imposed by Stalin, as well.

Sam did now comprehend the brutal reality that Stalin wanted total submission from his citizens. With that knowledge would come many sleepless nights, as Sam would wonder... was it the papers I sent?

Did I do irreparable damage?

Will Mariya bear the full brunt of my errors?

There would now be only one thing left to keep him going... his son still loved him... and he wanted to come to America. Sam decided to keep hope alive, against all the odds.

~

"Joe? Joe? Joe!!!!"

Danyk's shrieks of ecstasy at Joe's return reached him long before the boy actually did. Danyk's body, still broken and recovering, waddled efficiently continually gaining momentum until he reached Joe. Then, the two crashed into each other's embrace, Joe being the gentler of the two.

"Joe you are back!" Danyk announced his return.

Still hugging him possessively, his face turned upward from Joe's chest, adoringly searching his face, hoping to see the answers there that would bring him to his father.

"Did you take care of everything? Am I going to America?"

The boy's innocence was the poke of an arrow in his gut, and his trust was sharper still.

Joe's inadequacies left him openly vulnerable to feel the full sting of what was certain to come... Danyk's disappointment, not only in not going to America, but with him.

He'd met Danyk's father. That would be the easy part to share. Perhaps it was the best place to start. But how would he fill the spaces of the missing answers?

Knowing Danyk, Joe's own silence would fill it in for him. Somehow, the kid's natural perception, ability to read the truth no matter how devastating it was, saddened him greatly and neutralized his joy in seeing Danyk again. That kind of insight only came to those who had lived life at its worst... and that indeed seemed to be Danyk's lot.

Danyk's brilliance faded, and his smile grew somber. Silently, bravely, he let Joe know that he realized it would not all be so easy.

"Are you tired, Joe?" Danyk broke away. "I'm going to get you coffee, Joe. You sit and rest." He reached the door and gave Joe the best gift anyone had ever given him... the biggest, most genuine, welcome home smile he had ever seen.

It didn't matter to Danyk if he'd brought good news or not. Simply, the boy was glad he was home.

Home? Was this home? It had become Danyk's for sure. Everyone knew it was temporary, of course. While temporary and home aren't known to go together, for them, it worked just fine.

Joe, Jim and Danyk had managed to drape a bit of coziness and mirth over this dark, cold American fortress in downtown Moscow, USSR.

In the embassy's basement was a cell, wallpapered in cinder block and flaking paint chips that held the treasures of a thirteen-year-old boy. In so many ways, it was just like any other early adolescent boy's bedroom. The bed was made ... sometimes... after a few reminders from Joe. Clothes were heaped in a corner until laundry day..., which Jim had decided, was every Saturday. Movie scenes and car magazines, accumulated from American servicemen who were done with them, were propped upright and displayed neatly like conversation pieces for visitors to admire.

Most prominently and proudly displayed was an American flag that hung cleverly over the bed like a poster, illuminating Danyk's love for a country he couldn't remember seeing... and camouflaging a crack... a crater really, that meandered under it.

This was where the three of them, Danyk, Joe and Jim, spent time after dinner until lights out, shared stories of their lives and families, offered comfort and support when one was down or worried, divided chocolate candy bars and munched on popcorn. It was these moments shared there that softened the concrete, lessened the drafts from the holes in the wall and made it the most-comfy place to be if one had to be an American... a government official, a soldier, a spy or...a lost American child separated from his parents and otherwise alone in the world, vulnerable to sporadic interrogations and torture of the KGB in Moscow 1947.

Home? Yes. Temporary? Yes. But ironically, it was the one place

Joe and Danyk wanted to be... and the one place they wished didn't have to be.

Joe slammed the vehicle door leaving Jim behind. "Hey, you ought to go straight to bed!" Jim called out from a rolled down window.

"Well, yes, in a manner of speaking I'm doing just that. Going straight to bed... and working on a response to that telegram we got today."

"Are you sure you're up to it? It looks like you're coming down with the flu. I think you'd be better off resting up."

"Sure thing."

That's when Jim knew Joe would be doing anything but. Joe had one of those minds that never stopped working. Just when you thought he was quiet and calm, his observant, analytical mind came up with something that stopped you in your tracks.

He was "a thinking man's man" but not just book smart. Though he was thoroughly educated, he was mostly "people smart," something Jim deduced came from years and years of having a passion for... well... people.

He'd traveled the world and could learn more about a country or a people from taking an hour train ride with them than most could from prepping for a Princeton degree. It was a talent though respected, that hadn't quite yet gotten the full recognition it deserved from the higher ups, but Jim knew Joe was a force to be reckoned with and Joe's time was coming. When Joe finally let out all the steam he'd been holding in, they weren't going to know what hit them! Especially at this point in history with Washington scrambling to make sense of a country it had largely ignored but was becoming desperate to understand. Joe's command and acute understanding of the area would be a prized and sought out expertise.

Joe made his way up to the building, climbed the stairs to his apartment and used the last bit of strength to climb into bed. For the rest of the night, he nursed his flu as well as drafted a document for Washington. When he was done, he signed the document by a pseudonym. It was a security issue in terms of communication back with the states and was a common practice for those serving in the Foreign Service, especially those serving in Moscow.

He also had a personal and professional policy of never telling a Soviet citizen his real name... that was more for their protection than his; after all Stalin harshly punished any of his citizens who knowingly had contact with a western influence.

Joe turned out the light feeling satisfied that he'd still managed to get a full day's work in despite this bout of the flu. He had so much to accomplish and so little time in which to do it. It wasn't that he was a workaholic by any means, but he had a true sense of purpose and these days he hoped, if he contacted the right person, at the right time, with the right persuasion... it just might make a difference to the hundreds of Americans trapped in the Soviet Union who needed help. It was a small chance... but one he was still dedicated to, especially, perhaps most especially, because it could make all the difference to his young pal, Danyk.

Danyk was taken again, by the KGB, but there was a delay in telling Joe. It was for his own good.

If he had protested in any way, it would have diminished whatever influence he presently held with the Kremlin, and American officials might have questioned his vulnerability in remaining in his position. He had dedicated his life to preparing for his purpose here in the Soviet Union. He knew the history as well as any scholar, and for a Midwesterner he spoke impeccable Russian. All that talent and intellect could not be wasted. He was too valuable... so, perceptive friends required he not be told until two hours after Danyk had been taken by the KGB agents.

Those who had witnessed Danyk's departure had stood like observers of a funeral procession. Helpless, overcome with grief but knowing there was nothing they could do!

Danyk was not the only one who was taken for interrogation. All those who arrived at the embassy claiming United States citizenship eventually were. Almost all would be returned after giving up any claim to it. They would be terrified, broken and no longer American. The KGB would announce they had changed their minds, show the documentation they had signed agreeing to renounce their American citizenship, and then be on their way with or without the claimant, depending on their whim.

Repeatedly, it happened. It was a way of life at the embassy, and before this time period in history was over, it would be experienced by 1,900 people including twelve children separated from their parents.

The American Embassy simply had no power... no jurisdiction or influence, to stop them. This was Stalin's Russia and Stalin would have his way. Those at the embassy who had personally witnessed the dictatorship's treatment or brutality of its own citizens, perhaps understood this more astutely than those officials back in the states used to dealing with, if not reasonable, then sane heads of state.

Joe had witnessed the 'trials', which weren't really trials at all, convict average citizens without evidence or cause simply because Stalin had ordered it. He watched the blank facial expressions, the eyes that had given up hope, their confused pleas as they tried to defend themselves against charges they couldn't possibly have committed. Perhaps there were some real charges, such as, "Were you late for work?"

"Yes but... the bus never came, what was I to do? Please, I have a family and ill- parents."

"Guilty of crimes against the state."

As unbelievable as it might seem to an American, being late for work in the Soviet Union was considered a terrible offense. "You shall be imprisoned for a rehabilitation period of...," sometimes years. Sometimes for life. Sometimes they were to be executed. Why? Not for any real crime but because the officials had quotas to meet mandated by Stalin.

It was certainly a torturous two days for Danyk. He had been interrogated before, so now he knew full well what to anticipate. It would have been one of the few times in his life that it would have been better to be ignorant. "Do not look right, do not look left. No, no water until we are done. Straighten your back."

"Why do you want to be an American? Why do you want to be an American?"

Over and over, hour after hour the questions were asked and over and over again, hour after hour, the answers Danyk gave were never good enough.

Finally, they would beat him.

Joe was too well educated, too informed of Soviet methodology and mentality to not fully understand what Danyk was enduring and living through. He'd also been there for the aftermath of Danyk's first interrogation, the one that prompted him to visit Danyk's father in New York.

Since then, none of his efforts had borne fruit. Trying to get Danyk to his father in America was like trying to see through a cement wall.

He tried to hold on to the small bit of hope but mounting global evidence was fast leading to the conclusion that... there wasn't any.

No one was getting out. It just wasn't happening.

The mightiest nation in the world couldn't or wouldn't move Stalin's pinky finger if he was happy where it was, and Stalin didn't have any urge to move.

The nation that Joe loved chose to deal with all these injustices by paper pushing and turning the other way. He didn't quite get it. American citizens were not being protected by their government.

Did they fear Stalin?

He was a bully but just like other real-life bullies, he was more hot air than anything else. If the United States declared their serious intent to reclaim their citizens, he believed Stalin would back down. For all the country's bravado, the Soviet Union was in terrible shape, and it would be a long time before it recovered from the devastation of World War II. Now was the time to stand up to the Soviet Union, when it was at its weakest point!

Apparently, Washington didn't agree with him, but few politicians were as informed or as knowledgeable as he was. That wasn't ego... it was just an accurate observation.

For two days, time stood still. Joe couldn't feel his heart beating, but the lump in his throat and stomach never went away. He didn't dare step out of the embassy, worried that he would miss Danyk's return.

He thought for sure that Danyk wouldn't be able to bear it. Grown men couldn't.

He thought back to Danyk's first night at the embassy when the moaning of someone nearby had upset him and disturbed his sleep. He had not shared with him then that it was the result of the man being taken by the KGB for interrogation, for doing just what Danyk was trying to do... claim his American citizenship. Perhaps he should have told him then. Before Danyk's dreams had become larger than life, larger than the life he had been living back in his village in Gorodnitsa or the one he had now at the embassy.

Joe figured that when Danyk returned, he'd no longer be an American. Like all the others, he'd sign it away. Once that was done, it was over.

He would be free to return to his village and avoid more torture.

He wondered why Stalin didn't just forge his prisoners' signatures or declare it law that a claimant's signature was not required to limit Soviet citizenship to the Soviet Union alone. After all, Stalin knew, signature or not, that he had no intention of letting these people leave. Why must they be tortured, if they had no hope of winning?

Because Stalin enjoyed the mind games as much as he enjoyed the power.

The torture was just one strategy in how Stalin played his game. It would have been less fun if that aspect had been left out. Bullies don't just want to overpower; they want to see their opponent squirm.

When Danyk was ultimately returned, he was in a condition much like after the first episode.

Joe's spirits sank.

There was not much to do for a man used to taking action. It was a shredding of his manhood, but he managed to keep it to himself. Great men are able to do that.

Joe changed Danyk's bandages, soothed his forehead with cool cloths, slept on a cot in his room, and did whatever it took to keep him comfortable and feeling safe. Safe... what did that mean? That too, had become a term for a temporary condition.

The fact was that now fourteen-year-old Danyk had survived his second interrogation and still had not signed away his American citizenship.

Joe now knew that Danyk Szafranski... was more American than apple pie!

And then, it happened again...

And again...

And again...

Chapter 25

Coming to Terms

I t was a tremendous frustration to witness American citizens receiving inexcusable treatment by the Soviet authorities.

Did American leaders understand?

Diplomatic relations with the USSR had only begun in the 1930's and for most Americans, it was very unfamiliar territory. Joe and others had used the opportunity to join the Foreign Service to not only utilize but extend their knowledge and expertise of the area, which involved a complicated mix of politics, economics and philosophies, as well as historical events that couldn't be grasped quickly or with brief summaries.

So, when the Treasury Department telegrammed a request for an explanation as to why Stalin wasn't cooperating with regard to the newly created World Bank, George Kennan, acting charge d'affaires in temporary absence of Ambassador Harriman at the United States Embassy in Moscow, knew the opportunity had arrived to give Washington a complete education. Signing it "Mr. X.," he drafted a telegram, which would soon be known as, "The Long Telegram", a politically historical document, urging the United States government to recognize Stalin's brutal, dangerous and expansionist intentions directed by a core of paranoia and basic distrust of western and capitalistic ideology. He was forthright that the Soviet Union had no intention of coexisting and that their internal organization did not allow for realistic perceptions of themselves or the outside world. He urged timely assertiveness to minimize the damage while Stalin was still weakened and recovering from the war.

But would the response be to confront the bully... or back away to avoid conflict? And what would the price be... and who would pay it?

These questions would not be answered by those at the embassy with front ring seats to Stalin's philosophies and tactics, but by those back in Washington who knew him from secondary sources. The perspectives and resulting viewpoints could be quite different and would not always render the most satisfactory conclusions for those who stood to bear the brunt.

He'd now sat in the chair for twelve hours. Hot, thirsty, hungry and tired, he feared he still had a long way to go. Every muscle in his body worked against the tilt in the chair. The tremendous effort gave him a grimace that he couldn't have erased, if his life depended on it.

This was the fifth time the KGB had taken him into custody, and they hadn't killed him yet. Perhaps, this would be the time.

The building seemed empty, almost abandoned, unlike the other times.

Also, this time they seemed so furiously angry, so determined, but Danyk knew... if he signed the papers giving up his American citizenship... his hope, his dream of going to America was over. Joe had been very clear about that. As long as he held on, there was hope.

There wasn't a nerve in him that wasn't strained with fear. He'd been ordered, as the routine seemed to be, not to look right, not to look left, not to look up or down but only straight forward. Even blinking was forbidden for various lengths of time. He could feel his hands shake uncontrollably even though they were tied behind the chair.

He was now soaked from profuse sweat and excretion. He squirmed a bit, trying miserably to find a more comfortable position, but out of the darkness he was ordered to stop. If he didn't, it would mean another punch, maybe to the head or stomach. Even if he did stop, it could happen, as well.

They didn't just damage one's body; they played with one's mind. Over and over again, they placed documents in front of him.

"Sign!" they would say. "No." he would cry back.

"Why do you want to be an American? Soviet Union is not good enough for you?"

Over and over, hours and hours. They knew eventually he would give in; they always did. Danyk began to wonder, as well. He held on to what Joe had said... it would mean forever!

This would be temporary; eventually it would be over... if he lived. And then, he could go home to Joe... and maybe soon to America, and his father would greet him with open arms... and his dreams would come to life...and finally it would be over, and he could rest.

But not yet. He had to bear more. Just bear it. Just bear it. There are no choices to make.

His captors were growing more and more infuriated. It seemed they too were growing anxious and tired and wanted the deal done.

An order was given, and his hands were untied. The document was again slapped down in front of him and a pen placed in his hand.

"Sign!" The order was spat at him making it clear that they were expecting nothing less than total compliance. Their patience and game playing were over, and Danyk knew it.

I will lose everything! Everything!

He was hot, tired, thirsty, hungry, bruised, battered, bleeding and in actuality... just on the verge of giving up all hope. He was about to give in... give up all that was left to live for. He took a huge deep breath. Then...

Surprising even himself, he lunged to stand, though he was still tied to the chair, and he roared, "Nooooooooooooooooooo!"

He was not speaking to his captors. He was commanding himself and urging his angry, seething rage to materialize and find a strength so mighty that it would defy the KGB at least once more. "I won't sign it! I'll never sign it!!! No! No! No!"

Danyk did not know where his eruption had come from; some secret place deep within him that stores courage and the other things that make us the best of who we are. Then, he grabbed the document and tore it to shreds, letting its pieces feather to the floor.

For a moment, his captors were just as shocked.

But clearly, a fourteen-year-old boy was not going to be a match against the KGB, and after the second it took for them to recover, they beat Danyk until he was unconscious... and thought to be dead.

They left him there in his own pool of blood and waste, as they had thousands of others who didn't cooperate or swear allegiance to Stalin or were suspected of being traitors. It was a callous, heartless act and they had done it many, many, times before. If they had once been decent human beings, Stalinism had scared the decent part out of them. The gory reality was it was just another day at the office.

Sam was somber and bent over as he made his way up the steps to Miss Larned's office. It had been some time since he had seen her. He held his hand tight against his chest to keep safe the letter he had protected there since receiving it, an hour earlier.

When he reached her door, he gently knocked as was his general manner, and Miss Larned promptly responded, "Come in."

Sam nodded and gave a faint smile to greet her. When he quickly reached into his pocket rather than make polite conversation before getting down to business, she knew he had something serious to discuss with her. Over the years, she had come to know him well, and

Sam at times wondered if she understood him better than some of his closest friends did.

"How can I help you, Mr. Szafranski?"

She had barely completed her sentence when he presented the letter to her. Sam was not trying to be rude, and she didn't take it that way.

He quietly studied her as she reviewed the letter's contents, narrowing her eyes on occasion, indicating she was grasping the implications of the letter's content.

She took a moment after she completed reading, before she raised her eyes to address Sam. She needed to gather her thoughts and think of what to tell him, how to tell him.

Twice, she cleared her throat, but still adequate words didn't come to her. She knew the intimate details of this man's life, and together they had shared many ups and downs as Sam had tried to find and care for his family. At times, she had shared his joy and at others, her heart had broken, too. Today was one of those broken-hearted days.

"Mr. Szafranski, the letter says...the letter means... it says..."

Sam decided to make it easier for her. "Danyk not come here to America." He confirmed in a whisper, quiet and meek. Sam was grief-stricken and resigned.

"Yes." Her voice was soft and light, also just above a whisper because she could barely stand to verify the words.

In all the years she had known Mr. Szafranski, he had always gone forth with hope... of gaining his American citizenship, of finding his family, of bringing them back to America.

But he was now totally and utterly hopeless and defeated. An eerie silence fell over the room.

"Mr. Szafranski, it says...". She would have gone on to explain further that Danyk could remain at the embassy for a fee, and that they would continue any and all appropriate measures to gain Danyk's release, but Stalin was adamant concerning exit visas not being issued to Soviet citizens at this time or in the near future. However, Sam's blank and aimless departure stopped her.

Sam wasn't a pretty sight. He looked like a walking corpse as he had gently reclaimed the letter and exited the room. Ever the gentleman, she heard a faint, "Thank you," once he reached the hallway. The muffle of his shuffling footsteps echoed down the corridor until it was empty.

Sam followed his feet all the way home. He wasn't aware of much else.

The last two times the KGB had taken Danyk they had returned him a few days later. Each time, he was battered and bruised but not broken, at least not so broken that Joe and Jim couldn't put him back together.

A week had gone by and there had been no sign of Danyk. Joe was frantic. Maybe Danyk had signed away his American citizenship and the Soviets had forbidden him to return to the embassy ...or maybe he hadn't and just like so many other "visitors" at the United States Embassy claiming American citizenship, the KGB had executed him as a traitor just for trying to establish the claim. It happened, time and time again, right under their noses. They couldn't do anything about it. They couldn't interfere and stop the KGB from taking the "visitor" nor could they retaliate if the "visitor" was executed. N-O-T-H-I-N-G! They were utterly and humiliatingly powerless.

Joe and other high-level embassy staff members had recently learned that the U.S. Government State Department were resigned and didn't expect Danyk or any other citizen to be released. Stalin wasn't giving in. If anything, he was squeezing things tighter.

There wasn't much sleep going on at night. Joe and Jim could think of little else but Danyk, neither could the rest of the embassy, all of whom had grown quite fond of Danyk over the months of his stay.

"It's O.K. Danyk, just give in kid," Joe would say aloud to the darkness and then think it silently. "You're not going anywhere anyway, just give in and come home."

But could Danyk come home to the embassy if he lost his American citizenship? Who knew? Joe had never played this game before, neither had the world. Besides, it all went according to Stalin's rule book, and he was known to change it at any given time or for a momentary whim.

Should he tell Sam? What should he tell Sam? He knew he had the right to know, but it seemed plain cruel to tell a father his kid was half a world away being routinely tortured. He decided to wait until he could at least give him an outcome, one way or the other.

Another half a week went by, and Joe started to give up all hope. Could they actually have done it? Could they actually have killed Danyk? Joe resisted as long as he could, but finally he couldn't just fear that it was true, he had to take the thought seriously.

Maybe Danyk was dead.

Slowly Joe started the grieving process. He'd spend the evenings on Danyk's bed and would gently finger the treasures with which Danyk had surrounded himself. He'd flip through the pages of his magazines or count the money Danyk had saved from his job sweeping the embassy floors. He thought about Sam back in New York who would lose the son he loved but had never gotten to know.

He'd known Danyk and he was honored to be his friend. He wondered if the world would ever know about a little boy who dared to stand up to one of the world's worst monsters because he wanted to be an American... because he knew it was the greatest privilege he'd ever get.

He felt ashamed too... for being an American and sometimes taking it for granted. Sure, he was patriotic, he wouldn't be here in the Soviet Union doing what he was doing if he didn't love his country, but somehow... his measuring cup was smaller than Danyk's when it came to loving, no, appreciating his country. Danyk had never seen or even remembered America, but he sure knew what it stood for. Nothing makes you understand freedom more than not having it.

"I miss you kid." Then Joe looked upward, not talking to Danyk anymore.

"Hey, God... you up there? I know I don't check in with you enough, but I promise... you watch over him, and I'll check in more often. O.K.?"

"It was days before he could even lift his body." The American serviceman filled Jim in. "He doesn't remember most of it, but he said he managed to drink from puddles and beg for bread before a kind peasant woman decided to help him."

This is one heck of a miracle you know!" Jim almost mumbled it to himself because all he could think of doing was finding and telling Joe that Danyk was back.

They found Joe right away, as he was on the first floor when Danyk arrived.

"Where is it?" Joe was asking about Danyk, but he'd quite naturally, gone into coded conversation, in case the Soviet bugs that they all knew existed but couldn't always find, were in the same room with them.

"Doc's office. It's bad." Jim reached for Joe's collar to slow him down. "Joe... it's really bad."

"Alive?" Joe mouthed the words.

"Barely."

Joe gathered his composure and put an arm around Jim. "Let's go."

Jim didn't catch it, but Joe looked up and had a private conversation with God before he got to Danyk. If he listened once... maybe he'd listen again.

Chapter 26

Danyk Must Leave the Embassy

It was a slow-motion reunion with Danyk, so Joe was sure to move carefully and deliberately. His arms slid easily around the disoriented boy, and he comforted him the way he knew Sam might have if he could have been there. He closed his eyes and cautiously hugged the once again thin frame that had lengthened since his first arrival at the embassy.

Joe couldn't deny it any longer. He wanted to. With all of his being he wanted to. But denying the truth any longer would eventually cost the boy his life.

He couldn't help thinking about the nursery rhyme, Humpty Dumpty. Danyk had certainly been perched on a wall for quite some time. Each time he fell, Joe and Jim had worked their hardest to put him right back together again... and then, put him right back up on that wall. They could stand there and look official, do all the right things, but in the end, they were just decoration.

They weren't protecting Danyk; they were just making it possible for more damage to be done. How many more pieces could he be broken up into before he just didn't exist anymore? Just like all the king's horses and all the king's men, it was time to admit defeat. The

Danyk who had first arrived at the embassy so eager and intact after a war, though malnourished and abandoned, could be no more. Or perhaps it was they who had been the most changed. Regardless, it was time for them all to face the reality of what had to be.

He couldn't live through the boy being taken and tortured again... even if the boy could!

Telling Danyk to leave would be both the most selfish... and most selfless thing he had ever done.

First things first, though.

They would patch him up, tend to his wounds as they had always done but after, they would tell him, and sadly, Joe knew from the depths of his being that Danyk would never be just right again.

Joe and Jim quarreled about when to tell him. The night before sending him away? First thing that morning? After breakfast? Perhaps even the arguments themselves were a way to unconsciously stall.

Each wanted different things packed in the makeshift survival kit they had tried to put together with staples Danyk was sure to need on his way back to his village in Gorodnitsa, but when it was all assembled in the sturdy duffle, they realized it would be too heavy and cumbersome for the boy to manage. The canned goods seemed most important to sustain him but they might overburden the bag and target him for thieves? Maybe they should just give him cash? But what if there wasn't anywhere or anyone from whom anything could be purchased along the way?

They fussed and packed, then repacked, desperately trying to be smart about how they sent Danyk off into the world alone. Back in the states, it would have been unthinkable to send a fourteen-year-old boy off on his own in brutal territory. Here, it was all they thought about.

They tried to be meticulous, thinking through each detail as though it was a mission either one of them might have been going on, but in the end, they knew they had planned nothing. It was all a big question mark.

Would the KGB even allow him to leave? Would they pick him up soon after he did?

Joe and Jim would never know. Danyk would leave; contact with him would be over. Forever. They'd never know if he arrived safely back in his village or if a loyal neighbor had taken him in and helped him restart his life once he'd returned. Would he be marked and avoided by those desperate to avoid the attention of the authorities? It would never be known. There would be no closure.

Joe and Jim mourned guiltily together, each thinking there should be something they should be able to do, but the situation's reality was forcing them to come up empty.

Joe had overcome and lived through many of life's tribulations, once even being a prisoner of war in Nazi Germany. If it was happening only to him, it would have been different.

But it was happening to this child.

He felt as though he was letting Danyk down either way, as well as Sam, his father and maybe even God, too. He wasn't sure why, but he'd always expected so much of himself and since his early college years he'd always seemed to make good and deliver. This was a reverse direction, and it was throwing off his equilibrium. It was like putting on a pair of eyeglasses with too strong of a prescription, and now everything you looked at was different, distorted... unreal.

His Midwestern Presbyterian background had given him a foundation of faith and obligation to make the world a better place. He always had an ear for a neighbor's troubles, felt his fellow man's pain and suffering, thought about it, contemplated it. He pondered seriously his role in helping his country achieve greatness and be a leader of world peace. Somehow sending Danyk away contradicted all that. It was like being one of the bad guys and once it was done, it could never be undone.

He'd never be the same. The world would always be a little lopsided and he'd always be working to try to make it straight again.

Joe would come to terms with his frail humanness in a world

which was bigger than he and headed toward its own self-destruction because he had to. Because someone had to.

Because he wanted to shake the world and bring it back to its senses.

His unassuming character would keep him steadfast to his ideals and working hard to be a voice of reason for the world. Fortunately, history would, in the end, recognize all he had been right about. But for now, he was insignificant and had to send a child on his way into the depths of Stalin's Russia as an enemy of the state.

It was a good enough reason, he thought, to be grief-stricken. He didn't even try to hide his water-filled eyes from Jim. The tears were honest, and they spoke the words he just couldn't find.

Joe and Jim communicated best in silence around this time. When they did speak, they argued, so unlike both of their natural temperaments. But there was no place else to go with their frustrations, and the boy's situation strained both on such an emotional level that it brought out the worst in them.

Danyk eventually healed reasonably well as Joe and Jim were good nurses, learning from each torturous episode from which Danyk returned. They weighed his recovery further against waiting too long. Should the KGB discover his return, they'd be outraged and of course return for him.

Emotionally, Danyk was of course depressed, but he took great comfort whenever Joe or Jim kept him company. They noticed his spirits return, which in and of itself was miraculous considering what the boy had been through. Perhaps it was a defense mechanism or a strategy to survive that he'd learned during World War II. Perhaps it was just an adolescent's need for approval. Whatever. It was just one of the many factors they regarded helping them to decide that ... today was the day.

Today. They would tell him...for sure, today.

≈

At 6:30 AM the embassy came alive. Jim made Danyk eggs and bacon for breakfast in the embassy's kitchen. Danyk didn't leave a crumb on his plate.

While he was busy devouring his morning meal, Danyk's eyes never left Joe.

As Joe sipped his coffee, he uneasily played with the sugar bowl and his spoon, all the while knowing that Danyk's eyes were on him. He couldn't help himself. He couldn't look at Danyk. Jim busied himself with the clean-up.

He knows, Joe thought.

Joe picked up a muffin and tossed it in the air. He wanted to play. To change the mood.

He wanted just one more time being with the kid. "Here catch!" Joe tossed the muffin to Danyk. He caught it with a huge grin.

Maybe. Maybe he doesn't know. Joe suddenly wasn't sure. Then, again there was a long silence when Danyk stuffed the muffin into his mouth.

Joe had never known a kid to relish every bite he took. It didn't matter if it was a candy bar or brussels sprouts. The kid appreciated it all.

The words were forming in his head, getting ready to come out. Jim, wiping pots dry behind Danyk, stared at him awkwardly, waiting, nodding, silently telling him, "Now!"

Danyk took it all in. With a packed mouth, he munched and half smiled, but his eyes narrowed and aimed at Joe.

"What? Why are you both acting so strange?"

One more time, Joe tried to say the words. He took a deep breath, opened his mouth and a wounded sound came out instead.

Two sets of trusting eyes fell on him wondering, "What are you doing?"

Still, he couldn't find the words. Joe gave up, reached for another muffin and tossed it at Danyk. Then Joe left the room.

Jim and Danyk shrugged and gave each other a bewildered look, both pretending it was just another day. It would be anything but.

Joe left to contemplate things. He was a big contemplator. He sat at his desk playing with a pen most of the morning trying to put together the words that would send a young boy off alone to meet his destiny. Joe had never been a particularly outspoken person, but he did pride himself on being able to master the written word. He'd worked hard at it over the years... maybe writing it down first would help. But nothing significant came to mind and finally, frustrated with himself, he realized... he just had to do it. It would have to come to him on the spot because simply... time mattered and he was wasting it.

He went to find Jim who was piddling away the morning just as he was, staring off into space, not sure how to proceed. Neither one really wanted to be the one to initiate this, and each was waiting, hoping for the other to lead the way.

Maybe Joe would have continued to wait at least until Jim gave him the look that said, "We can't wait any longer. We have to tell him, now!" But finally, Joe was forced to deal with the fact it was in Danyk's best interest to leave sooner rather than later.

At any moment the KGB could return, wanting Danyk back into their custody. The only thing working for them was that the KGB thought they had left Danyk for dead after their last encounter. But somehow, they always learned what everyone was trying to keep secret... and Joe couldn't trust that they wouldn't come to at least check. That would be a more dreaded goodbye than sending Danyk back to his village.

Danyk was keeping himself occupied in his room when Joe emerged with Jim a close second. Joe sat his tall frame heavily down at the foot of the bed while Jim leaned on the door frame. It took only a second for Danyk to realize that this was not a typical visit.

The KGB had returned! Danyk felt panic and the blood drained from his face.

Joe was quick to pick up on his interpretation of their somber mood. "No, no Danyk! It isn't the KGB. They haven't returned."

Relief was immediate, but the fear remained, and Danyk lunged into Joe's arms for a bit of fatherly reassurance and comforting.

"It's O.K. pal, it's just us you have to deal with."

Danyk dropped backwards and searched Joe's face. "Did I do something wrong Joe?"

"No, no Danyk. That's not it either."

A long moment of silence fell while Joe gathered his courage.

Jim cowardly coughed to break the silence but didn't offer to start. Again, a moment passed while Joe summoned the words.

This is going to be bad, Danyk surmised, and he began to prepare himself. His blue eyes targeted Joe's, similarly blue and glistening. Patiently, he waited for life to smack him in the face again. This is going to hurt, he thought.

Could it be news of my mother?

It would be the worst news he could get, he thought, and emotionally he got ready.

Perhaps it was an automatic response, a conditioning after leading a particularly difficult life. "Danyk, you came here so you could go to America and be with your father..."

Danyk nodded, wondering now if the bad news concerned his father, not his mother. His nose wrinkled as his face squeezed tight trying to take in what was coming.

"We all wanted that for you. You know, I went to America and met your father. Many people have been working very hard to make it happen."

Again, Danyk nodded, this time with gratitude.

"You are an American citizen... a very brave American... and the United States of America recognizes your citizenship... but it has exhausted every possibility to get Soviet permission for you to go to America..."

"And I stayed an American citizen, Joe! I never signed the papers, I never gave it away." Danyk took pride in the accomplishment because he, more than anyone else, understood what he had endured to do so.

Joe detected Danyk's defiance, a part of him that did not often surface.

Joe's heart panged to know what the boy must have endured to exercise such pride and strength before him now.

"Danyk... you've shown such courage and you've handled everything... like a man. But... you are only fourteen years old and..."

Joe's voice broke. Danyk couldn't bear to see Joe obviously upset and again lunged into Joe's arms, which were quick to circle the boy tightly. Jim was drawn into the scene from the doorway and joined them on the bed, placing his hand on the back of Danyk's shoulder.

Joe's voice was still quivering but he was determined to go on and say what needed to be said.

"I'm sorry, Danyk, I'm so sorry." Joe's voice was filled with utter regret, but Danyk was still not certain what Joe had to tell him.

"Don't be sorry Joe, you do everything for me. I love you, Joe."

Now all three were undone, and they were a mass of tears and sobs, shaking shoulders and gasps for air.

"We love you too Danyk, which is why... this is ...so hard...so hard!"

It took every ounce of his being to pull Danyk away, look him square in the eye and say,

"You have to leave, leave the embassy."

"Leave. Leave? And go where? America?" Danyk's guess gave away his last measure of hope. But, even as he said it... he was quick to understand that there was none left. It was over.

"No, no back to Gorodnitsa... back to your village."

"No! No! No!!!" Danyk, fully comprehending and feeling betrayed, began to hit Joe's chest. Jim reached from behind and tried to slow the punches, but Danyk's tantrum was not to be stopped.

Then, Danyk turned the pounding on himself declaring loudly, "No... I go to America...

I see my father, I go to America and see my father."

Joe started to explain, over the yelling, and Danyk's anguished desires eventually simmered and sunk into deep sobs.

The more real it all was, the quieter the room became and then Joe felt no need to speak above a whisper. "We've tried... there is nothing else to do... and the KGB will be back, Danyk. They won't stop. There will always be a next time... they will always come again. Please, Danyk, know that is the only reason I would send you away. Please, know. Pleeeeeeeeeeease understand...for your own sake, more than mine."

Danyk continued to cry and cry, understanding everything they had said, but not being able to believe that they would actually send him away. They had been his lifeline, his protectors, his guardians, his companions, his family... and they were giving up on him!

Why?

Are they tired of me?

Did I do something wrong?

Did the KGB tell them to make me go? Is the KGB forcing them to make me go?

Joe and Jim did their best to provide the answers, but Danyk was not ready for them.

Though he had shown the courage of a man, he still had the heart of a child, and all it knew was that those he dearly loved had just turned him away.

By mid-afternoon, shortly after a lunch he had found difficult to swallow, Danyk began his journey back to his village. It would not be as long as the two-week journey he had taken to get to the embassy nine months earlier, as Jim had arranged for a Lincoln touring car that would drop him off in Skalat. From there, it would be up to Danyk to travel the few remaining kilometers to Gorodnitsa on his own.

Jim said his farewell at the embassy, as he chose to stay behind. He wanted to let Joe have his last bit of alone time with Danyk, understanding that they had a special bond and deserved to have a private goodbye.

The Lincoln was an open car, but a curtain had been put up to protect them from the misty day that was hanging over Moscow. It seemed even the sky wanted to cry but was holding back.

The chauffeur was a Russian who often worked as "the boiler man" for the embassy.

Although Stalin sent these men under the pretense of checking or repairing the boiler, it was well known to the American Foreign Service that they were, in reality spies sent to install and hide listening devices. Knowing that they were bugged, when Stalin didn't suspect that they had a clue, actually had many advantages in terms of what they did and didn't want Stalin to know.

However, this "boiler man" could be trusted, and he was perhaps chosen specifically for this chore, as he was likely to "forget" dropping off a Ukrainian boy, who was trying to avoid detection by the Soviet authorities in Skalat.

The Lincoln passed Bryansk station, which was full of commuters from every station of life, rushing from one line to another to buy their tickets. It was an odd mix of people, some carrying burlap bags or even primitive farming equipment. An old blind woman begged on a corner, a man with one leg hobbled as he leaned on a long stick. Buses went by full to capacity or overflowing.

Each meter they traveled took Danyk further and further away from the life he wanted and the one his mother had dreamed for him.

Where was his mother? Danyk was aching for security and couldn't help wondering and asking the same question that he had asked over and over again during the last few months.

Once they were out of the city, he saw the familiar views of peasants working the land, usually potato farms or "victory gardens", and stray livestock grazing the fields. He knew they were all signs that he was going back to his old life... but without his mother... without his father.

Soon, the car would stop, the door would open and he'd be

expected to walk away from the only bit of security left to him. Joe had become his everything! He was the father's arms that Danyk had never been allowed to know, and soon it would all vanish... all hope, all protection!

Only nothingness would be left... at least that was how he felt to the depth of his being.

He drew himself to Joe's side, not wanting to waste the minutes he did have left. He relished knowing he wasn't severed from him yet. He wanted the car to slow down... make the moment never end. He didn't want what he knew was to come next.

Joe was thinking likewise, and he stretched an arm around Danyk's shoulders, but there was nothing left to say. The car ride remained comfortably quiet and the two friends spent their last moments together in a joint silence that only true friends can share with ease.

The driver chose a quiet place to pull over when they reached Skalat and waited. "Joe, I'll never forget you!"

"I'm never going to forget you either... you know that." Danyk nodded sadly, knowing this was the end.

"When I get to America, I'll find you."

The boy hadn't given up. There was still a fight in him, and Joe once again felt an overwhelming pride and gratitude for having known him.

"We aren't ever going to leave each other, Pal. You're a part of me and I'm a part of you. You always remember that."

When you need to.

When it's too tough to go on.

When you need me, and I'm not there.

Danyk nodded and gave him one final hug. Then he was standing on a street in Skalat... fourteen, American and alone in Stalin's Russia. He wasn't in a good place.

All this, they had explained, was to keep him alive. Why then, did he feel as though he had died? Why did he feel empty?

He felt like he didn't exist.

Danyk's life had once been with his mother. Together they had faced everything. Now he didn't know where she was or if she was alive or dead. She lived only in his memories.

She promised him a life in America with his father. But it was just a dream, and he must now wake up.

For a while, the embassy had half satisfied him, nurtured him, fed him... provided love.

But had that too only been a dream? Was it all unreal?

Danyk held up his hands to examine them with blank eyes, to question his very existence.

He was like everyone else now. There was no hope of leaving Stalin's Russia, finding his mother or meeting his father. At least now, he knew. Consciously, there was no hope left, but subconsciously, one ember of hope still smoldered; it had not died.

Historically and statistically, most people with western ties living at the American Embassy in Moscow in the hopes of getting out, eventually gave up all rights to American citizenship, were killed by the KGB or committed suicide. Although Danyk did not yet realize his great fortune, he was indeed lucky to still be alive.

Sam had both letters spread open over his dresser. The official looking typewritten one was from the State Department in Washington and a handwritten note was from Joe. The first informed him "there is little hope that Danyk Szafransky will receive permission to depart the USSR in the near future." The second let him know that his son had left the embassy. The fight to bring him to America was basically over.

Each morning Sam scanned over them and fondled them gently pressing the pages out straight over the lace coverlet of his dresser. It was a way to mourn the loss – again - of his family. He supposed, finally, that they were gone forever.

His grief made him uncharacteristically outspoken, and he would share memories of his lost family with any friend who would listen. In his wallet, he carried a treasured photo of his wife and son. It appeared whenever he managed to find a particularly good listener, one willing to be patient and kind enough to listen, again and again, to the joy his family had given him, if even for a short time. He would share the immense heartache he felt at losing them. He knew he looked pitiful, but he, who under any other circumstance shared his feelings cautiously, was helpless to stop himself. His family, which had been his greatest strength, was now his greatest weakness.

Sam had good friends, and they endured him as best as they could for as long as they could. They understood and felt for Sam, after all, his situation was extraordinary. To live for years thinking your family had died in the war, then to hear from your son... be given hope... only to have it turn to dust, seemed an intolerable burden to bear.

So, they bore it with him.

Ann and Walter Romanuk were two of those good friends. They shared a similar background and had come from an area close to Sam's village back in the old country. Walter, in fact, had been a childhood friend. It helped them be particularly understanding and supportive.

"He is a lonely man!" Walter's wife, Ann, stated matter-of-factly between stitches while mending a pair of trousers.

"He has us." Walter defended but knew the offer was inadequate. "He needs a wife."

Men! She could not help but to be exasperated with him. They never see the obvious! "Maybe...we could find someone for him." She spoke as casually as possible. Walter should not know that she had already given this a lot of thought. "But he thinks of himself as married."

"Even if she is alive... God forgive me for saying this, but it is the truth...she is dead to him. He needs a wife for the here and now. I don't think he can take much more. It isn't fair to him. Life is going by, but he does not live it."

"So, you think a wife will change that! Nothing is going to make him forget."

"And he shouldn't. But that doesn't mean he shouldn't get on with life. His situation won't change... if he finds someone to make him happy... alright... just less unhappy. Could it hurt for him to have someone share his life? It could only help."

Walter knew his wife thought he had dismissed what she was saying, but he was actually giving it great consideration. After all, Sam was a good friend, and he wanted to see his friend happy. Or at least distracted.

"Would you... would it be alright if I introduced him to Tessie?"

When Walter looked up, she prepared to argue with him, but she didn't see any fight in him at all. Had she won so easily?

"She is a lonely woman. They might be good for each other."

"Maybe," Walter seriously considered. "Maybe he... he is just waiting for our blessing. Maybe we need to let him know it is alright to go on with life." Walter was resigned, it seemed, and his wife was similarly relieved.

"Ask him for dinner tomorrow night." After all, Tessie had already accepted the invitation.

"Shouldn't you check with Tessie first?"

"Of course... which is why I asked her yesterday."

Walter gave a big sigh. Why was this woman always ten steps ahead of him?

Danyk felt someone shaking him, and he awoke startled. He always needed to be ready and was quick to come to full alertness. It was how he had survived the last few years in hiding.

Kupetsky had cared for his grandmother all these years as he went from farm to farm, earning a place to sleep and scraps to eat. It was not that the farmers would not have paid him more fairly. They simply had little. He was grateful even for them letting him work on their farm.

Stalin had instituted collective farms, and the state was dictating much of day-to-day life. Even what he thought of as his neighbor's "farms" were not really theirs to do with as they wished. The state oversaw and controlled it all. Individuals were, however, allowed a very small plot to grow their very basic staples. But even this or the products they produced could be seized or taxed without any predictability.

Danyk wasn't certain how the government viewed him. Perhaps they continued to think he was dead, or maybe they knew he existed but thought of him as a simple peasant who had lost his fight to declare his American citizenship and was harmless. Or maybe he was still considered an enemy of the state with unknown whereabouts. He didn't want to take any chances of getting his neighbors into trouble with the authorities. Sheltering him could easily be seen as a betrayal. People were shot or sent to Siberia for less.

No friend or neighbor had ever betrayed him and given him away; however, rewards were given for reporting enemies of the state and one always had to remain cautious. Even implying a negative remark about Stalin or the government in one's own home could be considered a betrayal or reportable offense. The reality at this time in the Soviet Union was that neighbor betraying neighbor was common. This behavior was a result of years and years of brutality and abuse issued and commanded by Stalin himself to demand absolute and complete loyalty of his citizens, from his highest-ranking generals to his lowest, deprived peasantry. In part, it was his "paranoia" that drove him, but to a certain extent, his paranoia was based on the very real desire of his subjects and political opponents to overthrow him.

"You should go, it might be nothing, but soldiers are headed this way."

It was enough to set Danyk off into the forest, to hide until he was comfortable that the danger had passed. It was an awful way to live but the only way he knew how.

He did not have a particular hiding place pre-arranged, mostly because the need to hide could happen at any time or any place as he ventured from farm to farm looking for work. The possibility of danger or discovery generally passed quickly though, as the days of extended searches had long passed.

He tended to go into the forest as it provided a lot of natural cover, and there were numerous tunnels once exclusively used by the Underground that were now exposed due to bombings from the war.

They offered good protection and room to move around in case he did have to remain for a while. He was always careful to slide in without anyone noticing and if there was time and the right materials available, he would add extra camouflaging.

After he was safely in hiding, he would keep an eye out for a while, listen to his own heavy breathing and wait. Slowly his pounding heart and lungs would recover from the dash he'd taken to get there. When he felt enough time had passed, or Kupetsky had come to say the danger was gone, he would return to a farm... usually a different one, until once again, it was time to move on. And so on and so on.

The years passed and Danyk grew both tougher and gentler into manhood.

Gradually, he became a face in the crowd and blended into village life. By 1952, he believed the authorities had forgotten about him, and he was just one of many, working on collective farms instituted by Stalin. Much of his day and that of the other villagers was dictated by the state. They were paid little and only once a year, but they did receive a meager ration of food, if it was available.

It was impossible for Danyk to become anything more than a farmer as he had never been able to get any education. He had no papers or form of identification other than the ones his father had sent him years before proving his American citizenship, which of course he kept hidden away in a secret place.

Except for the support of the local villagers, he was alone, as well as unhappy. Any family, which still lived was difficult to see, and he preferred not to draw attention to them or remind officials that they were related to him - an American - forgotten perhaps by a chaotic regime, but American nevertheless and still an enemy of the state.

There was a girl though, who had caught his eye. Oddly, he had known of her most of his life, even attended school with her in the few early years that he had gone, but he'd never noticed her the way he had as of late. His pursuit of her was doused when he reasoned she'd have nothing to do with him. He was but a common laborer, less than a farmer and he had no hope of a future of any kind.

Still, it was difficult not to notice the sway of her skirts or her trim arms as they circled a bundle of laundry, and it made him long for more of a life than he had. He should be grateful, he chided himself just to live one more day, such was his humility. Even after all this time, the slightest betrayal or suspicion of betrayal sent people off to Siberia or the death squad. He at least, had been left alone... until the day the Soviet Army arrived.

The Soviet soldiers demanded the men between ages eighteen and twenty-five be loaded into the trucks.

It reminded Danyk of the days during the war when the villagers were rounded up at gunpoint by German soldiers and divided up. Mothers pulled from children, husbands pulled from wives... never sure why or for what purpose they were being taken.

At first, they thought they were needed for some specific farming chore or labor task.

But by evening, he realized he had been conscripted into the Soviet Army.

He did not dare to show what documents he had, although they were not on his person anyway. So, when he could not provide identification documents, the Soviets simply made him new ones. These new documents would list his date of birth as 1933, the year he arrived back in Poland when he was two years old. They would also certify his Soviet citizenship, a falsehood from his perspective, but a convenient way to establish an acceptable identity if he was to spend the rest of his days in the Soviet Union. In exchange, he would spend the next three years as a soldier in the Soviet army.

For so many years Sam had not been a happy man. His life had gone haywire. No matter what he did, he seemed unable to gain control of it. He did not know what had become of his mother or wife... both most likely dead. He knew at least his son lived, but how or where, he wasn't sure.

Many of his family members had been lost during the war, and he had little contact with those that had survived.

His only blessing and comfort was a small community of good friends, mostly immigrants like himself from the Ukraine.

One day, Walter's wife introduced him to a woman named Tessie. Sam made what he thought was a reasonable decision. It didn't involve passion; those days were long gone to him. Just reason. He was lonely. She was lonely. She seemed like a nice woman, and they shared a similar background.

What would his Mariya think if she were still alive? What would his Danyk think? It was not until all hope had died that he was able to do it. Finally, with a weathered heart he asked Tessie to marry him and she said, "Yes."

Chapter 27

A Reunion

S am saw that the letter was from France and he opened it eagerly, certain it was news from either Paulo or Marion, one of Mariya's brothers.

It seemed Marion would soon be arriving in Canada from eastern France. Marion's wife and daughter now knew that he had been taken as a POW at the start of the war but had learned nothing else since. Stalin's policy of repatriation would put his life in jeopardy should that information be shared with them and the Soviet authorities were somehow to get a hold of it.

He hoped that at some point Sam could cross the border and visit him after he was established.

"Who is the letter from?" Tessie casually asked.

"My brother-in-law... Mariya's brother." Tessie knew about his family back in the Soviet Union, but still it felt uncomfortable to mention Mariya or her family to Tessie.

I will have to tell Marion!

Sam had never told Marion or Paulo about Tessie. There had been no need as their lives were to go on separated by an ocean... and the thought that he was going on with life without Mariya, not yet knowing her fate, would be too hurtful for them... and too shameful for him. He could admit to himself that he wasn't totally sure who he was protecting, which in and of itself was another issue, a cloud hanging over him with which he was tired of dealing.

After so many years passing, his second wife had become more familiar to him than Mariya, who now seemed so disconnected from his day-to-day life. She was part of the old world, thousands of miles away that he had long ago left behind.

He had not seen or heard from Mariya for so many years. It was very likely she was dead, a fact he had only partially dealt with as he had never known with absolute certainty. The final stage of mourning, acceptance, he had never quite gotten to.

He did not want to give up on her life; that would be too much of a betrayal for a man of his character. Though he couldn't help feeling a sense of abandonment, he knew it was unreasonable to direct responsibility for it to her. If anything, he blamed himself and guilt kept him in an indistinct limbo, going on with the motion of life, but never really sure if he should be totally committed to it.

With Tessie, he had found companionship and a good friend. They shared their days and had a life together. His loyalties, just as the events of his life had been, were a jumbled mix of confused feelings that she somehow knew how to deal with naturally and with ease. Her sympathy and patience were calming, perhaps his greatest attraction to her. She never demanded his total loyalty, instinctively knowing that by refraining from doing so, she was gaining it.

Sam handed Tessie the letter, and she began to read it aloud. Suddenly, he was not there with Tessie any longer. He was at a different time and place, transported back to the day he was leaving for Canada and had to say goodbye to Mariya and her family. He was beginning a new life for his family. He had not known if he would ever see Marion again and had expected that his young wife would shortly join him after he had established a place for them. It was, he had thought, the beginning of all dreams and possibilities about to come true.

Tessie caught his distance. "What are you thinking?" She coaxed him to reveal himself to her, mostly because when he did, she sensed it lifted his burdens.

"So many things..." he said honestly, not sure where to begin. Tessie had never begrudged him concern over the family he had left behind in the old country, but he was always careful not to disturb the security she felt in their relationship either.

"I'm happy I may get to see Marion again... you would like him...I...I wonder..?"

"Wonder, what?"

"...if he has changed much?"

But the question really reflected Sam's unconscious issues about himself.

I don't think I'm the same man he will remember.

In 1952, Danyk had gotten a letter from his mother that she was "cutting the stones" in Siberia.

She had seven more years to serve.

He finally had closure on her whereabouts and though he was still concerned about her safety, he rejoiced that she still lived.

Serving his time as a Soviet soldier involved performing the duties of a laborer more than military preparation and was quite different from what Americans might have expected of military service.

Danyk accepted his lot without complaint or protest, as was expected by Soviet authorities, and reasoned that at least now he would have Soviet documents, which he'd had no way of getting before. Perhaps when his service was over, the documents would help him get some kind of training, as he'd never been allowed to go to school or... get a better job or even just a driver's license. All had been denied him before.

In his third year of service, Kupetsky had forwarded a letter, his second, from his mother saying, most unexpectedly, that she was home back in their village of Gorodnitsa!

He immediately asked for leave to go visit her, and when that was denied, he asked for permission for her to visit him. That, too, was denied. His boyish anticipation was crushed, and he felt pitifully heartbroken.

It was agonizing to wait six months until he was discharged. He counted down the days until finally... finally, he was on his way back to Gorodnitsa.

He tried not to think of the hours and minutes going by as he traveled closer and closer to his village. He had waited ten years to once again see his mother.

During their last encounter they had been in a small, over-crowded cell, hugging and holding on to each other for dear life, surrounded by unspeakable conditions and uncertain about what was to become of them. When they had come to take her from him, they had been holding each other so fiercely that they each left fingernail marks on the other as they desperately tried to clutch and hold on. Of course it was a fruitless effort, but one that neither, in the panic of the moment, could prevent themselves from doing.

The last thing he remembered was the look on his mother's face, the tears brimming in her eyes and falling like rain drops as they dragged her away. Her arms never stopped reaching out, yearning for the son she was to leave behind... to fend for himself.

To once again embrace her warmth and comfort seemed unreal and after living a lifetime of one disappointment after another, he dared not dwell on it.

But that was impossible.

What if the train broke down?

What if the authorities had changed their mind and taken her back by the time he got there?

His mind raced with "what if's".

Danyk knew that whatever he had endured in the last decade, it could not have compared to what his mother must have endured in

Siberia. Rarely had anyone returned, but what was known of it was that it was a hellhole on earth.

Over the past few months he had heard of other releases from Siberia, a hopeful indication that things might change as a result of what he considered a blessed event...the death of Stalin on March 5, 1953.!

It was as though a secret national celebration had erupted! Even national officials could not disguise their relief that he was finally gone.

Suddenly a rigid society relaxed and took a long breath. Prisoners were being released and sentences pardoned. His mother's release was clearly a direct result of brutal controls relenting. Literally, people felt like dancing in the streets, although decorum was still expected.

It was all Danyk could do to get out and push the train to hurry it along. Images of his mother played in his head... of her when he was young... of her in photos with his father... of her at their last tragic meeting, when he was torn from her arms.

He was confused at which image to hold on to... no matter...soon he would have a new precious image... her face, when he would finally come upon her to at long last hold, comfort and reassure her. He had dreamed of this moment for many years and ... it was finally here!

Kupetsky was at the train station to greet him, and he felt tremendous gratitude for his old friend who had come such a distance to give him a welcome. They embraced and watched as their spoken greeting clouded up into the frozen air. It was winter and bitter cold, yet, as Danyk greatly appreciated, Kupetsky had come anyway. He further displayed his gratitude with three firm manly pats on Kupetsky's back, which caused the new fallen flakes of snow to dislodge and sprinkle to the ground.

They still had a distance to go to get to his village and then to the mud-bricked house where his mother waited for him. Kupetsky was slow to move and Danyk assumed his aging body was less anxious to make the trek through the snow than his, which had grown strong and firm from maturity and hard long days of physical work.

Danyk did not want to hesitate for a moment, even if he had to carry Kupetsky himself on his back, so quickly they were on their way.

"How is she, her health?"

"How does she look?"

"Did she tell you about the 'cutting of the stone'? What conditions did she endure, did she speak of it?"

The whole way Kupetsky seemed breathless and gave quick minimal responses. Soon, Danyk tired of asking and focused on the fact that the answer to all his questions lay at the end of this journey. Soon, he thought, very soon.

Kupetsky had thought his first meeting with his mother should be private. So, alone he took the last few steps to his old mud house. Its thatched roof was covered with snow, and all the white of it and the snowy landscape made it look like a magical place. To him it was precious, all the ugly scenes of the war years and deprivation was for a moment, forgotten. He was truly home and in the bosom of his family!

He opened the door expecting his mother to fly into his arms!

Instead, an old bent woman stood behind a chair and didn't move. The room was dark as it had no windows and he could catch only a glimpse of her between the shadows of light created by a fire in the hearth.

His heart sank.

The woman did not look familiar, and obviously he did not look familiar to her, either. In fact, she seemed fearful of him. It was not his mother at all!

But then, the door opened, unhinged by a strong wind outside and the room lightened just enough to catch a distorted but familiar profile. The figure relaxed and turned more completely to him, as he closed the door and hit the latch... just as he had done a million times growing up in the house as a boy.

He felt oddly disconnected to the woman, but nevertheless he called to her. "Momma?" It truly was a question, and he waited, not sure what the woman would answer.

"Danyk?" The voice was not strong or convincing, but he knew it well enough to know...it was her! His heart broke all over again.

Because it was her... but not her.

Who was this woman... broken...old and ragged? Where was his mother's spirit, the part of her that made her Mariya, the part that her eyes could never hide? This woman's eyes were blank.

He struggled to make sense of it?

The woman, too, was struggling.

She didn't rush into his arms, instead she let him know that she was waiting for her own son.

"My son will be here soon."

She doesn't recognize me either?

He didn't know what was worse, that he did not recognize her or that she did not recognize him.

My mother does not know me.

He felt startled and cheated that the homecoming he had envisioned was not to be. And then, he remembered...

His mother's love! Even if he had changed... even if she had changed... the love could not be destroyed. It was his time to be unselfish, to be the one who gave more, nurtured and protected.

"It is me, Momma, your Danyk." His arms rose, reaching out to her but to avoid frightening her, he waited for her to come to him.

She stood frozen for a long moment and then the tears came. He couldn't wait any longer, but he approached her slowly, holding out his arms that waited for her to recognize him and enfold herself within them.

Still the woman didn't move and a long moment passed. Then suddenly, her eyes filled with tears and she began to sob helplessly. He held back no longer and ran to her, encircling her in his arms.

She had once been his towering figure, his protector against a cruel world. Now he stood above her and cradled her in his arms, whispering reassurances, letting her lean on his strength and telling her that he loved her.

It ended with a long but comfortable silence, a shared mourning for all the years lost... and an acknowledgement of a love that had endured.

Chapter 28

Prison Again

Even after Stalin's death, Soviet mail continued to be monitored and censored. All citizens carefully corresponded with foreigners, much to their frustration, choosing words carefully, limiting frankness and often hoping that the recipient could read between the lines. Trying not to offend authorities was a fact of life and dominated the mindset of any reasonable citizen, regardless of status or position.

~

1955 (Letter from Mariya to Sam, translated)

> *My Dear Szymon,*
> *...my heart does not permit me to tell you all that I have been through but now I am home with our Danyk and my mother who is frail and old. Our good neighbor and his wife cared for her when Danyk and I could not, for which we are most grateful. They looked after our Danyk as well,*

while I was away cutting the stones and being rehabili-
tated. I did not know how he maintained himself, nor could
I know, and it was always on my mind making me fearful
and distressed. He is a most loving son and I never fear
that he forgets his mother. He does not forget his father
either which I have made sure of as he was growing up.
The years I was away were most hard on him and I know
that he did not have or get what he needed. But I was not
there which I feel very badly about. He is most anxious to
fix our house, but he tries hard to find work which is not
always there for him. Always he has the farm but that does
not earn him money for extra things. He is a good son and
willing to do whatever he needs to do. He was a good Soviet
soldier but could not come to me right away when I got
home. I needed to wait a long time but when I finally saw
him, I was greatly relieved and he has been a comfort to
me. He will rely on you I am sure because you have never
forgotten him or your family. When you make everything
right, our family will rejoice again. When will that be? I
have never forgotten my most loving and devoted husband.
If all my dreams are fulfilled, I will see him again and feel
whole again. It is this hope that makes my days easier. We
are eager to hear words from you as we did after the war
and most anxious to know that you have been up-dated on
your family which longs for you...

God bless... Mariya

~

Danyk's love and devoted attention helped Mariya regain some semblance of her former life and self. But the mother with the tenacious spirit that he had known from before the war and before being taken into custody, had been worn down. No matter how he tried, she seemed unable to regain her full personhood.

Her sense of security was shattered, and she waited out the rest of her days, tormented by the shadow of her dreams, which were never to leave her... but couldn't fulfill themselves. They lived within her and she within them... sometimes to the exclusion of Danyk and the real world with which he still needed to cope.

Though his mother had returned, he was still often... quite alone. Only his father's letters occasionally brought her back, and he would see for a quick moment in time, the same mother who had nurtured him through his early years and a World War, full of hope and dreams as she once had been, uplifted by a promise that she was still holding his father to keep... the promise that one day, he would bring her and Danyk back to America.

Yet...

Mariya, though often depressed, still knew her man, and with what little she had of him, the censored letters that came sporadically, possibly due to governmental control or another reason, still had the keen perceptive intelligence that she had often relied on to keep herself alive.

Did Sam have another life?

She openly questioned this, in one letter to Szymon. So much time had passed. Had he forgotten her?

The correspondence that Mariya pulled from the opened envelope had already been reviewed and censored by authorities. First, she put the envelope down followed by the folded letter next to it, on the splintered table. As was her habit, she wiped her hands on her apron as though to remove the tainted regard for privacy that she'd touched, simply by handling the tampered letter.

Then, she proceeded to unfold it, daintily as though it might break into a million pieces. For regardless of how it had been altered, it was still her only connection to the love of her life, the husband she had once felt compelled to leave but for whom she still longed. It was proof that he was not an imagined figure but quite real, and there still remained some small hope, though with each passing day it grew more and more miniscule.

~

(Sam's letter to Mariya, translated)

Mariya, you are saying that I forgot you, but it is not the truth. I didn't forget you and I never will forget about you. I would like to tell you that after the war I wanted to bring both of you to America, but unfortunately it didn't work out. The American consul took Danyk to Moscow and he was there for a long time but he didn't succeed either, and I had to pay for everything, but I don't regret that. I only regret that I couldn't bring you here. Mariya, you are writing me asking me to send you a white scarf, but I don't know which scarf, and from which material you want it made. I think you know better what you want, so write to me again and please be more specific. Write me and tell me if Danyk can write and what are you doing... Also I would like to ask you if you received two packages I sent you... I bless you and all of my family.

Szymon

"What are you doing?" Tessie casually asked Sam.

Sam quickly folded the letter, not offering to share it with Tessie as he sometimes might.

Then, he placed it in the envelope and licked it shut.

"Just sending off a letter to my son. I haven't heard if they got the last two packages I sent. It is frustrating never to know if they get what I send!"

She was quick to notice his hurriedness but respected his privacy. However, she couldn't help but to notice that the envelope had not been addressed to Danyk but to Mariya. She kept the observance to herself.

Rather than feeling jealousy, she could only feel admiration for a husband who did his best to keep two wives happy under such strange circumstances. Though Sam knew that Tessie supported him in every way, there were still feelings that were his alone and not meant to be shared.

While Sam held the letter in one hand, Tessie surrounded his neck with her two plump but loving arms. "I've decided to make you something special for dinner. What would you like?"

"Beef stew?" "Perfect."

"No... you are what is perfect!"

He gave her such a look of appreciation for understanding him that her heart melted. She hugged him again and said a quick prayer.

God, bless and watch over Sam's Mariya and Danyk, for they lost this man, my husband, and that is enough suffering for one lifetime.

Danyk took the paper and squeezed it in his hand. If it had been a living thing, he would have squeezed it hard enough to make it bleed.

But it was just a damn Soviet document... worthless! At least that was what the officials had told him.

He descended the wooded steps stunned and began the path home. About a half hour later, color began to return to his cheeks, but his heart was still racing.

"Danyk, Danyk! Wait!"

He knew immediately, before even turning back, that it was Olga Shevchuk and to him, it was the sweetest voice on earth.

"Olga! Stop running; I'll stop and wait for you." He said it much more patiently than he was feeling.

Olga slowed and then approached holding her side and trying to catch her breath. "I'm so anxious to know... did...did they let you... did you get the driver's license?"

"No." Danyk didn't even sound disappointed. He had decided to just accept it.

"But you showed them your Soviet birth certificate, didn't you? You have papers. Why did they say you can't have a driver's license?"

"They didn't exactly say why...". Danyk stopped and turned to Olga who stopped too and looked at him with such hopeful eyes. "They never do, why can't I have an education? Same reason? And don't make me say it here! Others might hear us." Danyk was surprised to hear such anger in his own voice. It betrayed the deep hurt he was trying to deny. "You know why, too."

Olga's face dropped and suddenly, Danyk was devastated. It hit him like a horse kick!

There was no future for him whatsoever.

He had never been permitted schooling of any kind. He was qualified only to be a farmhand. He would not even be permitted a driver's license, which would have given him an opportunity to be promoted to a tractor driver. He had hoped to use the papers he had gotten in the Soviet Army. But still, his history followed him.

Somehow, they knew about his western ties. The only good part was they knew... but had not sent him to Siberia.

The driver's license had not been the only thing he had hoped to gain. Now, he knew there was no chance to ask Olga to marry him. How could he? He had nothing to offer.

His eyes welled up and he started to walk away disgusted... with himself... his life... the Soviet Union.

"No!" Olga cried and ran after him.

"Why are you walking away from me?" She was right on his heels and her skirt fluffed against her legs as her arms swung trying to hurry to keep up with him.

"Why? Because..." Again, Danyk stopped abruptly. So did Olga. Again, he looked into trusting blue eyes.

"Because we can never get married!"

He expected a tremendous reaction... surprise... shock, amusement. But she didn't deliver.

"I don't know if you would have said 'yes' but I would like to have found out. But I can't even ask. Because... I have nothing to offer you."

Why didn't she just walk away, now?

Why did she stay... just staring up at him?

At first, she was blank. Nothing registered. It was so far from the conversation she had expected to have with him. Then, she softly smiled, a dreamy shy smile that the girls of the village sometimes wore when they met their beaus after work hours.

"Why are you looking at me like that?" he demanded. After all, he was not familiar with the look of a girl admiring him. Generally, his days were too full with basic survival to be distracted with such entertainment.

He was angry, so much so that he interpreted her smile like a tease.

Did she think this was a joke?

On and on went her smile, and she began to rotate her body back and forth as though she were trying to stay warm. Her blue eyes continued to look up and blink at will. As hard as he could, he tried to avoid them, but they were so seductive that he couldn't help himself.

Finally, her smile vanished and she was serious, as serious as he. Then there was a long, long silence. Each went perfectly still while they busily calculated their next move and tried to read the thoughts of the other.

"If you want to know, why don't you ask?" Olga bravely spoke first.

Danyk just shook his head at the silly notion. It could never be, but at least now he didn't think she was mocking him.

"I'm the one that gets to answer. I'm the one that gets to say 'no'. Not you."

"Olga, why are you doing this?"

"I told you... I'm the one that gets to say 'no' or...or... 'yes'." Coyly she looked up at him again.

Is it possible that she cares for me? Danyk's heart danced! And then it plunged.

No, no, it is awful! I have to live knowing that she would have married me, but...

"Ask. Ask? Ask!!!" Danyk took a deep breath.

It didn't matter that this could go nowhere.

He wanted just the moment. Just this one moment...so he could remember it... treasure it!

"Would you marry me?" he asked from his heart. Then, more seriously emphasized, "... if I had a good job... if I could provide for a family?"

"Yes, Danyk Szafranski, I will marry you."

Danyk grew somber as he absorbed her words, hearing them over and over again in his mind... and heart.

He couldn't help himself and drew her to him. They held each other for a long moment and suddenly the tenseness of the day was washed away.

But then, he remembered it was all just pretend.

"Thank you, Olga, thank you." His appreciation was most sincere but spoken coldly.

Then, he let go and tried to walk away.

Olga wrapped her arms around his waist from the back.

"I'm never letting go. Nobody can make me... not even you! Not if you feel the same way about me."

He stood rigid in front of her, locked in Olga's arms. With each breath, he thought of all he would be gaining. Of all she would be losing.

347

One breath, ten breaths, twenty breaths, a hundred breaths and then finally, he turned toward her still locked in her arms.

"Well, maybe, we'll see." He reached for her chin and turned it fully upward to make sure she understood. "Maybe?"

"I have not yet surrendered. Do you understand Olga? This will not be easy."

At that moment there was nothing that would have convinced Olga that it was not worth it... and nothing that would have convinced Danyk that it was worth it.

Finally...at last... they kissed.

It may have been their first. Although they knew each other since childhood, their attraction had never before been acknowledged between them, nor had it been a secret to them either. .. or to others in the village who were keen observers of subtle adolescent behaviors.

Was it meant to be?

It was not only Danyk who would keep this question an issue between them... so would the Soviet police!

Soon, they would appear at Olga's home to warn her not to marry the American.

Everything was difficult.

To get supplies that he and his mother needed was always an ordeal. Papers were always lost. There would be delay upon delay. Others, too, had these difficulties, but for him it was always a bit worse. The government and police always let him know that he was still being watched and still under suspicion. A look, a comment, a harsh duty detail, the denial of any kind of work besides farm labor... were all meant to keep him in his place.

Every move was questioned. Danyk was a marked man.

His neighbors inquired, "Are you going to the festival?" knowing that Danyk tended to avoid appearing at any kind of public gathering.

"This time... maybe." He answered, thinking that the authorities knew who he was and where he was. If they wanted him, they merely had to come get him. Hiding would no longer do him any good. Besides, the authorities might be insulted if he didn't go and participate. No question ever had an easy answer, so he tried hard not to spend too much time worrying about it. His decision was made; he would go.

He thought perhaps it might even be an enjoyable day. Olga and her family would attend as well, and he would be surrounded by many people who had supported him over many difficult years, regardless of the possibilities of reprisals from the authorities.

His attitude was good, and he took in the festive air of people relaxing from long hard laborious days to enjoy a community gathering. It was such a rare occurrence, and he had decided to enjoy every moment.

He walked to the center of the activity, passed the area where the large posters of Lenin and Stalin were always respectfully displayed during any public occasion. In truth, there were no other kinds of occasions, such as holidays, vacations or religious observances. They were strictly controlled by the authorities.

It did not take long.

The posters were not in their usual place. Someone had torn down the pictures of Lenin and Stalin. Such disrespect was not to be tolerated and possible offenders were brought in for questioning; Danyk, the American, among them.

It was old, he told himself, and he was bored with the authorities. He sighed heavily in disgust.

It was new too, and it shook him to his very core to be questioned. He'd buried or managed to block from his everyday thoughts his days of being questioned and tortured at the American Embassy in Moscow as a child. He'd condensed all those memories into one fantastic nightmare, but being questioned again made the first time real all over again.

The trauma repeated, wreaked havoc on his sense of security, but there were no choices. One either crumbles or one survives. If you have enough reasons to go on, you choose the latter.

So, when Danyk was wrongly condemned for a crime he did not do, and sentenced to four months in prison, he chose to go on.

Upon his return...

Chapter 29

An Unexpected Return

He'd hoped Olga would be waiting for him. It was a selfish notion, he knew, but one he seemed unable to resist.

Now, he thought, at least she would understand what life with him might be like. There wouldn't be any guarantees or necessarily any stability. One day he might be working the fields and the next carted off to jail on a false charge. All because he was the American. He wondered if it had all been a set-up, just an excuse to arrest him and send him off to prison. Was he out of his mind to even allow her to consider a life with him?

He wanted to share his doubts with his father, as a son should be able to do, but it would not be appropriate, as his letter would be censored anyway and probably never make its way to America.

Instead, he only shared what was good in his letters to his father who now lived in Syosset, New York and hoped that his father did not believe that he was a communist.

(Danny's letter to his father, translated)

351

My dear father, I feel very blessed. Olga Shevchuk has answered me that she will be my wife. She is a very good woman who stands by my side. I have known her from childhood and feel it is a very good match. You may remember her family, my mother tells me. I only hope I can provide a good home for her. I will work hard to do my best and see that she has a good life with me and that our family will grow. I am only a farm laborer so our times may be difficult but she has shown a strong desire to work together with me. We will construct our own house if we are able to acquire the materials which are difficult to get. The bricks are not a difficult thing because we have plenty of mud and I am a good brick-maker but the other materials are not so easily gotten. My dear father, I would like you to give the marriage blessing so your son and his family will have good luck and prosper. I would like you to come visit and meet my new wife and see my home as I have never forgotten you as my father and would like to give you proper respect and the love you deserve from your son and his family...

Danyk

Sam's son was a good man and wanted to provide for his family, something he, himself, had ultimately never been able to do. Sam provided well for Tessie, but he had let down his first family. It was a defeat that never left him, never let him feel totally comfortable in his own skin. Tessie was not due home yet, and he allowed himself a luxury which rarely occurred to him. He cried. Loud, sobbing, anguished cries that shook his whole body.

At such joyous news, what father would cry?

Even what was joyful stabbed his heart. There seemed no way to live his life without pain, just at times there was mild relief. Tessie worked hard to bring him that, and he so appreciated whatever she offered.

Did that also make him a traitor? A cheater?

He answered his son by opening his heart. It was all he knew to do.

(Sam's letter to Danyk, translated)

My dear son, I received your letter and I am very happy and feel very sorry. It is a great happiness for me that my dear son is asking for a marriage blessing. I am sorry that I can't give a blessing in life, and only through the letter. My dear son, I am sending you my blessings... for a good married life, and let God bless you in your married life. I wish you a lot of happiness and I hope that you will stay healthy and will lead a good life. I pray to God that you would always be together and that you would always love each other and would never have any arguments.

My dear son I am very thankful to you that you treat me as a father and that you are inviting me to your house and thank you for your big heart, because you grew up without me. My dear son I will never forget your words as long as I live. My dear son, I would very much like to go to you to at least see you, but unfortunately I am not allowed but hopefully someday I will have a chance to come and see you...Also I would like to find out more about your construction. I know that you don't have enough materials, but don't worry, I will help you. In the summer it is easier, but I'm worried at how you are going to live in the winter when it is cold and snowing...

~

Olga had finished a long day of working at the farm collective and was trudging up the final dirt path to her family's mud-brick home. She was tired and distracted, but she came to an immediate and attentive alert when she realized the Soviet police were there. Somehow, she knew they were waiting for her.

Run? Where was there to go?

Besides, her mother must be frightened, and she couldn't leave knowing her mother might be facing a punishment for her sake. Danyk had warned her. For herself, she was quite certain of her decision, but she had not really thought of consequences for her family. If there were going to be repercussions to someone, it had to be to her and no one else.

It also might be nothing. At least that was what she prayed for as she took the final steps and entered her home.

The Soviet policeman sat comfortably in their one chair while her mother stood erect nearby. She looked disturbed but not terrified, which was a good sign.

"Good afternoon."

"Good afternoon. Olga Shevchuk?"

Olga nodded, acknowledging the identification. "Your papers, please."

Olga went to get them followed by her mother, eager to assist.

"Are you Olga Shevchuk, engaged to Danyk Szafranski, the American?"

She nodded affirmatively again.

"Excuse me?" The officer was indicating she should speak. "Yes," she answered timidly, "I am."

A second police officer now entered the room, and all eyes turned toward him briefly. It was difficult to miss his intimidating posture.

The first officer regained everyone's attention. "Do you understand that you are marrying an American and such an act will not be seen favorably by your government? Why would you want to marry an American?" The officer spit out the word American as though it were a disease.

"Because... because I love him." She was defensive and sounded somewhat like a defiant child. It wasn't how she had meant to sound. She wanted to be collected and poised so she tried again. "He hasn't done anything wrong. He was in the Soviet army and was a good soldier. He works hard at his job on the collective. There is never any trouble with him..."

The first officer interrupted..."He just got out of prison for disrespectful and treasonous behavior... tearing down pictures of Lenin and Stalin. This is the kind of man you wish to marry?"

"I'm marrying a good man! He didn't do any of that, why would he want to do that and call attention to himself? It was someone else and they allowed him to take the blame for it."

The first officer finally stood up and approached her. Without any hesitation, he slapped her across the face. Olga was stunned for a moment, but realized she shouldn't be. She took a long step backward and shielded her cheek from another blow.

"If you marry an American, you are a fool! You'll pay a great price. Think before you act and don't act impulsively like a child." The officer waited to see if she would respond.

Olga thought many things, but she didn't dare say any of them out loud. She simply returned the officer's stare, and after a few minutes she began to look at the dirt floor to help herself hold her tongue.

Finally, the officer marched out. Olga took a huge sigh of relief because she realized this could have been much worse. Her mother, however, did not see it that way.

"Maybe you need to think this through again, maybe...?" Olga did not mean to be disrespectful, and she knew that her mother had just been frightened. In fact, so had she, but she had already made up her mind. If neither Danyk, nor the Soviet officer had been unable to change her mind, neither would her mother.

"Tomorrow." Olga declared.

"What about tomorrow?"

"I'm meeting Danyk at the church. We are getting married."

In all ways, Olga was a sweet, loving, obedient daughter but she was young and in love... in some things she could be very stubborn. This was one of them. So, what was Olga's mother to do? She followed her to the church early the next morning.

Danyk, too, was there with his mother and grandmother. After their vows were spoken Danyk and Olga each went to finish their day's work. There was no real celebration to speak of other than a small family gathering at day's end.

Olga wore the special dress she had made anticipating the day and even carried a bouquet of flowers that her mother had picked that morning. She and Danyk were happy. This simplicity was all she had expected and all either had ever known. That night they went back to Mariya's mud-brick house and spent the night, all four of them, Danyk, Olga, Mariya and Danyk's grandmother.

The next morning and over the many days that followed, Danyk used all of his spare time and any of the money that Sam sent him to build their own house, which was in view of Mariya's.

Actually, it was more like a primitive compound... a hut for the animals that stored cutting utensils with a butcher's table and a cottage for the kitchen and oven which was separated by yards of open space from the main house where the family would sleep.

Even in winter it would be necessary to walk outside to use the outhouse or get water from the well as the house had no electricity or plumbing.

For Danyk, it was a palace. It was his own, and it would leave his family less vulnerable to the drafts and leaks caused by nature. And it had windows that let the sunlight in. His mother's house had only cut-outs, leaving the interior dark and damp even on hot summer days.

He was proud of his construction, though tired but so very grateful to his father in America for sending the money needed to make it possible.

~

It was just before dusk, and Danyk was up on a partially completed rooftop using the last bit of sunlight, when he noticed a lone hunched figure approaching. Instinctively, he knew to pay extra attention. The man's steps were familiar, but his bearded face was not, and he could not quickly determine if the man was friend or foe.

So, he watched, somewhat concealed by the thatching he was placing and studied the figure who had now taken solid footing. Slowly he circled his head in all directions, and for a frightful moment Danyk thought the figure was planning something devious. A thief perhaps, but then the man did something odd. He kneeled on the ground and kissed the dirt. The man's shoulders began to shake and Danyk had a surge of pity for him. Could he be lost, friendless, hungry?

What would cause a man to stop and carry on so, surrounded by strangers and unfamiliar houses, for certainly he'd never seen such a man before. Or had he?

It didn't matter. The man didn't seem to be leaving or getting up from the crumbled mess of old rags that he'd become on the dirt floor. Danyk realized he'd either need to offer help to a defenseless old man or prepare to protect his family from a mad one. So, he began a quiet descent down his crude ladder, still watching the man for a clue as to his disposition and intent.

When he was secure on the ground, he grabbed a pitchfork in his left hand before heading down the slight incline towards the man. Then, he called out, "Hey, are you alright?"

The stranger's head, a mass of gray hair, looked up and then his eyes aimed directly at Danyk's. They were piercing, scorching eyes and Danyk didn't dare look away.

They both needed a few minutes to recognize the other, for time had changed Danyk into a strong young man and life had changed the other as well.

But all the things that time could not change were the same. The build, the posture, the manner...suddenly, they both recognized the other and each had a sense of disbelief.

Without delay... Danyk took him to his mother.

She was sitting in the dark as she often did in the late afternoon. First, Danyk walked in and then the man. Danyk was not sure how his mother would handle his arrival, so he gently stepped aside and gave her a moment to adjust. She was much quicker to recognize who the man was than Danyk had been, and suddenly she drew in a huge mass of air at her own surprise followed by a large spreading of her arms to welcome him. Instantly, he was in her arms, cooing, "Mariya, Mariya".

"Uncle Mykhailo is home!" The whispered words were not needed... but it was a joyous thing to announce, nonetheless.

On February 25, 1956, Khrushchev denounced Stalin's rule. He also pointed a finger at Stalin's closest associates charging that many of their actions had been crimes against the general Soviet population.

These were bold and unexpected statements for a generation who had lived under rigid governmental authority, although they assumed the charges to be true. They simply had not expected anyone, certainly anyone in a high government office and an authority of the state, to announce or admit such a thing in public. Many had thought they would never live to see such a day and considered it with mixed relief and suspicion.

This changing of the guard was a blessing to Danyk and his family, first seeing the early release of his mother and then, later the temporary release of his Uncle Mykhailo from the gulag. De-Stalin-ization ultimately was responsible for amnesty and release of seven million prisoners from forced labor camps and various other relaxed restrictions. But still the Soviet Union was a communist state limiting private freedoms.

This was the Soviet Union that Danyk's three oldest children would remember.

Children were required to attend school seven days a week and exposed to regular and repeated Soviet propaganda. Authority and discipline were harsh and unbending. Dress and attitudes were stiff with austere educators who didn't dare break a rule themselves. Religious observation was greatly frowned upon, and church attendance was even recorded and tallied for review by authorities.

Big brother was always watching, and one was never sure just when one was stepping over the line and about to be called on by authorities. If one was accused, one would be punished; there was no real way to fight a charge. An excuse or defense was never even thought to be offered because of the mental upbringing of generations who had had their minds controlled and their wills nullified.

Khrushchev's verification was validating but for all intents and purposes, though it caused political upheaval, it created little economic or social change.

In all the years of Uncle Mykhailo's imprisonment, he had never learned of his own mother's fate, nor had anyone else in his family. Sometimes in his prayers, God had let him speak to her and, so he would think, surely, she had died and was now an angel watching over him, providing the only comfort he knew, talking to him, soothing him, expressing her pride in his bravery and courage. It helped Mykhailo go on to know she was at peace and not suffering.

The pill that was meant to end his life... apparently... did not!

It had come back up as dryly as it had gone down, which he had taken as a sign from his mother... from God...from fate- that it was not yet time to give up. Maybe it was never time to give up. Not for a man like him.

For his nephew, Danyk, his uncle's sudden unexpected arrival was a sign as well, and it rekindled his hopes and dreams that had simmered down a bit in the course of day-to-day life: starting a family of his own, raising children and struggling to put bread on the table each day.

Hope should never die! He had seen too much living evidence to deny that.

By 1969 Danyk and Olga had completed their family with the birth of a son named Bogdan. Earlier they had also had two daughters, Maria and Oksana, and another son named Mykhailo.

Having no other choices, Danyk had adjusted to his life as an American citizen living in the Soviet Union during the Cold War. Olga, who had chosen a life married to an American citizen, did as well.

Danyk's children were an oddity to this generation of Soviets, who considered themselves citizens of a world power, but lived an otherwise backward existence without much hope or expectation for improvement.

They co-existed, accepting that there were few consumer goods or new houses or the new modern conveniences that were now being marketed in more modernized nations, and at once, not accepting it, questioning it... but always and only in the privacy of their own home around the family dinner table.

While Danyk and Olga Szafranski's children would do what was rotely required of all other Soviets, their thinking was carefully guided by their father who was steadfast in his loyalty to America... and his dream that still persisted of someday going there.

It would be best put to say they had a rebellious nature, particularly their youngest, Bogdan, who due to his age, experienced the least effect of the Stalin years and its terror. Still, to an enormous extent his daily life was regimented by rigid Soviet standards.

Danyk had made certain his children's bedtime stories were much like those that his mother had told and retold him about America throughout the war. They contradicted everything the

Soviet propaganda tried to instill. Danyk was adamant that his children would not grow up to be Communists. They would know another way of life existed... a better way of life... and know that they too were American citizens, regardless of how much the Kremlin refused to recognize it.

They were equipped differently, ready to challenge and express themselves. At this time, in the Soviet Union, conformity was the expected rule in public as well as private life. Living and balancing on the divisor of two such different mindsets was not easy to say the least. Often, they needed to show great restraint and while they felt enormously blessed, they equally at times, felt tremendously burdened.

Bogdan, like other Soviet children typically began his school day with a morning drill:

Teacher: Who gives you the stars?
   Students: Stalin.
   Teacher: Who gives you bread?
   Students: Stalin.
   Teacher: Who gives you the day?
   Students: Stalin.

Then, he went home to his American father, who had been denied all these things... by that very same man when he was only a boy like himself.

And he began to have his own dreams......after all, he was an American, too.

Chapter 30

Many changes

S am hated everything about the hospital. The smell, the white walls, the metal furniture, the way the nurses ordered him about and told him he could have this but not that, and the way they told him he could see Tessie at these times but not at those.

However, he came every day, not missing one, and did whatever he could while he was there to make Tessie just a bit more comfortable. He thought every day that today would be the day they would tell him to take Tessie home and was most surprised when it did not work out that way.

On one particular day, he arrived as usual to find that Tessie was not in her room. They had taken her to a larger room crowded with other severely ill patients, many nurses and more of the wires and life-saving gadgets that tended to make him very nervous. It seemed they were on the look-out for him, and as soon as he arrived a young doctor called him over and began to explain to him all the things he did not want to hear.

When he went to Tessie's side, he acted the usual way and said all the usual things, but then realizing this might be his last opportunity, he sat especially close beside her. He took her hand and kissed it gently. She was very weak but still recognized the oddity of his behavior. And then she chose just to appreciate it. She gazed at him lovingly, too weak to make the effort to talk.

"I have always loved you, Tessie." He knew that she would be surprised by this. "It has not been easy, not for me... but not for you, too and I thank you, with all my heart, I thank you. You have been my best friend."

Tessie's eyes shut, thanking him for his loving words. She knew they were from his heart and in all their years together, she had not expected much more than this.

It took all of her effort, but she was determined to give her final farewell, too. She opened her eyes just long enough to say, "I love you too." Then, she drifted off for a long sleep.

Sam was allowed to stay by her side long after visiting hours were over. When they finally came to declare that she had passed away, he thanked the doctors, grabbed his hat and walked out of the hospital. He found his car and drove home, once forgetting to stop at a red light. It was 1970 and once again... Sam was alone.

In 1972, the Soviet Union began permitting controlled foreign visitation. Danyk was able to meet with Sam's dear friend, Walter Romanuk and his wife, Anna. They were in the Soviet Union to visit relatives who lived in Gorodnitsa.

It was a sign that times were changing. Of course, it was not permitted for the Romanuks to come to Danyk's village, but he was permitted to meet them in their hotel in Ternopil.

Twenty years before, this meeting would have been considered treasonous.

How wonderful it was to meet and talk with someone who knew his father and had seen him recently! He learned that his father was well and no longer living in Syosset but in New Paltz, New York.

Danyk felt filled with hope again that perhaps the Soviet Union had changed enough for another attempt. He begged Walter to convince his father to try again to bring him and his family to America. Walter assured him he would.

He waited and waited... and waited. But the letters that arrived from his father never mentioned a new attempt. He was disappointed, but it was just one more disappointment that blended in with a multitude of others that had filled his life.

Three years later, he decided to take the matter into his own hands.

"What are you doing?" Olga asked. Danyk had been sitting in a wooden chair staring off into space, when suddenly he jumped up and began to search through their papers and documents.

"I'm going to try again. I'm going to go to the local government office!"

"Try again for what?" She had no idea what he had just been thinking or talking about.

"I'm going to try to go to America!" They never discussed anything, as he left immediately, securing the door behind him.

His strides were wide as he tried to keep his momentum going. He walked into the local government office with his papers in his hand. He was feeling very brave.

For my wife and children, he thought. It was not really as impulsive a move as it may have seemed to Olga. He never really let the dream die. Deep inside him, he had never stopped believing that he would one day get to America. Walter's visit had stirred the desires and dreams now pushing him into action.

"Next..." the clerk called out to those waiting in line and Danyk came forward clutching a piece of paper.

"Yes?"

" I ...I was born in the United States. I... I am an American citizen. Here." He handed over his birth certificate issued from Manhattan, New York."

The clerk whispered something to another clerk who disappeared to the back offices. "One moment... stay right here."

The clerk placed the birth certificate on the counter but kept her hand over it so he could not retrieve it. After a minute, the clerk glanced over his shoulder and Danyk realized they were all waiting for someone. He had no idea who would ultimately appear, and it made his palms and forehead sweat. His heart picked up speed and suddenly he was fourteen-years old again waiting to be interrogated.

No, no! He focused on shutting everything out of his mind. He would not let the old fear return. He was a man! He had a family! He had to be brave!

Finally, a hard-faced man appeared. "You are the man claiming to be an American citizen?"

"Yes."

The man looked down at the counter and eyed the birth certificate that was still under the protective scrutiny of the clerk.

"Go home!"

That was all the man had to say. He offered no explanation and Danyk realized there was going to be no negotiating, not here and certainly not today.

Danyk reached for the birth certificate, surprising the clerk, but so did the man. Danyk had not taken a full grasp of it yet when the man forcefully ripped it from his hands.

Desperately, Danyk lunged to retrieve it, but the counter was in his way and then the man was quickly retreating back into the office from which he had come.

There was a stunning moment when Danyk didn't know what to do. He couldn't leave without the one piece of proof he had that identified him as an American citizen. But it had disappeared with the man. Just like that.

What had he done?

What had he done to his family? What would the consequences be?

Many weeks went by when all he could do was wait and worry. A suspicious sound, an unexpected knock could mean the authorities had finally decided to come for him. An even greater worry was that they would come for his family. For someone who had lived through all this before, these were very real concerns.

For all that the Soviet Union had changed since his youth, had it really changed at all? What else was there left to do?

~

Eventually, Sam took another wife.

It might have seemed to be a calculating move on his part, for he did indeed reason...I have been fortunate in at least one thing in life... my wives!

However, it was more a reflex, a tradition of his past, to provide and be needed. Mariya had been the love of his life, his Tessie, a good friend and tremendous comfort!

Vyktoria Henchuk, a practical woman, would find her own niche he was sure, and he, a practical, simple man, especially at this point in his life, had practical and simple expectations.

One evening, Sam sat at his desk and prepared to write Danyk a letter as he had many times before. He wanted to update him on his good friend, Walter Romanuk and his wife, who had gone to the Soviet Union and met up with Danyk in Ternopil for a visit.

Nearby was his wife, Vyktoria. "Are you going to tell him?"

"Of course... about Walter?" Sam pretended he hadn't known what she meant. "No... about us. He doesn't know yet that you have taken a wife?"

No! He doesn't know about you...or even Tessie, my first wife... and by the grace of God, I intend to keep it that way!

Sam was somewhat ready for the question and prepared to defend his position. "What sense would that make? He'll tell Mariya... and that would only hurt her. It is best if no one there knows."

"You don't think that is a little disrespectful to me? You have a family, and they don't even know I exist?"

"Why do you worry?" He tried to patronize her and make her feel silly for having such thoughts even occur to her. "We are worlds apart... a distance I couldn't overcome, though I tried for years and years." Sam didn't understand why Vyktoria couldn't be more like the way Tessie or his Mariya had been. They had always understood and never questioned him the way Vyktoria did. Those relationships had been different. This one was more, well ... aggravating.

At times Vyktoria grated on his nerves, but perhaps he was now just growing older and crankier as well.

"Things have changed, Sam. If Walter can go to the Soviet Union, then your family can make their way to our front door. What happens to me if they do?"

Always he had to reassure Vyktoria. It was tiring. "Don't you understand... that is a dream I have long ago given up on! Do you think, all of a sudden, poof... they will be permitted to leave? Walter could not even go to my family's village. It is off-limits to foreigners."

"But things change. Before, foreign visitors would never even have been a consideration... now, Americans can visit the Soviet Union. Next, they will be letting Soviet citizens visit America. You never know!"

"I only hope that is true." He looked at Vyktoria like she should be ashamed of herself, if she hoped for anything different.

But then he felt badly, remembering what an odd predicament his wife was in. Of course, her sense of security was threatened and he softened.

"I wish you could understand... I love my family. That I can not change for you, but... it has been a long time. I don't think that we are of the same worlds any more. We are all different people. I do what I can for them, I would not be a man if I didn't, but... my life has gone on. Should I be ashamed of that? Perhaps, but one day I will stand before God, and I will give my defense, and then... I will be judged. What more can I do?"

Sam wanted to say the right things. He wanted to say what

Vyktoria wanted to hear. He didn't want to live a life with her where she was always fearful of what might unexpectedly tear him away. He had lived with much uncertainty for many years of his life, and he knew how it wore away at one's reserves. To reassure her, he was admitting things to her that perhaps he had never before even admitted to himself.

The mid 1960's to the early 1980's was considered the Brezhnev era and the Soviet Union had tremendous economic growth during this time of unfamiliar calm and stability. The Soviet Union became the largest producer of oil and steel, began to produce large quantities of manufactured goods and constructed millions of very needed and sought after one-family apartments. Soviet consumers began to want and expect more, an aspect that was to later work against a nation trying to maintain itself. Things were changing, but still Soviet citizens were never quite sure which way was safest to sway. They just knew they were in a slightly better position than the generation before.

In 1981, at age 77, Mariya Szafranski died.

Danyk and Olga had taken care to give her a proper Ukrainian burial. In their home, the one they had built with the money sent from Danyk's father, they had laid her out in the spare bedroom set aside only for this purpose. For three days, family and friends came to view and show their respect.

Danyk knew that finally his mother was at rest, and he imagined that her spirit was now somewhere over America... looking down on his father. It was a peaceful thought, and it gave him great comfort. Until her last breath, she had hoped to return to America and be reunited with her husband.

Then, she was buried on the hill near her own mother who had passed away a few years before and the baby girl she had lost before leaving for America and having Danyk.

The day after, Danyk wrote his father a letter to let him know his Mariya now rested in eternal peace.

Soon after ... his father's letters stopped coming.

Danyk had decided to take his family to church in his mother's honor. The family prepared amongst all the chaos that is normal for a large family of four children, spanning the ages twenty-two to twelve, trying to feed, wash, dress and depart them all at the same time.

It had been a long time since he had visited a church, but this was a very special occasion. He had felt it would offer him comfort, and it was simply a decent thing to do. For many years it had been a restricted activity, but there seemed to be an easing of rules, and he thought he might try, since his purpose was so appropriate.

He herded his family down the path keeping everyone together, hoping to keep the youngest, Bogdan, somewhat clean as well, so they would make a proper presentation. He didn't know who else he might find there.

Up the stairs they went following Olga, who carried their first grandchild. She shushed them each as they passed her on their way in, and told them they should quiet down, which of course, being raised to be obedient and respectful, they did right away. Danyk lagged behind, keeping the group in order.

Danyk was the last to enter. He couldn't help but notice a young woman standing erect at the base of the stairs, making no motion to come in. He recognized her as a teacher at the local school but did not know her name.

It looked peculiar to see her holding a notebook and pencil, and she seemed to be taking notes. He reversed himself and quietly backed down the stairs, unnoticed by the woman who seemed intent on her note taking. There on the pad was his name and that of all his family members. Other names were there too, but his was the one that caught his attention.

He did not ask the young woman about the notepad or why she was taking notes. That he already knew. What he did not know was what the consequence of being a name on the notepad would be.

He knew she would be submitting the list to the authorities. Just because he was now permitted to go to church...did not mean the authorities would be happy that he and his family actually chose to go.

There was not much to do about it... there never was, but his children's names were on the list, and for a moment he stood pensively considering possibilities.

"May I hold the door for you?" Danyk startled the young woman as he was somewhat close, and he had said it rather loudly. He supposed she realized he was irritated, but she couldn't have cared less.

"No."

"Excuse me?" Danyk questioned innocently.

"No, I said."

"You won't join my family and me to pray? We've come, as the state permits, to pray for my mother? She recently passed away."

"No...no, I said, no... thank you!"

He was satisfied now that he had gotten her to thank him for bothering her and winked a victory at her.

"Then... we shall just have to pray... *for* you." It was either an offering or an accusation. "Don't worry... I will remember you." This time it was a promise.

The authorities chose not to disturb Danyk and his family perhaps because their hands were filled with other matters and concerns.

By the early 1980s the economy was stagnating. The population was demanding greater quantities of consumer goods, but they were producing less. This new generation of Soviets was growing dissatisfied with the government's sluggish response to change, supply shortages and a malfunctioning reward system for productivity.

Danyk's family encountered both joy and tragedy during this time.

Paraskenia, Sam's youngest sister, who had been just twelve years old when she and Sam's mother had been arrested, had given birth to a son.

Other than Danyk's own children and first grandchild, there had not been many other births to the family since the war. There was good reason for this...most of the men had relocated out of the Soviet Union, died in the war or been taken to Siberia and never heard from again.

As for the general population, there was a limited supply of men available to father children. It was taking a generation for the population to even out and continue on.

They had heard from a fellow prisoner of Uncle Mykailo's that he had recently passed away in Siberia.

They were grateful for the time they had been able to spend with him, when for a short time, he had been temporarily released from hard labor in Siberia to return to his village.

But his pardon, unlike Mariya's, had only been temporary and he had voluntarily returned, not wishing his family to bear any consequences. To Danyk and many of the people of his village that had known of his Uncle Mkyhailo's brave and courageous acts, he was a hero.

The world should note... for history... that he and men like him dedicated their entire lives unselfishly for the good of their people against incredible odds and obstacles.

It was their great misfortune to have lived at a time when the worst were in power and the best among men were considered their greatest threats. May they find peace knowing that, of all, Stalin feared them most.

"Bogdan, Bogdan! Hurry, you've overslept!!! You're going to be late for school." Olga called urgently to her youngest son.

Seconds before, fourteen-year-old Bogdan had been sleeping soundly, curled up in his warm bed. Now he was rushing, grabbing clothes, barely having both legs in his pants before he was out the door. He hadn't even tried to wash up or look for a packed lunch. He didn't dare take the chance that it would add more minutes to his lateness, which would be considered quite an offense. He was a blur to his parents as he dashed out the door and headed down the street.

Run. Runnnnnnn, he thought with great focus and determination. He yanked open the door to the school, feeling quite torn between opening it quietly and unnoticed or furiously and possibly gaining time.

As he entered there was a pitiful quiet and he knew... it was over!

The eyes of a hundred and ten students stared him down, each hovering over him from their place on the vestibule staircase. It was how each school day began, with everyone - students, teachers and administrators - assembling in the vestibule for the ritual of questions and expected answers. The staircase was massive and led up to the second floor, as did the students who had taken their assigned place on each of its steps, as it ascended.

The silence, as all eyes fell on him, was agonizing and seemed never to end. But he still needed to close the door, so he swallowed huge lumps of saliva and dared to close the door with a squeak that echoed throughout the hollow of the school's interior.

That seemed to be the last straw for the master of the school who had already begun the morning exercises.

"You are late!" It was a despicable charge, and he knew already this was not going to go well.

"Yes, I'm very sorry..." Bogdan thought quickly for an excuse, but he already knew it would not matter.

"Where is your Star of Lenin?"

Bogdan had forgotten it in his rush. He normally wore it in the middle of his chest as was required of everyone in the school. Again, he had done a despicable act.

For other children the worry would have been that the offenses would be reported to their parents, but Bogdan knew his father's only concern about pleasing the authorities was that he shouldn't call attention to himself or put himself in danger.

Bogdan's greater concern was that the master could use it as an excuse to embarrass and humiliate him in front of the other students. Though he never told his parents, in fact would have done anything to protect them from knowing, it happened frequently.

Bogdan looked down to where the Star of Lenin should have been and realizing he was trapped, felt too tongue-tied to answer. He knew the entire school was about to witness the master humiliating him. It was not going to be avoided, so it was best to be quiet and let it happen. The sooner it began, the sooner it would be over. At least that was what he hoped.

"I suppose you think you are above wearing it? Above getting to school on time and considering the others that you inconvenience with your lateness? I suppose your American father would approve, wouldn't he? He thinks he is privileged. I suppose you do too?"

This drew a degree of laughter from certain students who enjoyed it when he was embarrassed. The master looked up to see who it was that agreed with him, so he could show his approval.

"Soviet children know how to come to school on time. They show proper respect. I don't even know if it is worth it to try to teach you! Go home! Get your Star of Lenin... then maybe, maybe we will try to give you a good Soviet education! Let your American father know how you have disgraced him and your family."

Bogdan made his way back to the door, his head still down. As he did, he passed the teacher that Danyk had seen years earlier at their church, recording his name and those of his family members for the authorities. He had since learned her name. Miss Zemba's arms were

373

crossed over her chest, and she didn't appear at all sympathetic or ready to move out of his way.

"Excuse me, please." Bogdan requested politely.

First, she snickered and then hesitated a moment more before she decided she was good and ready to let him pass.

Bogdan slowly eased his way out, and then ran all the way home while his mind raced.

He hated the humiliation and the embarrassment of each episode, and the rigid authority that it represented. But he also knew and held on to the fact that it made him and his family stronger in their beliefs. In America, things were different.

When he reached home, Olga was just leaving for her job working in the fields. "Bogdan? Are you in trouble?"

"No, no, I just forgot my Star of Lenin, so they sent me home for it. Don't worry." he soothed.

A generation before Bogdan's father had carried many secrets alone... so now, it was his turn. And each time... it made him a bit angrier at his oppressors, more sure, more strong and more ready to do whatever would be needed for his family.

Their time would come, he vowed, just as his father had always told him.

When the time came at school to choose a foreign language to master, there was no other choice to consider. Bogdan, of course, chose English!

The Soviet soldier, a mature twenty-year old, sat in front of the computer completing his work. After years of studying English, he had become quite proficient and now translated incoming English documents into Russian for his superiors. As was necessary to perform his duties, he had clearance and access to classified documents.

One day, orders arrived.

His computer was abruptly turned off and he was notified that he was no longer to have access to classified materials. Apparently, it had only now been brought to light that ... his father was an American!

Bogdan didn't know if he should laugh that it had taken this long for the security of the Soviet Army to realize something that his entire village was long aware of ...or feel angry that despite his years of study and hard work, he could be demoted on the whim of a superior.

"Do they think I am a spy?"he shared with his family when he joined them for dinner that evening. As they had many times in the past, they tried to laugh themselves through another hurtful situation.

In May 1988, the Law of the Cooperatives permitted private ownership and generated further changes, such as greater freedom of speech. The national archives were opened, and the press was free to explore and publish what was found.

It was the beginning of the end of the Soviet Union.

Danyk and his family now regularly went to church on Sundays. There was no need any longer to fear reprisals and even those who had once considered themselves the gatekeepers, keeping track and reporting the habits of other private citizens for the authorities, began to enjoy such freedoms themselves.

One Sunday, Danyk and his family arrived at church in their usual duck formation including the new in-laws and grandchildren, with whom his family had been blessed.

They filed into a row just in front of a lone lady, now well recognized by them as the teacher from the local school, who at one time had taken it upon herself to be one of the gatekeepers.

Bogdan, now a man and still a soldier in the Soviet Army, straightened himself high without a care or courtesy for his former teacher, Miss Maria Zemba, who was seated behind him. If he blocked her view, well she could just move.

Danyk took a different view of it all and was not quick to seat himself. It would not have been mannerly, he thought, not to welcome the lady who had never before seen fit to join his family and the other churchgoers at Sunday service.

Who was he to judge? And perhaps he owed her his thanks. After all, though his concern had given him great anxiety, his family had never had to deal with the authorities for their occasional church attendance.

So, he bent to the back of the pew and drew her astonished attention with the wave of his hand. And then he used his pointed finger to make sure she regarded everything he had to say.

"You see... did you think I had forgotten?" Miss Zamba glared back confused.

Perhaps, she doesn't even remember our encounter years earlier, he thought.

"I told you on the steps of the church many years ago, when you were recording the names of my family like a true communist, that I would pray for you...and now those prayers have been answered." He pulled back with a satisfied smile.

"God, though..." he added slowly to punctuate his point and then leaned forward again, "sometimes... he takes his time... no?" Danyk nodded his head as though to show his amusement... and approval at God's antics.

Then, he waited patiently for her answer with a kind, knowing smile.

She had no answer, of course, and appeared somewhat unnerved by his attention. But that was a satisfactory response... as far as Danyk was concerned. In fact, it pleased him.

What broke the silence was Bogdan's choked coughing. He was using it to cover up his own amusement at what he had overheard, but it was quite an inadequate attempt and if anything, it displayed, not hid, his utter delight at his father's boldness.

Lastly, just before taking his seat, Danyk looked her in the eye and winked. For him, it brought closure as it was a significant gesture repeated from so many years before. When he had first given it, she had held the upper hand. At that time, it was a promise. Now, it was the mark of a promise-kept.

He turned and took his place next to Bogdan. Father and son knowingly glanced at each other, causing Danyk to give his son a confirming pat on the knee.

A moment passed and then Bogdan thought to turn to the woman, as well. It was as though he faced his childhood demon, for over the years the woman had taken it upon herself to be his tormentor many times. He had never told his parents, always trying to protect them from knowing that his father's American citizenship often made him a "marked man," especially in school and among his teachers and schoolmates.

Had my father known anyway? Bogdan couldn't help but wonder.

He probably did. But at the time, there had been nothing for him to do about it.

Except, to make me strong. Except, to keep me proud.

Except, to give me an example of a real man who never gave up.

So, he waited for the woman to give in and meet his gaze. When she did, she no longer frightened him, and he gave her a wink.

Like father...like son!

The Soviet Union was struggling and by 1990 had lost control of economic conditions.

Bogdan, now discharged from the army, had married and was trying to capitalize on free enterprise with a carpentry business, but knew their days in the Soviet Union were numbered.

"Now we go!" Bogdan told his father, but he did not get the response he had expected. "How can I go? I have no birth certificate. No proof! I am almost sixty years old! I have grandchildren!"

Also, Danyk had been fooled before into thinking the times were safe enough to pursue going. So far, they had not harmed his family. But would they the next time?

It was the first time Bogdan had ever heard his father express doubt.

But the torch had been passed, and he was fired up. His father had been the one to ignite it, and he wasn't going to let his father's dreams die now, not when the Soviet Union was about to fall.

Chapter 31

Life's Irony

Bogdan, the youngest of Danyk's children, had been born in the midst of the Brezhnev era and was part of a generation that viewed the world with a different set of eyes than those born even just ten years earlier.

They had never lived under a repressive Stalin regime with sadistic purges and the intentional starvation of millions of its own people or The Great Patriotic War (World War II) and its massive destruction and family loss.

Khrushchev and his commencement of "De-Stalinization" was ancient history, and they were the generation of wage increases, increased housing and modern conveniences.

It was not a perfect world by western standards but if they grumbled in the privacy of their own homes about sluggish, inadequate change or the government's mishandled response to meet the public's growing consumer desires and needs, they were not carted off to the gulag the following day. It was no small difference, and as human nature is known to do, this generation given more, expected more. Having less to fear, they were bolder in their requests, and began to test the perimeters of a barrier long ago designed by Stalin

379

to control the masses of those who lived during his time, through manipulation, terror and some of the worst brutality that the world had ever seen.

When one is not threatened, it is easy to be brave and feel entitled. Bogdan was aware of this, so his respect for his father was no less when Danyk made him wait a few days for his final answer.

"We go. We all go!"

Danyk had decided the conditions and Bogdan readily agreed.

Every family member had to be granted permission to leave, or no one went anywhere. It was all or nothing.

This time they would not go to the local government office. It would be a total effort.

They were going to the United States Embassy in Moscow!

For the second time in Danyk's life he was boarding a train for Moscow. He tried not to compare the two experiences because in doing so, he had to recall the grueling two-week journey he'd made as a thirteen-year-old traveling alone, surviving on rations of sugar-water.

Instead, he focused on his blessings and drew strength from them... the company of his strong and capable son, the adequate food, the shortened transport which was now just a twenty-two- hour train ride... and his family, which had flourished in spite of many obstacles, waiting for him at home, regardless of how this journey should end.

Perhaps, if he and his family made it to America, his father would take as much pride in his family as he did. It was just like Danyk to think not only of himself without a father but of his father without a son. How lonely his father must have been all these years without his family. It was a painful desire of Danyk's that he would at long last be able to share his family with his father. He prayed it would be so.

When they arrived at 6AM massive lines already surrounded the embassy, which was now not in the same location as when Danyk had arrived some fifty-odd years earlier. Yet, it was still a familiar feeling to be standing on such a line, clutching the documents he hoped to use to validate his claim that he was an American citizen. It seemed the waiting would be hours and they readied themselves to wait the course.

Just like a flashback of his first experience, the people were making their way to the front of the line giving their stories, only to be turned away. He remembered his run into the embassy passed the Soviet guard, who he had been sure was going to shoot him, and the wonderful welcome he had received instead, once securely inside.

He still had the photo that had been taken to commemorate his arrival at the old American Embassy when he was thirteen-years old. Sergeant Carber, an embassy staff member, was pictured on Danyk's right and the Soviet guard that had first let him enter the embassy was on his left.

And then, he thought of Joe and Jim, who together had mothered him and given him a temporary feeling of peace at a time when his life was in utter chaos.

If he ever got to America, he would find them... and give them chocolate candy bars, perhaps! They would be so happy for him... and he could give them the thanks they both deserved. It had been such a traumatic time when he had left the embassy. He had felt such a mixture of love, gratitude and maybe even ... betrayal that they were sending him away. He knew his last goodbye had been inadequate, and it had always bothered him that he had no way to go back and make it up to them.

He hoped one day he would get the chance to ask all the questions a man would ask. As a boy, his questions had been simple, and he realized now, with greater understanding of the world, all the odds Joe and Jim had put themselves up against and how so much of what they had done for him had been out of human kindness and not official duty.

After hours of waiting, they were finally coming closer to the front of the line. Danyk prepared to run for the entrance, if it was necessary, not sure if he was reliving another moment in time or if he actually intended to do so. It had worked once, perhaps it would work again.

Besides, now the guards were not heavily armed. It would be even safer to do so; however, the obstacle would be his aged frame. Reluctantly, he admitted to himself, it wouldn't move as quickly as it had back then.

"Look." Bogdan nudged him to look at a nearby notice. It read, "Those born in the United States of America should call ......" followed by a phone number. They thought twice about getting off the line to make the phone call until they heard a voice over the loudspeaker announcing it as well. The voice's instructions were to go to a certain place and call a certain phone number.

"Thank you." Danyk whispered his prayer to the heavens, thanking a God who had tested him his whole life but had never deserted him.

They left the line and called the number that they had been given. "A woman says to go to the front of the line." Danyk told his son. Could it be that easy?

"Just the front of the line?" Bogdan asked, confused.

"That's right."

So, they both went. Immediately, they were brought into the new Embassy, so different from the one Danyk had remembered and stayed in years earlier.

Staff in the embassy brought Bogdan and Danyk to a room and proceeded to ask Danyk a list of questions. He didn't have his birth certificate, but they seemed unconcerned, and continued with the questions they needed answered, to confirm his identity.

It seemed almost too easy to be true but by the end of the day, the embassy's consul had confirmed his citizenship.

"Would his wife be given citizenship?"

"Yes."

"And his children?"

"Yes."

"But... his grandchildren... would they...?"

"Yes."

Bogdan and Danyk looked at each other incredulously. Could it be? Not only was he a recognized American citizen but so were his children... and grandchildren. Everyone was covered. Everyone was going!

Danyk closed his eyes and took in the miraculous moment. I am going to see my father... finally!

Sam would be about 88 years old.

"What do I do next?"

"Go home and wait. We will send a copy of your birth certificate and travel documents."

"No! I will come back for them. I want them in my hand. What about my wife and my children?"

"They will take a little longer, but it shouldn't be a problem."

Before he left, feeling the euphoric effects of his dreams about to come true, he turned to the staff member and asked shyly... "Do you know the Americans, Joe Malaznik or Jim Mahoney? I would like to tell them I am going to America?"

"I'm sorry, I don't know them. How do you know them?" the official asked curiously.

"Many years ago, many years ago..."

Danyk mentally reminisced and for a moment was lost. "From when I first stayed in the embassy as a child. Do you know how I could find them?"

"I'm sorry, I don't. I only know they don't work for the embassy now. That would have been quite a long time ago."

Danyk nodded in agreement, feeling even a bit foolish to ask about them now, so many years later. But it had been something he had to do.

Well, that was a matter for another time perhaps. First things, first.

Danyk could have left immediately for the United States, once he returned with official documents from Moscow, after another twenty-two-hour train ride back home again... but he wasn't going to go alone.

The plan had been that everyone was going, or no one was going.

"I always knew I was going to America to see my father!" Danyk repeated many times to his family members. He sent off letters to his father to prepare him, but he had not yet received any response.

When documents for Olga were ready, Bogdan urged his father and mother to go on ahead. That way they could prepare the way. There was much that would have to be addressed and figured out by Bogdan.

Would his father and mother receive their retirement benefits? Danyk and Olga had worked long and hard for the state doing the lowliest of jobs. Shouldn't they be entitled? What would his father live on as he aged if there were no benefits?

What would they do with the house? For a short time Danyk's daughter and granddaughter would live there, but who then would take over the house and care for the livestock after they left to join him in the United States?

There were many other details that had to be worked out and the more thought they were given, the longer the list became.

Danyk could not help feeling anxious about leaving despite his tremendous desire to go. Though he could speak Ukrainian, Russian, Polish, and some German, he could remember only a little of the English that Joe had patiently taught him years before. Bogdan would need to brush him up a bit, at least enough to navigate the airport.

And another worry...how would he make a living?

Also...how long would it be before the rest of his family would join him? His early traumas had left him very protective of his family and feeling vulnerable to be parted from them. Always he liked to keep them close. And still another...and this would be a considerable one...*why hadn't his father written back?*

Never in his lifetime had he had the luxury to allow his anxieties to dominate him, so as before and always, he forged on. The arrangements were made, and he prepared for the fact that his arrival would be a surprise for his father. Perhaps, he thought, it was the mail system and the authorities, once again, preventing full communication with his father.

They still didn't want him to go to America... and they weren't going to let go easily.

~

On April 10, 1992, Danyk and Olga boarded the plane bound for the United States of America and decided not to look back.

Other than hoping his family would join him as soon as possible, Danyk felt no regrets leaving. In all these years, he had never bonded with the Soviet Union, nor had he let his children.

His mother had taught him early that there was a place called America and she had been there, lived there. It was real and gave its citizens rights and freedoms, and an opportunity to live their everyday life without fear of governmental brutality.

It was such a wonderful place that no matter what had been done to him, he never gave up his citizenship or thought to dishonor America in any way, even when it meant he would suffer for it greatly, and perhaps never even get to see it.

Even if he couldn't touch or see it ever, it was no less a part of him.

Danyk wanted his children to love it too and had used nearly every fathering moment to make it a fabric of their being.

His intense feeling had always left his children suspicious of Soviet authority and too, resentful of the tremendous tragedies and hurt that had befallen their family by the purposeful intent of those in charge.

At least, Danyk had always felt, his children would know another way existed.

He had given them special eyes from which to see the world and he knew it was an advantage... or perhaps even, at times...a burden, not shared with or understood by their peers.

Still, he felt it was the greatest gift he, a simple farm laborer, could ever have given them. It was his legacy to them, and he had taught them well, as his mother had taught him, to cherish it above all else.

And now they were going to this blessed place; they were going to America and soon *he would be with his father!*

~

Danyk clutched his passport in one hand and Olga in the other.

"Well..." he admitted to Olga. "I don't know what is happening... but I'm here! As long as I have my passport, I'm OK. "

They had expected to be met by someone from the Social Service Department... but they looked and waited... and waited...and waited...and it appeared no one was going to show up for them.

What to do now?

They didn't know the language or even how to go claim their luggage as they couldn't read any of the signs. In fact, it was the first time he or Olga had ever flown or been at an airport.

Danyk found a comfortable spot for Olga, who had grown very tired from the long flight, and told her not to move. He wandered for hours, occasionally checking back with Olga to let her know he hadn't forgotten her. Each time he could see her nervousness growing and admittedly, so was his.

He tried to start a conversation with anyone who looked responsive or kind, but no one could communicate with him due to the language barrier. He hoped to find someone who spoke Russian, Ukrainian or German but it seemed everyone was speaking English or some other language he didn't recognize.

Suddenly, a limousine driver holding a sign with a Ukrainian name appeared before him.

Danyk dashed for the man, almost startling him. "Oh, are you waiting for me?" Danyk was already feeling relieved. If nothing else this man spoke a language he understood. He hoped.

"I am looking for ..." The man gave a family name, which was obviously not Danyk's.

But... the man spoke Ukrainian.

"That's not me." Danyk sadly acknowledged. "But you are the only one here that I can talk to, so no matter what, I'm not leaving you. My wife and I have been here for six hours, and we need a place to sleep...you have to help me."

The driver agreed to take Danyk wherever he needed to go, especially since the people he had expected to meet had never shown up.

However, when he heard New Paltz, where Danyk believed his father now resided, he said that was too far. Was there somewhere else he could drop them off?

Danyk thought furiously and remembered he had taken Walter Romanuk's phone number with him. He showed it to the driver and asked for his help in dialing the phone.

He thought that he might need to remind Walter that he had met him twenty years earlier in Ternopil when he was there visiting relatives.

"I'm Szymon Szafransky's son, Danyk..."

But that was all that Walter needed to hear, he gave Danyk a warm Ukrainian greeting.

Then, Danyk explained that he was in the United States, finally here ...and here for good!

Walter, being a very old family friend and aware of all the struggles to get Danyk to America since boyhood, could not have been happier.

"And... and...I am at the airport here, but no one has come for us and... and we have no place to stay."

For a split second Danyk worried. His nerves and tiredness were getting the better of him. The silence on the other end of the phone was not helping to calm his fears. But then, Walter recovered from the surprise.

"Then you will come stay with us." Walter offered genuinely. "Is it you and Olga?"

"Yes... we, we thank you very much, Walter."

"Can you get a car, a taxi?"

"Yes, we have a driver here. He was not meant for us, but his people never showed up. He says he can drive us... but not so far as New Paltz, to my father." Walter was hesitant again, and there was another moment of silence.

"Yes, well... Let me speak to the driver, I will give him directions. Don't worry, we live in Syosset, we are not so far away."

With that assurance, Danyk's tense shoulders eased, and he felt enormous gratitude toward Walter.

Not only had he and Olga found a place to stay, but Walter would know how to contact his father.

Now, he could take pleasure in finally arriving in America!

They arrived just before midnight with all of their luggage in tow, but Walter was a gracious host, and he and his wife welcomed them warmly.

"Danyk... Olga. Remember my wife, Anna."

Danyk used a combination of English and Ukrainian to express his thanks, over and over again, until Walter would hear no more of it.

Walter, having lived in the Ukraine during his early life and still having relatives there, was able to communicate with Danyk fairly well.

Danyk had already explained how they came to be in their present predicament, so the next thing to be discussed was fairly obvious.

Danyk grew excited, preparing to hear an update on his father, but Walter was preoccupied with paying the driver and sending him on his way. "How much?" Walter asked the driver and then took out his own wallet to pay him.

"No, no..." Danyk rushed forward trying to refuse Walter's generosity. He held out a wad of bills, American dollars that he planned to use for his expenses. But Walter insisted, concerned that

Danyk shouldn't use up what he'd managed to save to make the trip just getting out of the airport.

Danyk at this point had no reserve to fight his hospitality. He was tired, hungry and recovering from being quite overwhelmed. He knew he would make it up to this generous man at another appropriate point in time.

Much of their luggage was left in the front hallway, too big to move at this hour. Walter and Anna showed them down a hallway to a guest room and showed them where they could put their smaller suitcases which they would need for the overnight.

Olga and Danyk couldn't help but notice the fine furnishings and thought that maybe Walter was a wealthy man... but for sure he was a good man to be so gracious and accommodating to them at such a late hour. He would be sure to tell his father what a good friend he had, and he knew it reflected his father's good character as well, to have chosen such a friend.

"You are both exhausted. Let's all get a good night's sleep and in the morning... we can talk."

There was so much to ask and discuss, but Walter had been correct. Danyk and Olga were beyond exhaustion, so everyone was happy to turn in.

The next morning, Danyk and Olga slept in. Their internal clocks needed to adjust, and they were still recovering from the anxiety of the day before. When they got up, the Romanuk's were waiting for them and had an elaborate brunch ready to be warmed up and served. They were the perfect hosts, and Danyk realized that a better first meal in the United States of America could not have been had.

Danyk didn't want to take advantage of their hospitality for too long, so after breakfast he asked Walter if they could please call his father. He was more than anxious; in fact, he could hardly control his excitement now that he was well rested.

When Danyk brought up his father, Walter grew silent and looked down.

"Danyk, Sam... your father passed away about ten months ago, on May 30th. I'm so very sorry."

The room started spinning and the words repeated themselves over and over again in his head. Did he understand correctly? His father was...dead?

It could not be. He was finally in America! His father had to be alive.

Danyk was stunned into silence and after Olga absorbed the news as well, she moved to his side to comfort him.

He spent the rest of the morning just going through the motions. His father had died just ten months before his arrival.

I am too late! Danyk thought with exasperation at life's many trials.

"Where is he buried?"

"In New Paltz, New York. He lived there with..." Walter stopped abruptly. "He lived there these last few years."

"My poor father...he never got to see me." Danyk felt for his father, not only because he had died but because he knew with all his heart, that their seeing each other again was as much a dream of his father's as it was his own.

"He... you should know... he had a wife. His wife Vyktoria still lives in the house they had together."

For some reason, Danyk had never even considered that his father would remarry. He had always been a stationary figure in a locked place that grounded his world. He had never really thought of his father in a dimensional way. This gave him more with which he must deal and come to terms with.

"He..." Walter felt it was best that he learned it all now, got it over with. "He had another wife as well. She died a few years back. Her name was Tessie." Walter noted the slump of Danyk's shoulder and felt the full measure of being the messenger of bad news.

390

Have I told him too much? Walter felt uncertainty and began to doubt his judgment at revealing everything at once.

"Ohhh...". Little to say, much to think about.

And then Danyk remembered, at times, packages his father sent enclosed greetings from someone named Tessie, but his father had never said that Tessie was his wife. He had assumed it was a good friend. Perhaps he had been in denial.

After a long pause it occurred to Danyk to ask, "Did he have any children?" He was numb already. It didn't matter what the answer would be, or did it?

"No... your father never had any other children, just you." "Oh."

He had never thought of America without his father.

What now? As Danyk had always done throughout his life, he put one foot in front of the other and went on.

Just three days later, back in what was still the Soviet Union (it would become the Russian Federation in December 1991), Danyk's family gathered at a Moscow airport. They were not there to give a farewell as they had to Danyk and Olga, leaving for America three days before, but to welcome back a family member.

Uncle Marion was returning to his village of Gorodnitsa to live out his old age with the wife and the daughter that he had been forced to leave behind when the war broke out.

For Danyk and his uncle, it would have been a monumental reunion. Other than Danyk; his father's sister, Aunt Paraskenia; his uncle's wife, Aunt Anastasia; and his uncle's daughter, Anna; no other family member had ever even met him before. To his daughter, he was only a vague memory as she had only been three years old when he'd left for war.

Marion had waited many years to let his family know that he had lived, due to Stalin's insistence that any Soviet soldier who had survived the war but been in contact with western influences be executed. At the end of The Great Patriotic War (World War II), Stalin had even sought them out, demanding that other nations repatriate them, so they could be eliminated, though he did not punctuate that last point.

Like many other Soviet soldiers who were lucky enough to learn in time that they must not return home, he had made a life for himself elsewhere without his loved ones or even contact with those still living in the Soviet Union.

His uncle had been more fortunate than others, having enough relatives outside the Soviet Union to act as go-betweens. While those in the Soviet Union could not be told of his survival for their own safety and his as well, his brother in France had been able to give him updates on his family from his own communications.

Marion had long before immigrated to Canada, which seemed far safer than staying with his brother in France. He had never remarried, nor had his wife. So, to learn so late in life that his wife and daughter both waited for him back in the old country and desired his return was quite a revelation and spiritual rejuvenation.

Now in his old age, he was returning home a retired Canadian. He wanted to die in the bosom of the family he had left unwillingly, so many years before. Perhaps they could have been bitter and held it against him that he had left and not returned until now... but they had never indicated that to him in any correspondence since learning of his existence.

Marion wondered how he would look to his wife. When last he'd seen her, he had been a big strapping young man preparing to go to war, to protect his country and his family. As a middle-aged man he had managed to recover some of the earlier vigor he had lost during the war, but now he was over seventy. He was wilted and wrinkled. He allowed himself to admit his greatest fear. *Might Anastasia reject me?*

It was all he could think about as he approached the observers, all waiting to spot their own friends and relatives departing the plane. He searched the crowd of faces, realizing that his wife's face would have changed over the years. But he had no trouble finding her. Hers was the most elated in the crowd, and it touched his heart. They zeroed in right for each other.

Before Marion was introduced to his daughter, he held his wife in a long-cherished embrace that offered the comfort and closure for which he had long hoped.

"Forgive me?" he softly begged.

We were all lambs led to the slaughter, she thought. She had long ago put blame in its proper place.

He was the lamb who had somehow managed to survive, and now he asked her to forgive him for it. She understood so much more than he thought she did because she too was a lamb that had survived almost fifty years in the Soviet Union. It gave one quite a perspective... but she couldn't convey that all to him now.

She squeezed the love of her life harder, so that without words he would know all that she was feeling... and then, only then... *Uncle Marion knew... he was home at last.*

Danyk and Olga had wanted to visit with Sam's widow, but she was not anxious for the meeting. It was beyond their understanding, but they didn't want to force themselves on her.

The Romanuks were kind enough to let them stay for a month. During this time, they had their initiation into the Western world and marveled at what Americans took for granted. Walter was a patient teacher as he was experienced and understood what would be unfamiliar to a typical Ukrainian immigrant.

Danyk and Olga were eventually able to get a place to stay at the St. Vladimir Ukrainian Church in Hempstead where he and Olga had been attending church with the Romanuks since they first arrived. They were immediately embraced and befriended by the American Ukrainian community.

Shortly after, Danyk got a job at the Ukrainian Community

Center in Uniondale as a night custodian cleaning and setting up for various functions like Bingo and dances. He now calls himself by his American name, Danny.

Four months after they arrived, Bogdan joined them. He left his own thriving business in the Soviet Union, a wood-working company, and almost immediately landed a job as a custodian in the East Meadow Union Free School District in NY. He, too, adjusted his name and introduced himself to his co-workers as Danny Jr.

By 1994, the entire Szafranski clan had arrived in New York. "Now", Danny thought, "it is time to visit my father."

It was a lovely Saturday morning. Danny Sr. had the entire family dress appropriately and prepared to make the trip a couple of hours north to New Paltz, New York. Everyone went... Olga... their sons and daughters, and all the grandchildren.

"Here, here he is,'" Bogdan announced, pointing to a particular gravestone.

This was not how Danny had envisioned his reunion with his father, not at all. He walked slowly in the direction that Bogdan had indicated, with his head bowed respectfully, both saying hello and good-bye to his father at the same time.

The moment, which seconds before had been filled with the enthusiastic voices of his family as they searched for Sam's grave, grew instantly solemn and everyone watched Danny to know how they should react.

Sam's headstone indicated his veteran status as an American soldier, which added pride to the tremendous mix of emotions that Danny was feeling.

If I had just been ten months earlier...

It was not just the loss of his father, it was the loss of his father meeting and knowing his family, seeing just once the pride and love in his father's eyes, to have his father hold him and reassure, "Now, you are safe my son. In America... I'm able to protect you."

And he knew it would have been closure for his father, as well. How his father must have ached and longed for him! As a father himself, he understood the great pain and unrest that Sam had endured.

He'd waited so long for all these things, but they now must be put to rest...unfulfilled. *If I had been just ten months earlier...*

Danny's family surrounded him to offer comfort and support as he honored and eulogized his father.

When he was done, the entire family posed in a semi-circle around Sam's headstone for a photograph to be taken. It would commemorate the only time Danny had to spend with the father he had spent his entire life trying to rejoin.

Danny tried once again to see his father's widow.

Walter had given him the address. Only Danny and his youngest son approached the door to knock. They had left the rest of the family packed in cars by the road hoping that Sam's widow might be convinced to offer them an invitation for a friendly meeting and exchange. It would have fulfilled their tradition of embracing a family member and showing proper respect.

"Yes, who are you?" The woman's hair was tied back and pulled on top of her head.

She hadn't opened the door all the way as though she feared the unfamiliar faces.

Somehow, though, Danny knew she had recognized him. Could that be the reason she was fearful? Could she think that Szymon's son would mean her harm in any way? It did not make any sense at all. Perhaps, she was just old, losing her faculties. In which case, he would want to take care of her, to honor his father's memory.

"I'm Danyk." Danny smiled thinking she would like him once she met and got to know him.

"I always told your father you would come one day." It was as though she was thinking aloud and hadn't thought to speak silently. From her tone, it didn't sound like something she had been looking forward to.

"I was hoping to visit with you and talk about my father." Certainly, she wouldn't refuse now. It would not be a neighborly thing to do, and his father would not have married someone without manners.

"I don't have much to tell you. He's dead now... and I'm alone."

It was hard for Danny to believe, but his father's widow was dismissing him. "Everything you see here is mine. I don't have anything to share, if that is what you are after."

Danny was still in denial and unable to alter his way of thinking to understand what she was implying, but Bogdan caught on quickly.

"We don't want anything. We only want to talk to you. Don't you want to know your husband's son and grandchildren?"

"Honestly, I have my own problems to worry about. I can't help you much."

Danny was still looking at her as though at any moment she would change her mind, realize he was a good man and invite him into her home... his father's home... from which he had probably written him many letters... and spent his final days still wishing he had met his son. He could not believe she would deny him this small favor.

"Come, we'll go." Bogdan was pulling his father by the arm.

"She doesn't understand." Danny wanted to try again and clearly wasn't ready to leave.

"We have to go, come on, everyone is waiting for us." You still have us ...your children...your grandchildren...your wife.

Bogdan felt incredible pain seeing his father denied. He understood how hurt he was and knew his denial came from years of longing and deprivation. He would be strong for his father.

Bogdan tugged harder and forced his father to realize that they had to go. They weren't wanted.

Halfway to the car, Bogdan turned to face his father and as gently as he could said, "She thinks we want an inheritance, money."

"I don't want her money!" What was Bogdan talking about? He just wanted to talk to her. She was a connection to his father.

"I know that. But she doesn't. She's scared."

"Let's go back. I'll make her understand."

"No. You can't force someone to understand when they don't want to."

Danny was not ready yet to give up completely... but perhaps his son was right. They would try again another time, after they had been here for a while, and she realized they were not a threat.

Vyktoria watched them leave from her kitchen window. Her husband's picture sat on the sill and she picked it up on impulse. It was not that she had not loved her husband, but she had been the least secure of his wives.

"I'm sorry, Sam." She said as she looked at the photo. "But they could take the house. Then, what would I do? Please, forgive me."

The Szafranski family was made up of hard workers. At first, they had lived in a rental in Uniondale, New York, but now, together, had bought a small house in nearby Westbury, New York for $166,000.

Danny had spent his life farming for the Soviet state. Now, he could grow what he liked on the tiny patch of his land in his West-bury backyard. Tomatoes, cucumbers, carrots, squash, all flourished under his experienced nurturance.

Both Danny, who worked the night shift, and Bogdan, who worked the day shift, now worked full-time at Woodland Middle School in East Meadow, New York.

It was physically demanding work especially for a man now in his mid-sixties, but there was little choice. He used his days to sleep and care for his garden, relaxing and enjoying the fresh air and greenery that had for most of his life been his "office". Now, it was a serious hobby and not a backbreaking labor to keep his family fed. He shared his vegetables with appreciative friends and took great joy that life was now abundant enough to be able to share his surplus.

Danny had lost his home and any pension he might have gotten from his life as a worker for the Soviet Union. Certainly, too, he would need to work many more years to claim any Social Security benefits here in the United States, but he could not help but to reflect..."Life is good."

Danny thought "...and now I am finally happy!"

Each of his children went about creating their own lives, but it helped at times to pool resources.

It was an adjustment for all, but a much desired one. Living in the United States with what others might have considered to be modest means was the equivalent of a luxurious one in the Soviet Union.

Toilets for one were a tremendously convenient feature to get accustomed to, running water, warm baths, getting meat at the grocery store rather than slaughtering it daily in your own backyard, paved roads, green mowed lawns, electricity and fast-food restaurants... although it would take years before the Szafranski's would ever think to try one!

They made friends with other Ukrainian families from their church and were finally living the American dream... at least that of your average-working class family.

Danny usually arrived at 3PM, anonymously passing the flurry of children dismissed from Woodland Middle School only moments earlier. He'd climb the stairs to the second floor and go to the supply closet in his section. He'd fill the rolling bucket with clean, hot water and a wet mop, and collect the other tools of his new trade, as well: an industrial garbage can, a broom, a dust cloth and some Windex. They'd all travel with him as he moved down the hallway, sweeping, dusting and mopping through most of the night into the next morning.

Sometimes, he'd see his son Bogdan, known to the teachers and staff as Danny Jr., before he ended his day shift, sometimes not. Generally, it was a solitary job, as the other custodians were in their own sections tending to their own duties. The most interaction took place before all the teachers left for the day, but if they were there after hours, it was because they had their own work to complete, so any conversation was generally a polite, quick greeting.

He'd say hello in his best English, which he practiced whenever given the opportunity to do so and they would ask him how he was. A few even got to know his name... his American name, Danny, of course, so that everyone would know, he too was a proud American!

He was quite a puzzlement to those who took extra notice of him. His childish curiosity was a contradiction to his alert, intelligent eyes and almost sponge-like desire to learn and absorb.

If he was given a second look, he'd use the opportunity to pose a list of questions. "What is this? What do you call it? How do you use this? What is "prop"? What is "mic-ro-scop?" And then back he went, back to the silent hallways, the empty classrooms, the building, lifeless with the exception of the cleaning crew, each far away in their own corner of the building absorbed in their own tasks.

Such had become the life of Danny Szafranski, the greatest American most of us would ever have the pleasure to know.

≈

However, most of us walked right by him, at most, offering a quick greeting. This was not how the story should end for a great, maybe the greatest American hero.

And it would not.

For, though Danny and his family are the people who lived this story... I am the keeper of the story.

And I, with a passion inspired by my dear friend, have become the culminating voice determined that it should be told... to be preserved for history ...and so that long overdue acknowledgement would be given to incredible individuals, particularly my friend, Danyk Szafranski, who I have come to believe are unsung heroes, deserving to be acknowledged and long remembered.

Danny displayed great courage and bravery throughout his life-time... first as a fourteen- year-old United States Citizen, defying the Soviet Union and the KGB to retain his American Citizenship and then in his day-to-day struggle to survive in the Soviet Union as an American, the first to be targeted or used as a scapegoat.

As noted by historians, America let him down big time. But he never reciprocated.

Danny always, even knowing it would probably never gain him anything, but a life of one trial after another, remained a faithful American in the Soviet Union even throughout the Cold War. That alon,e gives him a distinguished place in history.

Would Danny ever get even the smallest recognition? Such stories have a life and destiny of their own.

And Danny's was about to meet its fate.

On September 27, 1998, Danny was featured in a seven-page article in Newsday's Sunday edition (Long Island, New York). For a moment in time, Danny was the buzz of Woodland Middle School, where he worked.

Who was this great American hero who we saw each day sweeping our hallways?

Suddenly, people took the time to notice him, especially students who were awed and fascinated to have their assumptions about someone be so drastically contradicted.

Danny was no longer our hallway custodian. He was our school's hero, and he enjoyed every moment of it. He beamed through his day as students, teachers and administrators greeted and acknowledged him.

We have Mr. Rick Firstman, the Newsday journalist to thank for Danny's moment of fame. He painstakingly researched Danny's history and presented his complicated story with compassion and clarity. Finally, we all knew what Danny had endured and that in our midst was one of the greatest American heroes of all time!

How many of us can say that we would demonstrate the same courage or loyalty? He has raised the bar.

Though he had lived a life never expecting it (whoever dreamed the Soviet Union would fall), his loyalty ultimately paid off. Not only he, but his wife, children and grandchildren were recognized American citizens with all the rights and privileges. Of course, he lost his retirement benefits from the Soviet Union and had little time to build his Social Security once he arrived in the United States (something seems very unfair about that!). He worked until he collapsed at work and was forced to retire.

He and his wife then spent a little time living with each of their children. It was a day-to-day struggle, but the Szafranski's pooled resources and worked together. Danny and Olga were surrounded by a loving family until the end of their lives (Danny Sr. passed away on April 21, 2018, and Olga passed away on March 6, 2022). In many ways, they were more fortunate than many other people. They counted their blessings. At least, that is how my friend Danny would have seen it.

If you would like to find out more about how this story was recovered, please continue with The Author's Notes.

Mary Bruno Friedman

THE END

Author's Notes

It was unusual for me to be packed and ready to leave so early in the day, but I was hurrying home for my children, Adam and Lisa. I don't remember exactly why... maybe a dentist appointment or a sports event.

What I do remember was that rushed-mother-feeling with which the working mothers of my generation are so familiar.

It's like a stomachache that hasn't hit full force yet. It isn't going to stop you, but you know it isn't going away either. You feel the pulling, stretching, and straining attempt of your body to warn you that you are under stress, trying to do too much in too little time.

That was where I was at, the day that Danny approached me in the hallway of Woodland Middle School, just above the staircase that I had been fully intending to fly down, until he called out my name.

"Miss Mar-rie? Miss Mar-rie! Wait. Wait."

Like a fox in a chicken coop, I'd been caught. How to tell him I was hurrying... had to get home for the kids... had a load of laundry to do before I picked them up, plunked them into the car and got them wherever it was they had to be? How to tell him, indeed.

You see, we had a wonderful relationship, one that was a bit difficult to explain to an outsider, and it never involved being hurried or not having the time for some polite conversation.

Each day after school, Danny would make his way down to my classroom and bring his own unhurried world with him. He, being the custodian for my particular hallway at Woodland Middle School, would mix friendly chatter with his custodial duties as he tended to my dusty bookshelves and chalky blackboard.

His gentle, soothing conversation was a friction that distracted me from my focused, determined hurriedness and reminded me to slow down, which was quite necessary if the conversation was to go anywhere at all, as you see...Danny did not speak English, at least at first.

"What is this Miss Mar-rie?"

He would point to what was of interest to him, and I would struggle to explain in words he would understand that it was a microscope or a prop for a play. He always seemed to have one more question, which with my teacher's nature, always brought me back for more. And he knew it. He had a sharp eye for people and the world around him, and his radar was never turned off. It contradicted his lack of education and limited knowledge of the world, making him one of the most intriguing, interesting characters I've ever known.

And he was the sweetest.

How else can I explain my tolerance for a man who interrupted my work just at the point in my day when all I wanted to do was finish up and go home to my family.

And he was the kindest.

I could go on and on. The point is there was something about Danyk Szafranski that activated my radar, as well. There was something that made me zero in and take note. And not mind the time required to develop our friendship, always at the end of a busy school day, after at least eight hours of being a special education teacher with all the variety and devotion and exhaustion that entailed.

My radar, fine-tuned perhaps from years of teaching and keeping the eyes-in-the-back-of-my-head alert, told me Danyk Szafaranski was one special human being, and not only did he deserve my time and attention, but I should be honored to give it. Time would substantiate all this, that I somehow knew intuitively.

After many months, we had a pretty strong friendship. Danny's English had gotten better, not perfect by any means, but the strain and time it took to understand each other had lessened.

I guess he thought it was time.

"I...I have something to show you." Danny was still only halfway down the hallway, but his excitement carried and echoed through the empty corridor.

"Danny... can I see tomorrow..."

He held the box out to me like a gift and his eyes fell intently on me to register my degree of appreciation. She is going to like this, his expression read.

It wasn't unusual for Danyk to arrive bearing gifts. In fact, I'd gotten quite spoiled by his home-grown garden vegetables and bags of Ukrainian candy. But this gift appeared different. It didn't appear edible.

It was a box filled with pictures and documents, and I wasn't sure where to begin. My look must have reflected being overwhelmed, and he quickly decided he would have to do the digging for me. Momentarily, he held out one of the photos from the top of the pile.

"This... my mather...when she come back from Siberia." His careful speech always made me an attentive listener, in case he needed help and with that bit of focusing, I knew I wasn't going anywhere quickly. He always had a way of working that kind of magic on me... making me slow down when I was in high gear. And for the most part, I was always in high gear.

"Your mother was in Siberia?"

"Cutting the stone."

"Cutting stone? In Siberia?" The woman clutched a chair and stared off blankly as though her soul were empty. It was a sad picture, and it hurt me to know it was his mother, and she seemed to have suffered greatly.

"She was never the same mother after Siberia."

Then he held up another picture. "Me, in American Embassy... in Moscow. This is my room in the basement."

"You... lived in the American embassy in Moscow? How old were you?" The boy in the picture was obviously young.

Oddly, I felt like the boy in the photo was staring right at me... across time... beseeching help... and I had a strong desire to give it to him. It was a thunderstruck moment, powerful, moving and reflective.

Have you ever had one like that, a defining moment where you feel like a mighty power is revealing your purpose to you?

It is a little frightening, but you don't dare ignore it ...or reveal it to anyone because...well... it seems a bit preposterous, even to yourself! But that little charge gets stored, somewhere in you and you know, even when the moment passes, that you're not done with it yet.

"I... um... fourteen. My mother in Siberia... I alone. They take care of me at the embassy."

"What happened to your father?"

Danny pulls out another picture. It is the headstone of his father's grave, and it reads "American Veteran..."

"I don't understand... your father was an American soldier in WW II. How did he manage to meet your mother in the Soviet Union?"

" No... my mother, my father from Poland. My father an American citizen." "But you are Ukrainian. You are from Russia, the Soviet Union."

'Yes, but my mother, my father from Poland. I born in Manhattan."

"Danny... I'm getting confused. I thought you told me you came from the Soviet Union. You speak Ukrainian. How could you be born in Manhattan? Manhattan in New York? In the United States of America?"

That would mean Danny was an American citizen, too, naturally born. Things were not adding up. Everything I'd ever known about

Danny was that he was an immigrant from the Soviet Union. When the Soviet Union collapsed, he and his family had come to America.

Next out of the box was his birth certificate. Danyk Szafranski born on ... October 1931...place of birth... Manhattan...!!!

"Danny... are you an American citizen?"

"Yes," he was shaking his head. Eureka, she finally understands!

Had he tried to tell me this before? I searched my memory for similar conversations, but I came up empty. Had I just not had any context to understand what he was trying to explain to me? Now, a few things he had said to me in the past began to make sense.

The box was filled with puzzle pieces that contained a story Danny had been trying to tell me. They were artifacts of a life he had had before he spent his evenings sweeping school hallways, largely as an anonymous figure easily taken for granted or ignored by a school community as they dashed to their cars or buses.

"If you were born in Manhattan... how did you end up in the Soviet Union...alone... at the American Embassy in Moscow?" This was a pretty loaded question and way over the caliber and extent of questions that we generally passed back and forth between us in our usual conversations.

Danny gave me a satisfying smile like a fisherman who had just caught his fish. I've got her now, he conveyed with narrowing eyes that betrayed a keen intelligence usually more softly displayed for the rest of the world.

I knew it wasn't going to come out in a nutshell, so I began to prod and pull the pieces together. "So, you're an American citizen, fourteen-years old at the time... and you're ... for whatever reason...in Moscow. Your mother is sent to Siberia (I'm thinking from my limited knowledge of Soviet history that it has something to do with Stalin's purges), so you go to the American Embassy?"

"Yes, they take care of me... let me show you..." Danny reaches again and out comes two separate wallet-sized pictures. One is of a man holding a dog and another is a standard portrait. "This one is Joe...Joe Malaznick and this is Jim Mahonney." It seemed odd to hear the Irish name pronounced in a deep Ukrainian accent. "They take good care of me. They give me their pictures so I can always remember them." A sad nostalgia washes over Danny and his excitement at educating and unveiling so much to me is lost for a moment while he reflects. The strength of the emotion he is feeling distorts his face.

Now, I get it!

A child alone, abandoned, in trouble.

I'm picking it up... of course, on my own radar ... deet .. ta.. deet... ta.. deet.. deet. The signals are coming in loud and clear, and I've been unconsciously picking them up all along. It makes sense to me now, why Danny has always been a soft spot for me, captures my attention and heart.

"I want to find them; you help me?"

"You want to find the two men that took care of you at the embassy?" "Yes."

My first instinct was to tell him, "Impossible!" After all I wouldn't even know where to begin; I was a teacher not an investigator. But his beseeching look matched the young boy's in the photo at the American Embassy, and for whatever ludicrous reason, I didn't dismiss him. I wasn't yet done with that thunderstruck moment of thinking that I had some purpose here, some part in this story that wasn't yet over.

I hadn't realized it yet, but this was the final episode of closure that Danny needed to get on with things after a very complicated, troubled and courageous life.

Really only a few minutes had passed since Danny had spotted me preparing to take flight, yet the groundwork for what was to take place over the next many months, years and even decades, had been laid.

We said our ritualistic good-byes.

"Have a good night, Miss Mar-rie, have a good everything!" Danny liked to cover all the bases.

"Night Dan, have a good everything, too."

I'm home cooking dinner and the phone rings; early spring, I think. "May I speak to Mary Friedman, please?"

"Yes, speaking." Another sales call; why are they always calling when I'm trying to prepare dinner.

"I'm Rick Firstman, a freelance journalist and I would like to do your friend's story for *Newsday* (a Long Island newspaper)."

Stop everything. Stop my heart, stop the spaghetti! Somebody is interested in Danny's story!

I should have known that sooner or later the odds were in our favor. I'd written to everyone I could think of...politicians all the way from Congresswoman Carolyn McCarthy to President Clinton and his wife, Hillary Clinton (whom I'd later meet and try to interest in acknowledging Danny), newspapers, magazines, T.V. news shows like 20/20 and Dateline, Steven Spielberg and Oprah. I stopped short of the Pope.

But this was the first real contact back.

"Yes..." Oh please, please, please, please...help! Somebody else take notice that in our midst is one of the greatest American heroes of our time. Somebody else gets what I'm getting!

And to my absolute amazement, oh me of little faith... he did.

For the next several months, I had a buddy, a comrade who was as passionate about Danny's story as I was.

If memory serves me correctly, at least six other journalists at *Newsday* called thereafter with interest in Danny's story, but Mr. Firstman had our loyalty, which if you haven't figured it out by now, means he was our man, and we were sticking with him.

Rick began by interviewing Danny. At first his story was delivered in bits and pieces, helter-skelter, the way he had first told it to me using broken English, hand gestures and even getting on the floor to demonstrate how so many people could be forced to fit into a tiny jail cell, one sitting between the legs of the person behind them.

Danny Jr. (Bogdan) was helpful in interpreting what Danny

couldn't express in English and at each interview I learned more amazing details of his life. Some haunted me and made it difficult to sleep at night, and there were times it broke my heart to use Danny Jr. as the interpreter. He too, heard stories for the first time, the ones his father had not had the heart to share with him before and at times...we all cried.

The biggest question of all, the one that Rick Firstman and I wondered about and couldn't stop shaking our heads over, was, why?

We just didn't get it. As Americans, we were even a little ashamed of ourselves, but still...we just didn't get it.

Why didn't he give up his American citizenship? Look what it cost him... a lifetime of suffering.

If he'd known that one day the Soviet Union would collapse and that there would be some pay off, we might have understood. But to us, it just didn't make sense. Because he couldn't have known that. In fact, through most of Danny's life, the Soviet Union was a fire- breathing dragon, and it wasn't letting him go anywhere, ever!

Did he really remain American, defy Stalin, defy the KGB, sacrifice his education, standard of living and entire life... never expecting any personal gain?

Rick went to Washington D.C. to begin the extensive research that would put Danny's story into historical, as well as personal context, and began to interview historians and even people who had been there at the embassy at the same time as Danny.

It was pretty unanimous...Danny was a rare historical find.

To the amazement of historians, Danny is one of a few or perhaps the only person to have survived and share his story of not only being a lone American in that particular place and time but of remaining an American! Most, under extreme duress and torture, submitted and signed their American citizenship away, were driven to suicide or were executed.

On Sunday, September 27, 1998, *Newsday* featured a seven-page article called, "Born in the USA" by Mr. Rick Firstman. It was a magnificent piece of journalism, revealing Danny's personal history within the context of American and world events for the first time.

The reaction to the article spanned a tremendous spectrum and I thought it quite telling in what our society valued.

I'm quite proud of the fact that my students and most of those attending Woodland Middle School were almost starstruck. For a time, Danny was quite a celebrity and truly appreciated for being the heroic role model that he was.

The faculty, too, were in awe though somewhat shy about expressing themselves to Danny, no matter how much I encouraged it. Some were concerned about the language barrier. But if we'd been able to communicate back and forth to reveal his extensive history, I thought surely, they could communicate their admiration and congratulations. And many did (which greatly warmed my heart toward certain individuals).

His own Ukrainian community celebrated, of course, and he was cheered on and received pats of congratulations on the back.

The buzz created did a lot to satisfy my own desire to have Danny recognized, and I loved seeing him smile and look like he was floating from all the attention. A burden appeared to be lifted from his shoulders.

But it just didn't seem to be on the scale that he truly deserved. I just didn't feel done with it yet and neither did Mr. Firstman.

Rick approached his publishers for permission to write a book. In a reluctant, impulsive move, I mentioned to Danny one day that if Rick Firstman's publishers didn't give him permission to write a book about his life story, that I would write it.

Danny with his impeccable memory never forgot those words. As I filled him in on the replies to correspondence I had written on his behalf, and shared with him what I thought was disappointing news... that Mr. Firstman had not gotten permission to write the book from his publisher, he would toss my words back at me.

"Miss Mar-rie, you write book, I want you do it." He'd say the words shaking his head at first, meaning their refusal meant nothing to him. Then, he would bob his head up and down, smiling as though he had caught a huge fish. From the very first, he was sure that I would one day write his book for him. From the evidence that sits before me on my word processor, I should perhaps rename myself Flounder.

Danny's gentle stance gives no hint of the hero within. Neither does his soft smile give away his heroic proportion! In fact, there is not much about Danny's appearance to suggest a man who has demonstrated such courage and lived through many of history's most brutal events. Only his story itself does. And, of course historians and experts on the time period, one who happened to be at the U.S. embassy at the same time Danny lived there...and documents at the National Archives once classified "secret."

No one word or paragraph or book could represent Danny. I only hope they serve to honor him. It is recognition long overdue. His strong character, sense of honor, and degree of integrity can be represented only by the man himself, in the way he treated all others and lived his life.

In 1949, there were 1,900 American citizens with unresolved cases - including 21 children separated from parents in the United States being held by Soviet officials against their will. Much to my dismay, there was nothing the United States officials could do to protect them...or perhaps more accurately, there was nothing their superiors would allow them to do. Which leads me to Danny's friends and advocates: Joe Malaznick and Jim Mahoney.

What first initiated Danny telling me his story was his overwhelming desire to find these two men. It was a chapter not finished for him and he longed for closure. Rick Firstman did his best, but he wasn't able to find any records or any evidence that they ever existed.

Rick believed what was suggested to him by a historian at Princeton, that they were spies and that their names would never be found amongst the names of the American servicemen serving in Moscow at the time. In fact, from my research, I've come to understand that even if the United States didn't consider the servicemen serving in

Moscow at this time to be spies in the James Bond sense, Stalin did! And to a certain extent...he would have been correct. They were certainly there to pick up as much understanding and knowledge of this evasive and mystifying nation as possible without letting Stalin realize or prevent it.

However, it is my belief that Danny's friends at the embassy never gave Danny their real names; not to protect themselves but to protect him. It would be easier for him or any other Soviet citizen to deny or acknowledge familiarizing with western influences, should they be interrogated, if they truly did not know with whom exactly it was that they were fraternizing. These men probably felt it was the kindest and wisest thing to do, considering Stalin's brutal view of anything touched by western influence. It is one more fact that monumentalizes Danny's survival. Once exposed to the western world (such as returning Soviet soldiers from German Prisoner of War camps), you were considered an enemy of the state and targeted for execution.

Danny lived for nine months amongst American citizens. To say that his survival was miraculous is an understatement.

In addition, it should be noted that due to the historical method of record keeping, at times names were recorded inaccurately, with misspellings or variations. I did my best to keep them consistent for the reader. Also, there are a few instances where names were switched or simply created.

I'm not the journalist or expert investigator that Rick Firstman was, and I absolutely must make readers aware that this is not the non-fictional accounting of Danyk Szafranski's story that Mr. Firstman might have written had his publisher granted him permission to do so.

I spent years conversing, questioning and re-questioning Danny with follow-up questions.

I spent decades becoming familiar with these events, time periods and documents on Danny's specific profile from the United States Department of Justice, and Immigration and Naturalization Service.

Although I was as accurate and factual as I could be to tell Danny's story, wherever Danny's story fell short... it was my imaginings that took over.

The characters were real people in my mind, and I tried to make them come to life as I felt Danny saw them. In my heart, I journeyed with them and did my best to portray them, relying mostly on my heart's eye and their mingled voices reaching out across time and dimension, beseeching me to help the boy get his just deserves.

I hope I have done their story justice.

I hope the boy gets his just deserves and the man finally has closure.

I hope each reader is inspired to find their hero within... grander and of greater proportion than any fear they must face.

And I hope each and every American wakes up tomorrow morning holding dear their citizenship and prouder to be an American. Because that's what Danny would have wanted.

Now, at last on my final page, All the voices have been heard.

They may now rest... Not in silence... But at peace.

Mary Bruno Friedman

NOTE:

If you would like BOOK CLUB Discussion Questions or to contact the author, go to:

www.of-heroic-proportion.com

I would like to thank...

...first and foremost, Danny Szafranski for living a life that deserved recognition and appreciation. He spent many hours with me sharing and reliving some of the hardest moments in his life and I am deeply appreciative of his patience and tolerance while we, together, stumbled through the intricacies of his personal journey and a mountain of historical facts which were often difficult for me to absorb. He, a man with limited formal education, has been my greatest teacher and given me a great blessing... a hero to believe in!

Danny's son, Danyk Jr. (also known as Bogdan Shafranski), and Danny's granddaughter, Olha Perito Shafranski, were instrumental as our translators, and at times, exposed to hearing the raw details of Danny's life that he might otherwise not have chosen to share with them. They, brave and tireless, offered endless support and love to their father and grandfather, not only towards the completion of this endeavor, but on a daily basis.

If not for Rick Firstman, I would never have had the detailed framework for the story. He provided the valuable historical context which enabled me to get started. Thanks so much, Rick!

There have been many other friends and family members over

the years that have, in one way or another, contributed to this book. The list of amateur editors and critics is fairly endless but most notable and in order of their review would be my sister-in-law, Janet Boltax; my cousin, Cathy Eighmy; my dear late aunt, Kay Ferrara Gloster and Sue Gold. I'd also like to thank the many friends who previewed the book (especially Paul Lieberman) who never doubted its value and gave me endless encouragement. They have listened to my discoveries, allowed me to vent frustrations or just permitted me to talk and talk and talk about something they have heard all before. A very big thanks to the gang!

A special mention goes to Holly Curtis for all her efforts designing a memorable book cover.

Now, for some of the most important people in my life, my daughter, Lisa; my son, Adam (whose invaluable help and persistence is the reason this book has finally been published!!!) and my devoted husband, Steve, who always has my back.

Other than Danny and the story itself, you are the people I did it all for. At times, you had a wife and mom whose mind was elsewhere or a wife who didn't really want to be cooking dinner... she just wanted to get back to typing because, let's face it, she was a little obsessed. But I knew that was what it was going to take to get it done.

And it needed to be done. And I needed to do it.

And I did it.

I did something worthwhile, and I hope it makes you realize you can do something, too. Anything you want... just make it... worthwhile.

If you do, I promise to be proud of you.

Photos

Danny's early life with this family while living in Manhattan, New York.

Photos that Mariya sent to Sam from what was then Poland.

The day Danny arrived at the US Embassy in Moscow the US Staff member on Danny's right insisted that he go outside to take a photo with the Soviet soldier that allowed him to pass into the embassy. According to Danny, he was terrified to leave the embassy's safety. But, he obeyed and went. Danny was never sure if it was kindness or apathy that motivated the Soviet soldier to let him enter when so many others were being denied.

This first photo of Danny on his bed in the embassy with the American flag and boyish magazines proudly displayed is what first intrigued the author to have Danny's story known.

Photos

The man holding the dog is one of the servicemen that cared for Danny while at the embassy. Danny desperately wanted to locate him and believed his name to be Jim Mahoney. He also wanted to find Joe Malaznick.

This serviceman took the photos of Danny below during outings to Spaso House.

Danny and Olga on their farm in the Ukraine.

Sam's brothers at the start of WWII.

Paulo and Marion (Mariya's brothers) are on the left. This photo was taken post WWII in France before Marion left for Canada. The man on the right is unidentified.

Mykhailo and Mariya after Mariya's release and Mykhailo's temporary release from Siberia.

Paulo and Marion upon Marion's return from Canada to Ukraine.

Photos

Danny and his entire extended family visit Sam's grave shortly after they arrive to New York. You may notice the different spelling of the last name.

Author's Biography

 Ms. Friedman began her teaching career as a special educator with a degree in Emotional Disturbance and Neurological Impairment at Bellevue Psychiatric Hospital in Manhattan. Her unique experiences while teaching there began her life-long desire to advocate for the underdog and cheer for imperfect characters that manage to get it right anyway.

She suspended her teaching career briefly to raise her family. Upon her return to education, she became a departmental teacher at Woodland Middle School in East Meadow, NY, which is where she met and befriended Mr. Danyk Szafranski. Further, earning certification as a Wilson Language Systems teacher, she spent many years teaching dyslexic students to master reading. As well, spanning over her thirty-year teaching career, her other positions included teaching special elementary students and High School English.

In 1996, Of HEROIC PROPORTION began to take form as the narrative nonfiction account of Mr. Szafranski's life. Once told to Ms. Friedman through Danyk's tears and written though her heart's eye, it became her passion to share this up-lifting and inspiring story so that others might also see that true heroes really do walk among us.

Ms. Friedman also utilized her love of writing, drama and story-telling to motivate young people toward self-expression, publication and a life of learning with purpose for nearly ten years by writing and producing her own plays for school-wide audiences and guiding her students to write and produce their own, as well.

In January 2007, Ms. Friedman's dedication was recognized by New York State District Kiwanis, and an EVERYDAY HERO Award was presented to her by the students of Woodland Middle School's Builders Club.

In 2018, Ms. Friedman retired from the East Meadow Union Free School District and enjoyed time as a docent at Old Bethpage Village Restoration in Bethpage, NY. She presently resides in Melville, New York with her husband, Steve. Their greatest joy is spending time with their expanding family, especially their children, Adam and Lisa, their significant others, Deb and Jonathan and five grandchildren (Evie, Maddie, Brie, Lenny and Mariella).

Bibliography

Books

Bennett, J. (1989). *Behind the Urals: An American worker in Russia's city of steel.* Indiana University Press.

Britton, S. (Ed.). (2007). *800 Days on the Eastern Front: A Russian soldier remembers World War II.* Greenhill Books.

Church, G. J., Peterzel, J., & Samghabad, R. (1987, April 20). The art of high-tech snooping. *Time.*

Firstman, Rick. "I Am An American", *Newsday*, 27 Sept. 1998, pp. G14-20

Friedman, I. R. (1975). *The Other Victim.* Random House.

Gitelman, Z. (2001). *A Century of Ambivalence: The Jews of Russia and the Soviet Union.* Indiana University Press.

Hahn Beer, E., & Dworkin, S. (2000). *The Nazi Officer's Wife.* William Morrow.

Herman, V. (1979). *Coming Out of the Ice.* Harcourt Brace Jovanovich.

Keegan, J. (1990). *The Second World War.* Viking Penguin.

Kennan, G. (1967). *Memoirs 1925-1950.* Little, Brown and Company.

Marrin, A. (1985). *The Secret Armies: Spies, counterspies, and saboteurs in WWII.* Atheneum Publishing.

Miller, R. (1979). *The Resistance, World War II Collectors Edition.* Time Life Inc.

Miscamble, W. D. (1976). *George Kennan: A life in the foreign service.* Vantage Press.

Moynahan, B. (1994). *The Russian Century: A photographic history of Russia 100 years.* Random House.

Nir, Y., & Lukas, R. C. (1989). *The Lost Childhood*. Scholastic.

Paldiel, M. (2007). *Diplomat Heroes of the Holocaust*. Rabbi Arthur Scheier Center for International Affairs of Yeshiva University.

Paldiel, M. (2007). *The Righteous Among the Nations*. The Jerusalem Publishing House.

Pettit, J. (1987). *A Time to Fight Back*. Faber and Faber.

Rieul, R. (1986). *Escape from Espionage: The true story of a French patriot*. Walker Publishing.

Scott, J. (1989). *Behind the Urals: An American worker in Russia's city of steel*. Indiana University Press.

Seaton, A. (1971). *The Russo-German War 1941-1945*. Praeger Publishers.

Seliger, M. (1996). *When They Came to Take My Father*. Arcade Publishing.

Sevander, M., & Hertzer, L. (1992). *They Took My Father: Finnish Americans in Stalin's Russia*. University of Minnesota Press.

Sevareid, E. (1977). *WWII-Life Books History of the Second World War*. Preston Hall Press.

Shuter, J. (2001). *Resistance to the Nazis*. Heinemann Library.

Sherrow, V. (1996). *The Righteous Gentile*. Lucent Books.
Stein, C. (2000). *World War II in Europe*. Enslow Publishing.

Tobien, K. (2006). *Dancing Under the Stars*. Tyndale House Publishers.

Van Dee, E. H. (2004). *Sleeping Dogs and Popsicles: The Vatican versus the KGB*. University Press of America.

Various authors. (1990). *Sources for Soviet History, The USSR Since 1945*. Elizabeth Campling. HarperCollins Publishers.

Winston, K. (2004). *Letters from a World War II GI*. Franklin Watts Publishing.

World War II. (1999). *World War II: A Visual Encyclopedia*. PRC Publishing LTD.

Websites

Army Quartermaster Museum. (2007, April 22). *Rations in Review, The Quarter-master Review, May-June 1946*. Retrieved from http://www.qmmuseum.lee.army. mil/history/

Bridges, P. S. (1964). *Spaso House*. Foreign Service Journal. Retrieved from http://moscow.usembassy.gov/embassy/embassy.php?record_id=spaso

Bug Sweeps. (2007, April 22). *The Art of High-Tech Snooping*. Retrieved from http://www.bugssweeps.com

Cold War. (2007, August 8). *Kennan interviews*. Retrieved from http://www.gwu. edu/~nsarchiv/coldwar/interviews/IronCurtain.episode-2/tucker6.html

Cold War. (2007, August 8). *Interview with Professor George F. Kennan*. Retrieved from http://www.gwu.edu/runsarchi/coldwar/interviews/episode-1/kennan.4html

Cold War. (2007, August 8). *National Security Archives*. Retrieved from http://www.gwu.edu/~nsarchiv/National Security Archives

Cold War. (2007, August 8). *Kennan interviews*. Retrieved from http://www.cnn. com/SPECIALS/ColdWar/episodes/01/interview/kennan

Darby's Rangers. (2005, June 28). *Stalag IIB: The Final Report*. Retrieved from http://darbysrangers.tripod.com/id64.htm

DP Camps. (2004, March 2). *Histukr3*. Retrieved from http://www.dpccamps. org/dpcamps/histukr3.html

History Guide. (2007, August 8). *Kennan*. Retrieved from http://www.histo ryguide.org/europe/kennan.html

JewishGen. (2005, June 28). *Cemetery Project*. Retrieved from http://www.jewish gen.org/cemetery/

Litopys UPA. (2008, March 21). *Chronicle of the Ukrainian Insurgent Army, Ukrainians in World War II Military Formations: An Overview by Peter J. Potichnyj*. Retrieved from http://infoukes.com/upa/relatedmilitary.html

Mazur, M. (2004, February 29). *Wolf*. Retrieved from http://web.mit.edu/maz/ wolf/65-179/wolf169.txt

Mazur, M. (2004, February 29). *Wolf*. Retrieved from http://web.mit.edu/maz/wolf/65-179/wolf1.txt

Mazur, M. (2004, February 29). *Wolf*. Retrieved from http://web.mit.edu/maz/wolf/65-179/wolf166.txt

Mazur, M. (2004, February 29). *Wolf*. Retrieved from http://web.mit.edu/maz/wolf/65-179/wolf170.txt

Mazur, M. (2004, February 29). *Wolf*. Retrieved from http://web.mit.edu/maz/wolf/65-179/wolf171.txt

Mazur, M. (2004, February 29). *Wolf*. Retrieved from http://web.mit.edu/maz/wolf/65-179/wolf172.txt

Mazur, M. (2004, February 29). *Wolf*. Retrieved from http://web.mit.edu/maz/wolf/65-179/wolf173.txt

Mazur, M. (2004, February 29). *Wolf*. Retrieved from http://web.mit.edu/maz/wolf/65-179/wolf174.txt

Mazur, M. (2004, February 29). *Wolf*. Retrieved from http://web.mit.edu/maz/wolf/65-179/wolf175.txt

Mazur, M. (2004, February 29). *Wolf*. Retrieved from http://web.mit.edu/maz/wolf/65-179/wolf176.txt

Mazur, M. (2004, February 29). *Wolf*. Retrieved from http://web.mit.edu/maz/wolf/65-179/wolf177.txt

Mazur, M. (2004, February 29). *Wolf*. Retrieved from http://web.mit.edu/maz/wolf/65-179/wolf178.txt

Mazur, M. (2004, February 29). *Wolf*. Retrieved from http://mit.edu/maz/wolf/65-179/wolf179.txt

PBS. (2007, April 8). *Kennan on the Web*. Retrieved from http://www.pbs.org/newshour/gergen/kennan.html

Traces. (2007, August 8). *Kennan's letters*. Retrieved from http://www.traces.org/kennansletters.html#occupiedcountries

University of North Carolina. (2007, August 8). *George Frost Kennan*. Retrieved

Bibliography

from http://www.unc.edu/depts/diplomat/archives_roll/2004-04/miscambie-kennan/miscambie-kennan.html

U.S. Archives. (2008, April 21). *Guide to Federal Records*. Retrieved from http://www.archives.gov/research/guide-fed-records/groups/092.html

Washington Post. (n.d.). *The Paradox of George Frost Kennan*. Retrieved from http://www.washingtonpost.com